The Isles of Shoals

By Lyman V. Rutledge

Ten miles off Portsmouth, New Hampshire lie nine small islands whose total area barely reaches 205 acres. These are the Isles of Shoals, and this is their history by a man who has spent half a century on and around them. Tiny as they are, their influence has been unusually widespread and surprisingly profound in their effect upon the commercial, political, religious and cultural life of mainland America during three and a half centuries. The book represents the most complete interpretation of this "Kingdom in the Sea" yet published.

The story covers island life from the first recorded sighting by Samuel de Champlain in 1605, Captain John Smith's first visit in 1614 and the early fishing villages; the Haley dynasty which transformed these islands into a well-known summer resort early in the 19th century to be broadened and deepened later by the Laighton family and its illustrious daughter, Celia, who became one of the best known writers of her generation; to the summer religious and educational meetings which are still very much alive today.

The lore and legend in this book covers storm and shipwreck, pirates and buried treasure, ghosts and apparitions, murder, tragedy, romance and village life.

Thirty-two pages of illustrations, by themselves, provide a chronologically photographic history of the Isles of Shoals.

THE ISLES OF SHOALS
IN
LORE AND LEGEND

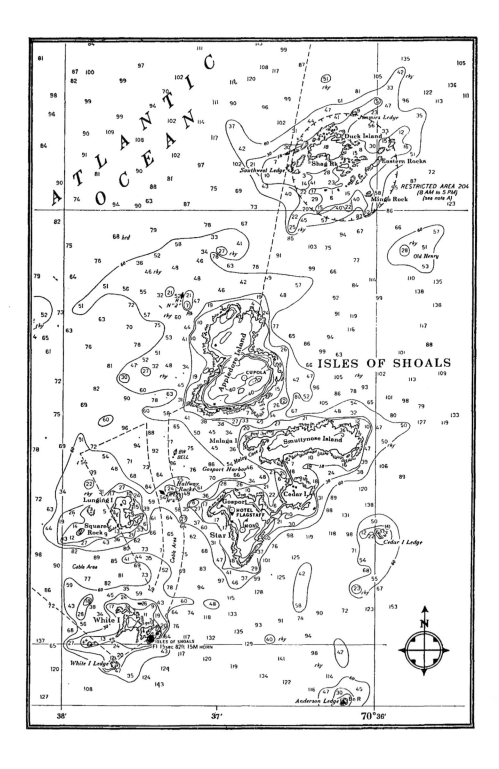

THE ISLES OF SHOALS
IN
LORE AND LEGEND

by Lyman V. Rutledge

The Isles of Shoals Association (Unitarian-Universalist)
Portsmouth, New Hampshire

Copyright © 1965, 1971 Lyman V. Rutledge, © Lyman V. Rutledge 2011
All Rights Reserved
Composed and printed in The United States of America

ISBN 13: 978-0-9742414-2-5

Reprinted in 2011 for The Isles of Shoals Association (Unitarian-Universalist)
by Peter E. Randall Publisher
5 Greenleaf Woods Drive #102, Portsmouth, NH 03801
www.perpublisher.com

Copies are available from:
The Isles of Shoals Association (Unitarian-Universalist)
c/o Star Island Book Store, P.O. Box 1409, Portsmouth, NH 03802
www.shopsonstar.com

Reprinted in 1971 by THE STAR ISLAND CORPORATION

Morton-Benedict House, 30 Middle Street, Portsmouth, NH 03801
www.starisland.org

ACKNOWLEDGMENTS

With grateful appreciation we acknowledge our indebtedness to friends and institutions whose combined inspiration and assistance have filled these pages. A summary of their benefactions would add a long chapter to the volume. It is our privilege, however, to extend special thanks to a limited few, with the assurance to those whose names do not appear that their helpfulness is not forgotten. We have in mind a multitude of devoted Shoalers who have sent in clippings, photographs, anecdotes, and memorabilia of every sort to enrich the "living history" of the Islands. They deserve our warmest thanks.

From the larger throng the following are selected because of special services rendered.

For research and personal assistance: Katharine Fowler-Billings (Mrs. Marland P.), research in geology; Lewis M. Bragdon, Atty., York, Me.; Raymond A. Brighton of the *Portsmouth Herald;* Hilda M. Camp, Waterbury, Ct.; Robert Choate and Russell Grush of the *Boston Herald;* Barbara Durant (Mrs. William B.) of the Laighton family; Mrs. Earl Flanders, Dover, N.H.; Clifford A. Follansbee, John Hancock Co., Boston; Hildreth Frost (Mrs. Robert V.), Newton and Wellesley, Mass.; Mabel Hale (Mrs. Albert), descendant of Rev. John Weiss; the late Elizabeth Hoxie, Newburyport, Mass.; Prof. C. F. Jackson, former dean of the University of N. H.; Aimee Lamb, Milton, Mass., and Dublin, N.H.; Charles Lawrance, Kingston, Mass., and Mary Lawrance, Claremont, Cal; Prof. Frederick T. McGill of Rutgers University; the late Frederic G. Melcher, owner of *Publishers Weekly,* N.Y.; Marjorie Spiller Neagle, (Mrs. George E.), Newton, Mass.; Rosamond Thaxter, Champernowne, Kittery, Me.; Rev. Frederick L. Weis of the Unitarian Historical Society; Betty Wood (Mrs. Howard D.) West Newton, Mass.; Mrs. Wilson F. Payne, Needham, Mass.

For assistance in editing this manuscript and finding a publisher: Lawrence M. Conant, Dublin, N.H.; Edward Darling, Director of the Beacon Press; Edward R. Knowlton, Charlton, Mass.; Prof. and Mrs. Robert S. Illingworth, Barre Mass.; Mr. and Mrs. Edward A. Dame, Concord, N.H.

v

For extended research facilities: The American Antiquarian Soc., Worcester, Mass., kindness of Mr. Clifford K. Shipton; The Boston Athenaeum; Boston Public Library; Congregational Library, Boston, kindness of Rev. Vaughan Dabney; Dublin, N.H., Public Library, kindness of Dorothy Worcester (Mrs. Millard); Houghton Library of Rare Books and Mss., Harvard University; Huntington Library, San Marino, Cal.; Longfellow House, Cambridge, kindness of Thomas Valcour; Mass. Historical and Genealogical Soc., Boston; N.H. Historical Soc.; North Middlesex Co. Registry of Deeds; Harrison Gray Otis House, Boston; Portsmouth Historical Soc., Mrs. Richard T. Call; Portsmouth Public Library, Dorothy Vaughan; Rockingham Co. Records, Exeter, N.H.; Unitarian Historical Library, Mrs. Martha S. C. Wilson; York Co. Records, Alfred, Me.; Watertown Public Library.

Special tribute is paid to Thea Wheelwright for editing the manuscript and to Barbara Ellis for lending her artistic skill.

We are indebted to J. B. Lippincott Co. for permission to quote from *Captain John Smith* by Bradford Smith. Copyright 1953 by Bradford Smith.

CONTENTS

Frontispiece	ii
Acknowledgements	v
Contents	vii
Introduction	ix

PART I
THE EARLY FISHING VILLAGE

1.	"They live on a Rock in the Sea."	1
2.	Captain John Smith — Admiral of New England	6
3.	The Island Empire	
4.	Whose Utopia?	14
5.	An Era of Vilification	19
6.	The Townships of Appledore and Gosport	23
7.	Pirates and Ghosts	30
8.	The Church and the Gospel	39
9.	The Era of John Tucke	43
10.	The Haley Dynasty	46
11.	Building the Stone Meetinghouse	50
12.	Island Culture	55

PART II
THE LAIGHTON SAGA

1.	The Advent of Thomas B. Laighton	61
2.	Shattered Hopes and a New Venture	67
3.	The Laighton-Thaxter Partnership	71
4.	The Long Engagement	77
5.	The Nomads	81
6.	Suddenly a New Career	85
7.	Celia's Problems	92
	Poor Little Spud	95
	Levi's Failing Health	96
	The Passing of Thomas and Eliza	99
8.	A Book, a Hotel and a Murder	103
9.	The Passing of William Morris Hunt and Levi Thaxter	115
10.	Celia's Parlor at Appledore	120
11.	Whittier	129
12.	From Turbulence to Calm	133
13.	The Twilight of Appledore	140

PART III
THE CONFERENCE ERA

1.	As it was in the Beginning	147
2.	Tragedy of the Waitresses	153
3.	The Purchase of Star Island	157
	L'envoi	164

Appendices

I.	Oscar and Cedric View Star Island	167
II.	The Islands	169
	Area and Altitude	169
	Flora and Fauna	170
	Geology	171
III.	Ministers, Missionaries, Teachers and Agents	173
IV.	Roster of Appledorians	175
V.	Western Skyline from Star Island	185
	Chart of the Hills	190
VI.	Erratic Spelling	192
	Bibliography	194
	Pictures Credits	197
	Index	198
Illustrations		following page 114

viii

INTRODUCTION

POINT OF DEPARTURE

As in life elsewhere, there is the illusion and there is the reality of island living, only on the island the illusion is more evident. It is the illusion of freedom, of independence. The reality is the learning of relationships.

Spend a winter on Star Island alone with wife and child in the era before two-way radio communication and you learn that the reality of such living can be summed up in a single sentence: one does not, in actuality, live *on* the island; one learns to live *with* it.

Strangely enough, once the arrogance of the independence idea — man standing giant size and dominating his universe — is fully dissipated by the physical necessities of survival, a real and thrilling freedom generates. It is more than survival. It is a positive knowledge of proportion, of one's minute but definite role in the scheme of things. Call it, if you will, a sense of values, or, as Lyman Rutledge put it to this writer many years ago on the rocks of Star Island: the ability to take delight in the inevitable.

The island then becomes a point of departure, firmly fixed geographically and spiritually, for all manner of voyages and adventures. And the sense of proportion learned on the island has a unique and pervasive power wherever the voyage might lead.

It is, therefore, not in the least surprising that this volume which represents the distillation of half a century of dedication to and intense study of the Isles of Shoals should reveal some odd and seemingly disproportionate relationships between the infinitesimal groups of islands and their sometimes profound influences upon places and people far removed from them both in time and space. The attitude which they engender, the tough resiliency which must be part of any Shoaler's nature, are not attributes common to the world ashore. They leave their mark. Hence, their impact on events from the earliest days of the discovery and settling of New England to the summers of yesterday and today is an impact of values sometimes well-known and clearly seen, at other times totally unexpected and subtle both to the historian and to the casual reader.

What is most fortunate is that the book came to be researched and written. Fifty years of intimacy with the odd little configuration of peaks of submerged mountains off the coasts of Maine and New Hampshire have made the Shoals a point of departure for countless voyages in space and time. The author invites you to cruise with him through the enchanting lore and legends of this "Kingdom in the Sea."

EDWARD R. KNOWLTON

February 2, 1965
Charlton City
Massachusetts

SHOALS-FEVER

(Adapted from Sea-Fever by John Masefield)

I must down to the Shoals again,
To the lonely sea and the sky,
And all I ask is a tall ship,
And a star to steer her by,
And a strong hand, and the wind's song,
And the white sail shaking,
And the gull's cry, and the moon's wake,
And the gray dawn breaking.

History rightly composed is a musical instrument which restores to us the melodies of long ago. Celia Thaxter's *Among the Isles of Shoals* is a Stradivarius whose tones grow richer with the years.

PART I

EARLY FISHING VILLAGES

1

"THEY LIVE ON A ROCK IN THE SEA"

PICTURE them there, a huddle of fishermen on nine lonely islands ten miles southeast from Portsmouth Harbor. Their life is rugged enough without the added burden of a Province tax. Their selectmen have gathered around the kitchen table of their minister, Reverend Joshua Moody, and drawn up a petition addressed to the Honorable Samuel Shute, Governor of New Hampshire, asking that they "be excused from the Province tax."

It was a sunny day in April of 1721 when Richard Yeaton, "a Selectman of the Isles of Shoals," set sail in a brisk breeze with the petition in his leather wallet. He could not be sure of a friendly reception since landlubbers had little regard for islanders who didn't know enough to winter on mainland. That these fishermen were not only respectable citizens, but passionately devoted to their island home was simply incredible. More than a hundred years later, when Celia Thaxter wrote her amazing story about life at the islands — summer and winter — Charles Dickens wrote to James T. Fields: "I think Mrs. Thaxter's prose is very admirable, but I don't believe it! No, I do *not*. My conviction is that those Islanders get frightfully bored by their Islands, and wish they had never set eyes on them." On reading this, Whittier wrote to Celia, "I wish he could have seen them as I have."

In approaching Governor Shute, Yeaton did not humble himself. "The people are very few in number," the petition said, "and most of them are men of no substance, live only by their daily fishing, and near one third of them are single men and threaten to remove and leave us, if the tax be laid, which will prove our utter ruin if our ffishermen leave us . . . They live on a rock in the Sea and have not any privilege or right in Common Lands as other Inhabitants in the respective Towns have."

Their old meetinghouse, built on Star Island in 1680, had served its time, and during the winter of 1720-21 a new one had been built. The petition continued: "The charge and expense which they are at in the support of the ministry is as great as the people can bear at present, it having cost them but lately the sum

ISLES OF SHOALS

of Two Hundred pounds for that end in building a Meeting House — which is not yet all paid."

Their appeal was for elemental justice. The Province gave them nothing in the way of roads, schools, churches, or police protection. Why then should they be charged with this nefarious tax? All they wanted was to be left alone. The selectmen were voicing the one characteristic which gave the islands their chief claim on history — the spirit of self-reliant independence.

Nothing more is heard of Richard Yeaton except that the petition was granted.

But who were these Islanders? Whence came they? How did they come by that fierce love of freedom and loyal devotion to the "rock in the Sea?" Their story adds a long-neglected chapter to American lore and legend.

The Shoals tradition goes back to the early explorers, and beyond them to the nameless and unrecorded fishermen of the North Atlantic. From the time of Leif Ericson in the year 1000, fleets of fishing boats drifted from European waters ever westward in quest of better fishing grounds. History traces them past the British Isles, the Orkneys, Shetlands, Faeroes, Iceland, Greenland, Labrador, and even down to Ericson's Vinland, which is now said to be on the south shore of Cape Cod or on the island of Martha's Vineyard.

Centuries later explorers whose names are familiar followed the fishermen, and from Columbus on, their exploits fill the pages of history. Study the dates from Bjarni Herjulfson in 985 to John Smith in 1614 and imagine the flags of many nations unfurled to the breezes of the Gulf of Maine. Then picture the unrecorded fishermen who had discovered that these waters were the best fishing ground in the Atlantic. Contemplating these, John Scribner Jenness said:

"Indeed, when we consider that during the entire sixteenth century, fleets of fishing vessels yearly visited our eastern waters, we are justified in conjecturing that for many lustres of years anterior to the settlement of New England, the commodiousness of the Isles of Shoals for the prosecution of the fisheries must have, summer after summer, attracted thither the Doggers and Pinckes of the English; the clumsy Busses of Holland and Zealand, the light Fly-boats of Flanders, the Biskiner, and the Portingal and many another of those high-peaked vessels whose models seem so

ISLES OF SHOALS

quaint, and whose rig is so incomprehensible to us of the present day."

These nameless fishermen were not explorers or colonizers or settlers, but transients. They cured their fish on the sun-bleached rocks, filled their barrels with fresh water from the spring on the south shore of the largest island, gathered wild berries from the thickets, and felt the heady freedom of these unchartered islands. Their lookout stood on a rocky summit commanding the complete circle of the horizon. No Indian canoe ventured near them. No pirate ships molested them. They were a law unto themselves. The English sailors among them called the archipelago "The Isles of Shoals" and gave most of the islands the earthy names which they still bear. The largest was *Hog* because of its fancied resemblance to a corpulent hog wallowing in the brine. The long narrow island near *Hog* was *Smuttynose* because of a smutch of dark seaweed on a nose of rock extending into the sea from the southeast corner — or was it the elongated proboscis of Hog Island? *Cedar* derived its name from a few scrubby old cedars found there in 1614 — the only trees visible on any of the islands. *Star* was so named because its broken crags extended in all directions like the spangles of a star. *Duck Island* had in its center a swampy fresh-water pond where wild ducks in migration paused for a rest. *Malaga* was named by Spanish sailors who remembered the vineyards of Spain.

The remaining three were named for owners. *Londoner's,* later contracted to *Lunging,* was named for a ship, the *Londoner,* wrecked on its savage rocks, or for the London Company, which sent over a fleet of four ships in 1615 and at some unrecorded date established a trading post there. *White* and *Seavey* are one at low tide and two at high. No one has as yet identified the Seavey who gave his name to the western hump, but the eastern rock, which has borne the lighthouse since 1820, was named for an ancestor of Captain Joseph White, born on Hog Island about 1750 and brutally murdered in Salem, Massachusetts on April 6th, 1830.

Scattered here and there among the islands are "hiding rock and treacherous shoal." Nine of these bear names appropriate to their character, location, or incident. Offshore from *Duck* are *Shag, Eastern, Mingo,* and *South West Ledge; Babb's Rock,* named for Philip Babb, lies west of *Hog; Square Rock* is southwest *of Londoner's; White Island Ledge* is southwest *of White; Cedar Island*

3

ISLES OF SHOALS

Ledge, southeast of *Cedar; Anderson's Ledge,* southeast of *Star.* Nine islands and nine surrounding ledges, eighteen in all.

Some historians have undertaken to date the naming of the islands by noting the first appearance of the names in any document. That misguided ambition gives a wrong impression. They say, for example, that the name *Star Island* first appears in 1650, as if it had been nameless until accidentally mentioned in a court record. It is only fair to say that we have no dates for the naming of any island or rock or even for the archipelago. We know that they were called the Isles of Shoals before 1614, but not how long before. And this uncertainty adds to the charm and mystery of these "enchanted islands."

When the first rude shacks were thrown together will never be known. It is certain only that the early European explorers found fishermen already familiar with these islands. Who, then, was the first explorer to mention them?

The seventeenth century opened with a voyage by Bartholomew Gosnold, sailing for Sir Walter Raleigh in 1602, but with no results other than the naming of Cape Cod.

Now began the eleven voyages of Samuel Champlain, who sailed first as geographer for Aymar de Chastes in 1603. That year Pierre du Guast, sieur de Monts the Huguenot, was granted the charter vacated by de Chastes, and received from Henry IV of France a charter for all territory between 40° and 46° N (roughly from Philadelphia to Newfoundland), which he called Acadia. In his patent it was noted that he had already made several voyages to this and other countries. In 1604 he built a fort on St. Croix Island, later moved to Port Royal, and the next spring coasted down the shore looking for a warmer climate. Champlain, who became his geographer, noted in his log: "July 15, 1605. We saw a cape, bearing south, a quarter east from us, distant some eighteen miles [Cape Ann]; on the east two leagues distant we saw three or four rather prominent islands, and on the west a large bay [Ipswich]."

This is accepted as the first definite mention of the Isles of Shoals by any European.

George Weymouth, sponsored by the Earl of Southampton, visited the Maine coast in 1605. His enthusiastic report led to the formation of two Virginia companies in 1606: the London, or South Virginia Company (from Cape Feare to New York) and the Plymouth or North Virginia Company (from Philadelphia to the

ISLES OF SHOALS

St. Croix River). The overlapping area of 200 miles was to be a buffer zone in which neither was to settle within 100 miles of the other. That summer Sir John Popham sponsored an expedition for the Plymouth Company, which explored from the coast of Maine southward. In 1607 Sir Ferdinando Gorges, chief figure in the Plymouth Company, fitted out the *Gift of God* for George Popham, brother of Sir John, and the *Mary and John* for Raleigh Gilbert. They built a fort on the Sagadahoc (Kennebec) River, but during the hard winter George Popham died and the settlement was abandoned. The area is still known as Popham's Beach.

By this time France, Spain, Portugal, Holland, and England were in feverish haste to plant their various flags on the new continent. How the Cross of St. George happened to prevail is a fascinating story that centers more in the Isles of Shoals than in Jamestown, Virginia.

In 1607, as every school child knows, the South Virginia or London Company established the first permanent settlement in America at Jamestown. The success of this venture is credited to an obscure Englishman whose character and achievements shine with increasing lustre as modern historians delve into his past — Captain John Smith.

2

CAPTAIN JOHN SMITH
ADMIRAL OF NEW ENGLAND

JOHN SMITH'S story is so fantastic that last-century writers denounced both author and narrative, but it is now conceded that he was the most remarkable figure in colonial history, and though a bachelor, the most romantic. Mr. Bradford Smith, who admits no relationship to the Captain, says in his biography:

"Recent historians, with every advantage of documentary evidence in hand, have revalued the Captain at a much higher level. Charles M. Andrews credits him with opening up the whole New England area to settlement. Wesley Frank Craven finds his judgments about Virginia supported by a careful study of the sources now available. Hamilton Basso (*Mainstream,* 1940) thinks him 'the only early colonial leader who fully understood the reality of the struggle in Virginia and who grasped the essential nature of the colonial economy,' and 'one of the greatest contributors' to English colonization. H. Wood Jarvis (*Let the Great Story be Told,* 1946) picks Smith as one of the founders of the British Empire, ranking him with Clive, Warren Hastings and Rhodes. Harold Stannard goes even farther 'Since it was he who first proved that a permanent colony could be established across the Atlantic, he may be hailed as the real founder of the British Empire overseas' (*Makers of Empire*)."

As to personal character, Smith was "one of Nature's Noblemen." "There is a strain of medieval idealism in Smith," says the biographer, "a strain which can be found in those romances of chivalry which required a true knight to be pure as well as brave. No breath of scandal ever touched John Smith. As Thomas Carleton, one of his companions at arms in Transylvania put it,

'I never knew a Warrior yet, but thee,
From wine, Tobacco, debts, dice, oaths so free.' "

Smith had returned to England after his amazing adventures on the new continent when the London merchants under their South Virginia grant were planning their first settlement. Included

ISLES OF SHOALS

among the settlers as a member of the Council, soon after arrival in Jamestown Smith rose to leadership and was named captain of the colony. His career in Jamestown ended suddenly when he was severely wounded by the explosion of his powder bag and was compelled to take the next boat to England. After a long convalescence, he was commissioned by Sir Ferdinando Gorges to explore that mysterious land already claimed by France but known to the English as North Virginia or Norumbega. The full account of this voyage is given in Smith's *Description of New England* published in 1616, from which we quote:

"With two shippes I went from the Downs, the third of March 1614 and arrived in New England the last of April — at the Ile of Monahigan: our plot was there to take Whales and make tryalls of a Myne of Gold and Copper. If those failed, Fish and Furres was then our refuge. — I had but fortie five men and boyes; we built seven boates, 37 did fish; myself with eight others ranging the coast in a small boat. We got for trifles [from the Indians] 1100 Bever skinnes, 100 Martins, and neer as many Otters . . .

"I have had six or seven severall plots of those Northern parts, so unlike each to other, and most so differing from any true proportion or resemblance of the Countrey, as they did mee no more good then so much waste paper, though they cost me more. . . I have drawen a Map from Point to Point, Ile to Ile, and Harbour to Harbour, with Soundings, Sands, Rocks, and Landmarks as I passed close aboard the Shore in a little Boat. . .

"The remarkeablest Iles and mountains for Landmarks are these . . . Smyths Iles are a heape together, none neere them, against Accominticus . . . a many of barren rocks, the most overgrowne with such shrubs and sharpe whins you can hardly passe them; without either grasse or wood but three or foure short shrubby old Cedars . . .

"And of all foure parts of the world that I have yet seene not inhabited, could I have but meanes to transport a Colonie, I would rather live here then any where; and if it did not maintaine it selfe, were wee but once indifferently well fitted, let us starve . . . .

"By that acquaintance I have of them, I may call them my children; for they have bin my wife, my hawks, my hounds, my cards, my dice, and in totall my best content."

In the years that followed, the Captain made repeated efforts to win his way back to his beloved New England, but each venture ended in shipwreck, capture by pirates, or thwarting intrigue. His

ISLES OF SHOALS

now famous map of New England was published in 1616 and carefully studied by the Pilgrims before they embarked for New Plymouth.

The major ambition of his later years was to write a history of the sea from the time of Noah's Ark. This dream also was to remain unfulfilled.

In answer to the question raised by some historians, notably Samuel Adams Drake and B. F. DeCosta, as to whether Captain Smith ever made a landing at the Shoals, we only ask: How else could he have counted them so accurately or known about the "shrubs and sharpe whins and two or three shrubby old Cedars"? Charles W. Tuttle, New England antiquarian, says that Smith's original map shows eighteen islands and rocks — the exact number visible today. We are inclined to say from a close examination of the text that he landed, surveyed the archipelago from the summit of Hog Island, discovered the spring of fresh water on the south shore, and thought well enough of the place to take possession in his own name. All historians agree that he was the first European to indicate the islands on any map and that his was not only the best up to his time, but was accepted by geographers as standard for many years, establishing for all time "New England." Except for him, this would have been New France.

On Star Island is a monument erected by Reverend Daniel Austin of Portsmouth to commemorate the two hundredth anniversary of Smith's visit to the Shoals. The triangular base was originally surmounted by a marble shaft bearing three small effigies of Turk's heads. These represented the three Turks, Turbashaw, Grualgo and Bonnie Mulgro, who were beheaded in single combat by Captain John Smith in Transylvania. The shaft was destroyed in a storm and the three effigies lost in the rubble. Fifty years later the New Hampshire Society of Colonial Wars restored the foundation and capped it with a granite block bearing a modest inscription. This was presented to the owners of the island.

As a reward for his loyal services in severing the Turks' heads, Smith was permitted to engrave on his shield of arms "the figure and description of those Turks' heads." Those who visit St. Sepulchre's Church in London will find the Turks' heads carved in a stone over his grave. John Smith died on June 21st, 1631, at the age of fifty-three, and over his tomb is engraved: *"Here lies one conquered who has conquered Kings."*

3

THE ISLAND EMPIRE

FISHING industry at the Shoals developed rapidly during the decade following John Smith's arrival. The trading post on Londoners prospered. The islands were well known by 1623, and Sir Christopher Levett came to anchor there on his way to the Maine coast. He had a patent for six thousand acres of his own choosing in the Province of Maine, and was commissioned by Gorges to start a settlement and establish a church. His brief notes show clearly that he took for granted the development which he found at the Shoals. It is significant too that he did not use the name "Smith's Isles." He wrote:

"The first place I set my foot upon in New England was the Isles of Shoulds, being islands in the sea about two leagues from the main.

"Upon these islands I neither could see one good timber tree, nor so much ground as to make a garden.

"The place is found to be a good fishing place for six ships, but more cannot well be there, for want of convenient stage room, as this year's experience hath proved.

"The harbour is but indifferent good. Upon these islands are no savages at all."

Captain Levett observed also that each of the six ships carried a crew of at least fifty men, which meant that the islands were then inhabited by three hundred or more fishermen. About a third of the men lived ashore to cure and store fish products, while the rest cruised about fishing. There must have been a village and numerous cabins for shore living, but no mention is made of these.

Somtime during these early years the industrious fishermen at the Shoals developed a superior product called "dunfish," or "dumbfish," which captured the market both in the budding American settlements and in Europe. The process known as "dunning" was much the same as for drying fish on wooden "flakes" or "frames," but was carried out with much greater care. When a boat came to dock with the day's catch, the fish were immediately put

9

ISLES OF SHOALS

ashore and taken up by the cutter, who ripped them open and passed them on to the header, who in turn cut off the heads and removed the viscera. The splitter then cut out the backbone and passed the two halves on to the salter to be rubbed with salt and piled in bulk to cure for ten to twenty hours. After that, the shoremen washed and laid them out on flakes and frames to dry slightly. Then followed a long period of alternate drying in the sun and "sweating" in the storehouse until the product was ready for market. In the words of Celia Thaxter, "A real dunfish is handsome, cut in transparent strips, the color of brown sherry wine."

The discovery, or development, of dunfish turned out to be one of the most important items in New England economy. For decades the price of fish in the world market was quoted from the Isles of Shoals. As late as 1822 it was $8.00 a hundred pounds while other fish was selling at $2.40. Fishermen from the best grounds brought their catches to the islands for dunning and reshipment to Bilbao, Talloon, Rochel, and other foreign ports. Returning cargoes of wine, sugar, and commodities in general were imported for new settlements from Martha's Vineyard to Acadia. In 1636 Thomas Mayhew was commissioned to buy eighty hogsheads of provisions and spend a hundred pounds for "rugges and coates" for Martha's Vineyard. The Shoals had become a port of call between the Old World and the New.

The thriving village at the islands was in the truest sense a settlement, although it had no leader or colonizer known to history. Even the names of the seamen, the fishermen, and artisans are lost. Whoever they may have been, they came without grant or patent, took possession without question from any source, developed their industry, and passed from the scene with no official recognition from colonial leaders, councils, or courts. There has been nothing like it in our history. We should erect a monument to our nameless Shoalers.

Having no official recognition, the Islanders were under no government but their own. Law and order were maintained by ship's command until colonial governments were formed. Shoalers had no truck with the political life of the mainland. Orders from the Crown and from the Massachusetts Bay Colony were ignored. Even in later years, when they perforce had to accept the authority of Maine, Massachusetts, and New Hampshire, they continued to be the most independent of all colonials. Without oath or ceremony

ISLES OF SHOALS

they owned first allegiance to their island empire, and to the customs which had grown up among them as islanders.

The question of legal ownership of the islands began with the first patent issued in the King's name to the North Virginia or Plymouth Company in 1606. This put them under command of Sir Ferdinando Gorges and his council, but the Shoalers knew nothing of that. Then in 1620 Gorges formed a partnership with his friend John Mason, who resigned from his post as Governor of Newfound Land to help colonize New England. They owned the Shoals jointly but did not interfere with the fishing industry. Their chief ambition was to establish settlements on the mainland and develop the hidden resources which Captain Smith had assured them would be found there.

Mason and Gorges had much in common. Both administered their colonial possessions as absentee landlords, from their headquarters in England. It is doubted by some historians whether either of them ever visited the shores of America south of Newfound Land, although some of their nearest kin were sent over as agents to care for their vast holdings. Both had wealth and local distinction. Mason was a merchant shipmaster in his youth, then commander of a small fleet for His Royal Highness, James I. He was Governor of Portsmouth, England, and for six years (1615-21) Governor of Newfound Land.

Sir Ferdinando Gorges was a sailor and a soldier of fortune, knighted in 1591 for distinguished military service in France and commissioned Captain and Keeper of the Castle, Fort, and Island at Plymouth (England). He was a charter member of the Plymouth Company.

Both were Royalists in high favor with the King, and equally devoted to the Established Church. Both were violently opposed to Puritans, Separatists, and any other democratic independents. They were by nature and culture aristocrats, and viewed the growth of American colonies as a source of wealth and strength to the aristocracy of England. Their joint ambition was to revive the fading glory of the archaic feudal system. They saw themselves by the King's favor Lord Proprietors in Utopia. By securing large grants of land in the teeming wilderness they would exercise their lordship by subletting lesser grants to relatives, friends, and tenants. There would be royal titles, baronies, and lordships, and all major industries would be held by the Lord Proprietors as monopolies.

11

ISLES OF SHOALS

Both were largehearted and generous, willing to bestow their private fortunes on the colonies, and genuinely interested in the welfare of their tenants. They were not tyrannical in their own administration although they gave full support to cruel and tyrannical monarchs.

Mason and Gorges together were an interesting contrast to Captain John Smith, whom they knew. Captain Smith had three points in common with the other two — he was a Royalist, an Anglican, and an ardent colonist. In other respects he was their extreme opposite. There would be no feudalism in Smith's Utopia. He was at heart a democrat, with high regard for the character and ability of the horney hands of toil . . . "What pleasure can there bee more than contriving their owne grounds to the pleasure of their owne minds?"

Mason and Gorges were burning with zeal to save this new world from Commoners and Puritans. They invested their large fortunes in this enterprise, and while they lost their fortunes, they succeeded in planting a few Anglican churches and Royalist settlements, and wrote their names high in the roster of American colonizers. Maine and New Hampshire proudly honor them as founders, and history names them with John Smith as men who saved the North American continent for the English speaking people.

We see them now in the years 1619 to 1635 throwing themselves unreservedly into their fight for church, King and personal fortunes. Their first move was to gain control of all New England under grants and patents to various colonizers, and they therefore welcomed the Leyden group, afterward known as Pilgrims, little dreaming that this small band would ever have the courage or foresight to write "The Mayflower Compact," and to establish local government once their feet touched the soil of New Plymouth.

Gorges led a petition signed by forty noblemen, knights, and gentlemen for a patent under the name of "The Council Established at Plymouth in the County of Devon, for planting, ruling and governing New England in America." All rights and privileges of the Charter of 1606 were to be continued, but the northern boundary was extended to the St. Lawrence River. This was granted on November 13th, 1620. Mason took out a patent for all territory between Naumkeag (Salem) and Merrimack rivers, calling it Mariana (March 9, 1622) . A few months later, Mason and Gorges had the Plymouth Company give them a patent for all territory between

ISLES OF SHOALS

the Merrimack and the Kennebec rivers, calling it the Province of Maine. Thus the settlements from Salem to the Kennebec would be under their joint command. They had already begun to recruit colonists who would, they hoped, develop all the resources and soon be paying large rents to their landlords.

In that fateful year (1623) the Plymouth Council appointed Robert Gorges and Francis West to serve as Governor and Lieutenant Governor of all New England. The first administrative duty assigned to them was to collect a tax of five pounds for every thirty tons of shipping in New England ports. This would be the first taste of revenue, the first returns to Mason and Gorges for their heavy investment in America. It seemed to them right, just, and inevitable, but not so to the settlers at New Plymouth and the Isles of Shoals! The response was violent. Most of the tonnage was in fish products, and the Shoals fishermen would have none of it. Gorges and West returned to England defeated. Young Gorges died that winter, and nothing more was done about the tax, but Shoalers were now alerted to a new situation. Their independence had been challenged.

They did not know, and the world did not know until long afterward, that this tiny rebellion among Shoals fishermen against the five-pound tax touched off an explosion which blasted Parliament out of its House, and kept it out for eleven years. The Commoners were accusing the King and his Royalist supporters of arbitrary monopolistic administration. They objected to the powers granted to Mason and Gorges in the New England charter, and had hailed Sir Ferdinando into court and charged him with conducting an illegal monopoly. The King knew that this shot was aimed at his own regal person and in a rage he dissolved Parliament and sent the leaders — Pym, Coke and Selden — to the scaffold. The New England charter remained in effect, but Mason and Gorges were thereafter more discreet, though no less determined in their efforts to establish Royalist colonies with Anglican churches.

4

WHOSE UTOPIA?

NEW RESIDENTS who came to the Shoals after 1623 were mostly young unmarried men from England who had been induced by Mason, Gorges, and Smith to seek their fortune in the untouched wealth of New England. The well-established independence of the fishermen and their sense of personal ownership of this island empire caught the imagination of the newcomers, who were happy to be members of such a community. On the other hand, the loyalty of the newcomers to church and Crown did not offend the fishermen, since they were all under one flag and spoke the same language. However, there were some differences.

Perhaps the most interesting conflict was over the residence of women at the islands. True to the ancient tradition among seamen that females aboard ship bring bad luck, the fishermen had not thought of bringing women to their far-off fishing grounds. But the young men of the new dispensation were sent out as colonists and were expected to become permanent settlers with families. This alarmed the fishermen. There must have been "rip-roarin' knock-down-drag-out arguments" on the subject, with the immediate result that "a court order" was brought out forbidding women to reside at the Shoals. What court issued it has never been made known. In fact, the only evidence that it ever existed is the acknowledgement by later courts that it had become obsolete around 1635.

In 1647 Richard Cutt, absentee landlord of Star Island, and John Cutting, whose name appears nowhere else, presented the following to the court held at Pascataquack, Maine:

"The humble petition of Richard Cutt and John Cutting sheweth: that John Renolds, contrary to an Act in Court, that no woman shall live upon the Isles of Shoals, hath brought his wife thither, with an intention there to live and abide; and hath brought upon Hog Island a great stock of goats and hogs, which doth not only spoile and destroy much fish . . . but also doth spoile the spring of water, etc. . . .

"Your petitioners, therefore, pray that the said Renolds may be ordered to remove his said goats . . . from the Islands forthwith.

ISLES OF SHOALS

Also, that the Act of Court, before mentioned, may be put in execution, to the removal of all women from inhabiting there . . . etc."

The court ordered that "Mr. Renolds shall, within twenty days, remove his swine and goats . . . And as for the removal of his wife, it is thought fit, if no further complaint come against her, she may as yet enjoy the company of her husband."

This was obviously an act of spite on the part of some disgruntled fishermen and Richard Cutt, who had moved into the "great house at Strawbery Banke." These unhappy men must have taken their feud to Boston, for the record there shows that John Seeley and Antipas Maverick of the Isles of Shoals were ordered by the Boston magistrates "to attach the wife of William Wormwood and bring her before the magistrates of Boston" (October 27, 1647). Three years later, Wormwood presented an appeal to the Court of Gorgeana, in behalf of many Shoalers, that the infamous "Act of Court" against women should be repealed. It was noted that this Act was already obsolete before 1635 and had not been invoked for more than fifteen years except for the two women, Mrs. Renolds and Jane Wormwood. The court now ordered (1650) that "upon the petition of William Wormwood, that as the fishermen of the Isles of Shoals *will* entertaine womanhood, they have liberty to sit down there, provided they shall not sell neither wine, beare, nor liquor."

Another interesting tradition clung to the rocks for many generations. It was that men could — and should — settle their differences by personal combat. Courts were to be avoided and their orders ignored. Jenness, writing in 1873, rehearses an amusing incident to the point:

"We may mention, in illustration of this spirit among the Islands, that some years ago, one of these stalwart Shoals fishermen was arraigned before the author, as a magistrate, upon a charge of "assault and battery." The man admitted frankly that he had severely beaten the complainant in a square stand-up fight, but he set up, as a complete defence, that, in his own language, 'they had agreed to heave the law one side.' His rude sense of Shoals justice was sensibly shocked at a judgment against the sufficiency of his plea."

These independent Shoalers were so completely absorbed in their own affairs that their contacts with Mother England or the new settlements in America seemed as tenuous as the tangled

ISLES OF SHOALS

threads of a broken cobweb. They gave little attention to the turmoil in Parliament or the beheading of a king, except as it affected their fishing industry. It meant nothing to them that Miles Standish of Plymouth sailed into their harbor one summer day in 1628 with a prisoner, one Thomas Morton, who was being sent back to England because he had danced around a maypole somewhere down in the wilderness near New Plymouth.

Two men, Jeffrey and Burslem, taverners at the Shoals, accepted the responsibility of holding him, but they must have said many "badd words" when the Plymouth Fathers presented a bill of two pounds to go toward the expense of deportation, on the grounds that Morton was a menace to the new settlements. If they had only known it, this was their bid for immortality since the presence of their names on that bill identifies them as the first settlers at the Shoals whose names appear on any document!

Shoalers were equally indifferent to John Winthrop, who sailed by (June 11, 1630) in the *Arbella,* leading his fleet of four ships on their way to Salem. They did not know how much their own destiny was wrapped up in the Massachusetts Bay Company charter he carried, which failed to state where the new governor, his assistants and officers of court should hold their meeting. The King's Bench had fully intended it to be in England, as designated in the original draft, but in the copy issued by the King and now held as a priceless possession by the Company, the clause stipulating the place for annual meeting was omitted. Hence on September 2nd, 1630, GovernorWinthrop and his assistants held their first meeting on American soil and established independent local government, following the pattern of the Mayflower Compact.

There was also a clause in the charter to the effect that the Bay Colony was to have the area from three miles south of the Charles River to three miles north of the Merrimack. All parties to the contract supposed that both rivers flowed eastward to the sea, but the new settlers soon discovered that the Merrimack makes a sharp turn northward about thirty miles inland (at Lowell, Massachusetts) and has its source in Lake Winnipesaukee. With amazing speed they drew their line east and west from three miles north of the lake and found that it came out at Casco Bay (near Portland) , giving them virtually all the settlements on the Maine and New Hampshire coasts, including the Isles of Shoals.

Mainland boundaries were of no consequence to Shoalers,

ISLES OF SHOALS

however, until 1635 when a line was drawn through the harbor splitting their empire in half. They demanded a reason for this outrage and the answer unraveled a yarn longer than any of their own spinning. They might have known what was coming if they had caught the meaning of events that were passing before their inattentive eyes. They knew in a general way that Mason and Gorges held virtually the entire coastline of the Gulf of Maine jointly, and that the Shoals were included in that domain. They knew that the proprietors had organized the Laconia Company and been granted all the rich timber and fur-trading country around Lake Champlain, together with rights and privileges at the mouth of the Piscataqua and at the Isles of Shoals; and that the ambitious outfit had set about building "factories" on the banks of the river to make salt and wood products and handle the great shipments of fur they expected from the north. Both projects failed. The explorers sent by the new Company up the Piscataqua expected to reach Lake Champlain in a few days but found themselves in an impassable wilderness and returned in sorry condition. A ship, the *Lions' Whelp*, of London, which sailed for the Isles of Shoals in 1633 on a fishing expedition for the Company, returned at the end of the season battered and beaten — a total loss.

The Company dissolved, and in 1635 Mason and Gorges set about to divide their assets. The Isles of Shoals had turned out to be their most valuable holding. The fishing industry there had not been affected by all these maneuvers. So the Lord Proprietors extended their boundary line down the Piscataqua, through the Shoals harbor, and out to the wide ocean. Mason took the south portion — Star, Londoners, and White — into the Province of New Hampshire; Gorges took the north — Cedar, Smuttynose, Malaga, Hog, and Duck — into the Province of Maine. The line thus drawn has been confirmed by succeeding governments, and to this day citizens north of the line pay taxes in Kittery, Maine, those to the south in Rye, New Hampshire, in tribute to the fact that in 1635 neither Mason nor Gorges was willing to give up the islands entirely.

Mason died that year, shortly after the division of properties, and Gorges was left in his declining years to fight the battle alone against Massachusetts for possession of the Shoals area. His strategy was to have the obnoxious Bay Colony Charter revoked and himself made Governor General of all New England. The King gladly did his part and ordered the charter to be canceled (May

ISLES OF SHOALS

1637). Gorges was to sail for America at once with the revocation in his pocket, but his ship broke up in launching, and the charter revocation was never delivered. Massachusetts held her precious document and now proceeded to bring the Maine and New Hampshire settlements into submission.

While this was going on, settlers were thronging to New England. Between 1620 and 1640 more than 20,000 immigrants arrived in America, and prosperity was in the air. These new settlers — Puritans, Separatists, Anglican Royalists and free lancers — wandered from place to place, each following the line of his own personal advantage regardless of prior commitments. They selected their own plantations, traded where most convenient, and found that it was easier and quicker to bring their disputes before the Massachusetts courts than to brook the long delays of the King's courts in Maine and New Hampshire. When therefore it became known among them that Mason had died, that Gorges was not coming to America, and that the Massachusetts Bay Charter was not to be surrendered, the settlements in Maine and New Hampshire began to vote reluctantly to accept Massachusetts rule. When in 1640 Massachusetts confidently extended her northern boundary to Casco Bay, the opposition was too weak to resist. And the next year settlers in the Piscataqua area signed a petition to be taken under her protection. Hampton voted to join in 1639, Strawbery Banke and Dover in 1641, Exeter in 1643. The Province of Maine held out until King Charles was beheaded in 1649.

It was during the memorable summer of 1635 that the severest storm in colonial history swept the Atlantic Coast.

According to *Morton's Memorial* (no relation to Thomas Morton): "it was such a mighty storm of wind and rain, as none now living in these parts, either English or Indian, has seen the like, being like unto those hurricanes or tuffins that writers mention to be in the Indies."

There is no record of loss or damage at the Shoals other than the strange voyage of the house of Tucker, the tailor. It was washed from the shelving rocks of Smuttynose, and drifted on to Cape Cod, where it was hauled ashore and identified by a box of linens and papers. The Tuckers had fled uninjured as their house was wrenched from its foundations.

18

5

AN ERA OF VILIFICATION

THE EARLY Shoalers from date unknown to 1640 had built up a fishing industry and developed their famous dunfish which commanded a world-wide market. They had established trading posts on their islands which supplied the budding settlements in times of greatest need. They had built substantial homes and had maintained on Hog Island an academy for boys which was patronized by the best of the new colonists. The foundations of that academy and of about seventy houses are still to be found on the southwestern hillside. On Smuttynose they had built a brick church about 1640, a courthouse, and comfortable dwellings. They had made for themselves modest fortunes somewhat in advance of any known among settlers on the mainland. The village at the Shoals was for many years said to be stronger in wealth and resources than the New Plymouth Colony, and when all New England was called upon (1677), to ransom the wretched citizens of Hatfield, Massachusetts, who had been carried captive to Canada by the Indians during King Philip's War, the Shoalers contributed more generously than the rest — more even than Salem. These are not the acts of people described by John Scribner Jenness as "the motley shifting community of fishermen, seal hunters, sailors, smugglers and picaroons who made the Isles of Shoals their rendezvous, and their home." To support his condemnation, he offers the following:

"For instance, we read in York County Records, how that Samuel Matthews and Abraham Kelly, of the Shoals, were indicted for abusing and reviling the constable there." Nicholas Hodges, Robert Mace, Richard Oliver were indicted for the same offense.

Stephen Forde, "for abusing the constable and calling him rogue and rascall"; William Curtis, for assaulting his majesty's officer; Gabriel Grubb, for saying "he could find it in his heart to kill the constable," and Bartholomew Mitchell, Rebora Downs, and Bartholomew Burrington were charged with assailing the Shoals'

19

ISLES OF SHOALS

constable "by words and blows, and threatening to break his neck on the rocks, and pulling off his neck cloth."

Jenness cites other instances: In 1669 Mary Kelley, wife of Roger Kelley, was presented "for abusing of her neighbours in an unseemly manner with badd words." In 1666 Richard Down's wife was presented "for scoulding and abusing of her neighbours," and Gabriel Grubb's wife "for slandering and abusing her husband." Joane Andrews was sentenced to "ten lashes on the bare skin at the whipping-post," and Grace Tucker was convicted of abusing her neighbors "by evill and rayling speeches."

At this point Jenness throws away his argument against the Shoalers by saying:

"So serious and prevalent, indeed, was this sort of offence, that a law was enacted by the General Court, held at Gorgeana in 1649, 'that any woman, that shall abuse her husband, or neighborhood, or any other by opprobrious language, being lawfully convicted, for her 1st offence, shall be put in the stocks for two hours; for her 2nd offence, to be doucked: and if incorrigible, for to be whipped.' The court ordered each town in Maine to erect a cucking stool."

In other words, these laws and regulations against the "common scold" were not aimed at Shoalers, but at the general public. There is nothing to show that women at the islands were more vicious than their inland neighbors. Moreover, the Shoalers refused to erect a ducking stool, nor did they administer the stripes, leaving that to the mainland officials.

When it comes to "badd words" the women had interesting patterns to follow: for instance, the Puritans of the Bay Colony and the Anglicans of the north colonies hated each other with such pure and burning hatred that they went beyond language in expressing their feelings. Dr. Henry Greenland of Kittery, a staunch Royalist, was accused by Richard Cutt, the Puritan, of conspiring with pirates to have him kidnapped and his property stolen. Dr. Greenland said it would be worth 10,000 pounds, and he would take care of the legal side of it by accusing Cutt of treason against the King. The vicious plot was betrayed to Cutt by his Puritan friends, and the pirate ship *Mermaiden,* which was to have taken him to England was seized and taken to Boston and tried for piracy. Plenty of "badd words" were spoken.

In 1640 Reverend Thomas Jenner, Puritan, said "the people of the Eastern settlements are generally very ignorant, superstitious,

ISLES OF SHOALS

and vicious, and scarce any religious." Captain Underhill of Dover was brought to trial in a Massachusetts court for saying that "they at Boston are zealous as the Scribes and Pharisees."

A Piscataqua man said in England (1632) that the Massachusetts planters "would be a peculiar people to God, but all go to the Devil."

John Josselyn wrote of the founders of Boston: "some are of a Linsie-woolsie disposition, of several professions in religion; all are like the Aethiopians, white in the teeth only, full of ludification and injurious dealing, and cruelty, the extremest of all vices . . . and savagely factious among themselves."

Thomas Warnerton, of Strawbery Banke, said; "They are all rogues and knaves at the Bay, and I hope to see all their throats cut."

In brief, the argument Jenness advances against the Shoalers applies with even greater force to the high and mighty dignitaries of the mainland.

But Jenness, the barrister historian, takes one more step downward before he is through. He quotes Hubbard's *History of New England* in a long passage about drunken sailors and fishermen, as if all came from the Shoals, whereas only five out of eleven are said by Hubbard to be from the Shoals. The other six were from Strawbery Banke. But more to the point, Hubbard was strongly puritanic, hated the eastern provinces and all Anglicans, and gave them only a scant review in his history. He was deliberately vilifying the whole seaboard, but Jenness by inference makes it apply to the Shoals only.

He overlooked one item that reveals Shoals character much more truly than the sordid incidents in his diatribe. In the York County Records for June 30, 1653, is the tragic story of Stephen Forde:

"Whereas Stephen Forde by a soore providence of God through a violent storme at sea 18 moenths since had his hands and leggs so frozen that a great part of them were rotted off, whereby he was uncapable to use either his hands or leggs to get his subsistance. In commisseration whereof the inhabitants of the Yles of Shoales out of their charetable minds and good will, for his subsistance, have contributed there-unto the sum of fifty-six pounds or thereabouts, which is in the hands of Peter Gee.

"The court being unwilling that a person so deeply suffering should be neglected or the estate soe given by such well-minded per-

21

ISLES OF SHOALS

sons should be either Imbesseled or mispent, Do order that Capt. Bryan Pendleton and Phillip Babb shall demand and receave the said some of 56 pounds soe charitably bestowed from the sayd Peter Gee and to improve the same In the sayd Ford's behalf, giving security for what they receave unto Capt. Nicho. Shapleigh and Mr. Edw. Rishworth, which shall be returned into the next Court and out of the revenue thereof to Mantayne the sayd Stephen Ford with necessary food and Rayment. And if this syad revenue bee not sufficient to mantayne him the Court shall and is hereby Injoined to make that up which is comfortable for him."

This was twelve years before his wife Joane was sentenced to nine stripes for calling the constable a horn-headed rogue. Perhaps he was.

6

THE TOWNSHIPS OF APPLEDORE
AND GOSPORT

AFTER the visit of John Smith the population of Hog Island increased rapidly. The ever-flowing spring of fresh water on its south shore drew the first "settlers" and held them until wells were dug on Star and Smuttynose. Two of these are still in use after more than three centuries of service.

Names of Shoalers began to emerge from obscurity soon after the deportation of Thomas Morton in 1628. By that time the population had spread over several of the islands and within a few years was said to number at least a thousand. That is doubtless an exaggeration. More authentic estimates place the maximum at six hundred.

Philip Babb was one of the earliest and most important. He was constable, taverner, and general factotum, kept cattle, sheep, and hogs in the valley back of his butcher shop. He died in 1671, leaving an estate of 200 pounds, a tidy sum for those days. His ghost still haunts the cove where his hogs were rendered.

The first and most prominent names on Smuttynose were John, Richard, and Robert Cutt, three young men from a well-to-do family in England. They were sharply divided in religion and politics. Robert was a Royalist Episcopalian, John and Richard were, or became, Puritans. All three were prosperous at the islands, but in 1647 moved to the mainland, without giving up their island holdings, and became wealthy. Richard and John, as Puritans, were welcomed by the Massachusetts Bay authorities, who gave them the chief offices in the Piscataqua area. Richard made his home at Strawbery Banke, but bought up most of Star Island, which he administered through his son-in-law, William Vaughan. John seems to have won the confidence of both Puritans and Royalists, and when New Hampshire was created a royal province, was commissioned to serve as president. He was thereupon "cast out of all Publick Employments by the Government of Boston," but to the end of his life enjoyed full compensation from the King.

23

ISLES OF SHOALS

Three young brothers from England, William, Richard, and John Seeley, settled on Smuttynose before 1640. They were true islanders and were given chief positions as magistrates, constables, deputies, and merchants.

The three Kelly brothers, William, Roger, and John, and the three Oliver brothers, William, Benedict, and Richard, bought or built "dwelling houses, housings, staging and stage-room, flakes and flake room and mooring places" at the Shoals, and later took land on the main.

Most notable among them all was a young fisherman named William Pepperrell, who settled on Hog Island in 1676. Soon he fell in love with an island girl, but she refused to marry him until he was skipper of his own brig. He accepted the terms. In a few years as Captain Pepperrell he married her and built a substantial house on the western slope of the great hill. Here in 1696, according to the cherished tradition of all Shoalers, his son William was born — the son who became famous as victor in the Battle of Louisburg in 1745 and was afterward knighted by the King. Sir William's biographers say he was born in Kittery and show a marker on the house there. But there is also a bronze plaque on the foundation of the Pepperrell house at Hog Island. The undisputed fact is that the Pepperells moved from their island home over to Kittery in June of 1696 about the time young William was born.

As citizens of Kittery, father and son prospered in many enterprises. They were importers, exporters, and large landowners. They could drive thirty miles to the northward without leaving their own domain. Their ships were known in the seven seas. They built the largest and finest mansion of their era and were glamorous entertainers. The father died in 1734. The son was commissioned captain in 1717, then major, lieutenant colonel, and colonel of the militia. He served in the Massachusetts General Court for two seasons, and was on the Governor's Council for over thirty years, eighteen years as president.

The prosperous villagers at the Shoals began early to think of erecting a town government of their own.

With both Charles I and Ferdinando Gorges out of the way, Massachusetts Bay became fearlessly aggressive in taking control of the northern provinces, and in 1652, having declared herself an independent Commonwealth, assumed complete authority over

ISLES OF SHOALS

Maine. Up to this time the Shoals had openly rebelled against Massachusetts government, but now accepting the yoke, they began to plead for more local government. Their first approach was a petition signed by twenty Shoalers, that the "Honored Court held at Boston, . . . mought be pleased to take our condition into your serious and sage consideration & to grant us the privilege of a Townshipp . . . that we may have amongst us a Clarke of the Writts & some others authorized to have the hearing & issuing of such causes as may fall out under the summe of Ten pounds. . . .

"Alsoe . . . that, you would be pleased to make us a distinct company in that respect, wee being upwards of a hundred men at this time, & that our loving friends John Arthur Lieut. & William Sealy Ensigne so chosen amongst us, to beginne that service." . . .

The "Clark of the Writts" was authorized, but the other requests were ignored.

After five years of restless waiting, the Shoalers presented a second petition (1659) to be made a separate town, and were a second time refused, on the ground that "The Court doe not judge the persons petitioning to be in a capacity at present to make a township." In response to a third petition it was ordered that the whole group "shall be reputed and hereby allowed to be a township called Appledore, and shall have equall power to regulate their towne affairs, as other towns of this jurisdiction have."

Note that the Town of Appledore comprised all the islands, which meant that the town was divided between Maine and New Hampshire.

The name Appledore was from the fishing village on Barnstable Bay in England. It stands directly across the bay from Portsmouth, which name had replaced Strawbery Banke in 1653.

In 1662 came the Reverend Samuel Belcher whose pastorate of thirty years covered many changes at the islands. During his first decade the villagers on Hog and Smuttynose moved from one island to another, some going to the mainland. We hear virtually nothing from Star, but the record shows that a few highly respected Shoalers lived there as tenants of Richard Cutt, the Puritan. The line drawn through the harbor thirty years earlier seems now to have taken on new meaning — it divided the Anglican Royalists on the north from the Puritans on the south. They were all under

25

ISLES OF SHOALS

Massachusetts government, but the north half went naturally to the Maine courts, while the south went to New Hampshire.

Sometime during Belcher's pastorate, forty families migrated in a body from Hog to Star for no assigned reason. Historians since have been vague as to both time and cause, placing the date between 1660 and 1670. They suggest the fear of Indian raids, better shore facilities at Star, and the like as the cause. However, a brief glance at chronology suggests a more plausible reason and a later date.

First of all, Massachusetts had held full control of the Province of Maine since 1652.

Second, the Township of Appledore created in 1661 included all the islands, hence moving from one island to another had no effect on local government.

Third, in 1672, the Islanders petitioned the general court to be "adjoined to the same county unto which Star Island belongs." The petition was granted.

Fourth, the Province of Maine under Massachusetts rule was bearing down on taxes, while John Tufton Mason, grandson of the original colonizer, was appealing to the King for recognition of his claim to the New Hampshire lands bequeathed to him by his grandfather.

Fifth, Richard Cutt, who owned Star Island died in 1676, and new homes were now available on Star.

Sixth, in 1677 the Massachusetts authorities undertook to tax Shoalers toward government expenses. The Shoalers rebelled. Walter Randall challenged the constable. Henry Joslyn climbed to the belfry of the meetinghouse on Smuttynose and rang the alarm; Islanders gathered in the church and united in open resistance, solemnly declaring that they would not pay a penny unless the Governor and Council would guarantee that money raised should be "laid out upon the Isles of Shoals." And this was the end of the meeting.

Seventh, New Hampshire was made a royal province in 1679, and the Puritan John Cutt was transformed into the Royalist President of the new Province.

A reasonable conclusion is that residents on Hog Island were eager to get out from under Massachusetts rule, had looked longingly over to Star Island, found long-desired homes there available after the death of Richard Cutt, and were incensed by the new tax imposed by Massachusetts. Therefore when New Hampshire was

ISLES OF SHOALS

given royal status with their own John Cutt as president, they cast off from the shores of Hog Island almost as one fleet, paddling half a mile across the harbor with all their household goods. The date would be the summer of 1679 or 1680.

Reverend Mr. Belcher must have watched the migration from his window on Smuttynose and observed that a new meetinghouse would do well on Star. Under his hand the first meetinghouse, with tower and bell, was erected on the highest hill, where its successors have since stood.

The Town of Appledore was dissolved in 1682, and the Council of New Hampshire represented to King Charles II that the Shoals were "not at present under any government at all." In 1685 the northern half were presented at court "for their neglect in not maintaining a sufficient Meeting House for the worship of God," an order that was ignored with scorn, since the new meetinghouse on Star, "28 x 48 feet, with belfry and bell," was adequate for all the islands. The old building on Smuttynose fell apart and was forgotten.

In 1701 the same Council ordered James Blagdon, a Shoaler, "to settle the inhabitants, where he lives, under this government, and to call them together to appoint a Representative for said place to sit in General Assembly."

Following their tradition of independence, the Shoalers ignored the order and were served in 1711 with a warrant, and another in 1716, whereupon the Government saw fit to annex Star Island to New Castle (Rye) for election and assessment purposes, but the Islanders neither attended elections nor paid the taxes.

However in 1715 the New Hampshire Provincial Assembly elevated Star Island to the status of township and named it Gosport — a name brought over from a hamlet on the south shore of England near Portsmouth and Appledore.

Shoalers were never terrified by threats of Indian raids, and they asked for protection only when more formidable enemies seemed to threaten. Celia Thaxter's surmise that the mass migration to Star Island was from fear of Indian attacks has been shared by many writers who have not consulted the record. The first and most telling observation is that Indian threats did not come until a decade after the migration.

27

ISLES OF SHOALS

In 1691 a small army of eastern Indians came down the coast with the intention of sacking the Isles of Shoals, but were intercepted by English forces under Captain March, and their plan thwarted.

There is also an account of three deserters from Canada, who came down into our colonies in 1692 and told Governor Fletcher that two French men-of-war were fitting out at Quebec "with a design to fall on Wells, Isles of Shoals, Piscataqua etc." Again the raid was thwarted, but in this story nothing is said about Indians.

Shoalers had petitioned the government for protection in 1653 and were granted "two great guns," to be mounted at their own expense. They had thrown up a rough stone fort on the western hill of Star commanding the harbor mouth, but it had not been kept up. The stones were scattered and the guns left buried in rubble. In 1692 when a new generation of Shoalers petitioned for a corps of 40 men under competent officers to rebuild their fort, they were granted a crew of workmen under Captain Edward Willy on condition that the Islanders would provide bed and board for the men.

In the petition signed by eight responsible Shoalers it was agreed that food, shelter, and wages would be provided for 40 soldiers, but when the men arrived Captain Willy found that three absentee landlords, Andrew Diamond, Francis Wanewright and Nathaniel Baker, of Ipswich and Boston, had indignantly refused to pay any part of the cost. They were three of the wealthiest Shoalers of the time and owned a lion's share of Shoals property, including much fishing equipment, yet they curtly instructed their tenants, servants, and employees at the islands to pay nothing and do nothing toward the project.

Captain Willy, judging by his correspondence and general conduct in this affair, was as good a diplomat as soldier, and withal a fine-spirited gentleman. He kept his men at the islands a full month, laid up the rude walls of the fort — DeCosta says it was about 50 feet square — and reconditioned the two guns and charged the account to the New Hampshire Province to which Star Island belonged. The Islanders paid what they could and the Province covered the deficit. At some time, either during this reconstruction or shortly after, nine four-pounders were added to the fort, but Willy mentions none in this correspondence.

In all the history of the islands there is only one authentic

ISLES OF SHOALS

account of an Indian raid. In 1724 during Lovewell's War, the savages made up a flotilla of fifty canoes and cruised the mainland coast to the terror of all settlements. They captured twenty-two vessels — several of good size, one armed with swivel-guns — and made a foray on the Isles of Shoals, where they cut out two shallops but committed no other depredations.

The old fort on Star Island was manned by Shoalers, and the whole village must have assembled there, except for Betty Moody who hid with her small children in a tiny cave at the opposite side of the island. The long-accepted tradition is that once in the cave the smallest child would not stop crying, and the distraught mother in attempting to stifle its cries stifled its life.

7

PIRATES AND GHOSTS

THIS WAS the age of pirates bold, and buccaneers and privateers, and sea rovers generally. So it is that writers who love the roar of pirate guns and the drip of innocent blood, and the mystery of treasure buried at midnight in some lonely place, try to make out that the Shoalers too might have been pirates, or at least have given friendly nods to pirate ships. Surely these islands would have made a "bally good" rendezvous where pirates could haul down their skull and crossbones and h'ist the King's banners while lying in port, offering threats to the Shoalers if a word or sign of a word ever got to the main. Yet in spite of all this there was exceeding little piracy at the islands — a few visiting ships were suspected and an untold amount of treasure was hidden away in true Treasure Island style, but Shoalers never turned to piracy.

The King's Navy and his mainland officers kept a weather eye out for unidentified ships and offered rewards to Shoalers who would spy out pirates for them. In response one Robert Saunders, in 1724, brought intelligence of a ship haunting these waters. The General Court allowed him forty shillings "to be paid by the constable of Gosport, as he is behind in the payment of his Province rates for the year 1723." No more intelligence of this nature was advanced by Shoalers!

Jenness offers the gratuitous comment, "There is strong ground for suspicion, indeed, that the Islanders were generally indulgent, and sometimes friendly and serviceable in their intercourse with the numerous pirate ships which visited their harbor."

We remember Dr. Greenland fifty years earlier had engaged the Captain of the *Mermaiden,* then at anchor in the Shoals harbor, to kidnap John Cutt and confiscate his property. The Captain was a pirate, but not a Shoaler.

From first to last, twenty or more sea rovers are known to have cruised the Bay of Maine. Most of them were pirates, but some were loyal privateers accused of piracy. Samuel Argall and William Kidd, for example, were privateers who became a little careless about identifying their prizes. Argall was never accused of piracy,

ISLES OF SHOALS

but Kidd, though a privateer commissioned by the King, was accused of piracy and hanged.

Many of these names are familiar to later generations: Edward Teach (Blackbeard), Major Stede Bonnet, Dixie Bull, Henry Avery, William Fly, Samuel Cole, Henry Granville, Thomas Hawkins, Thomas Pound, Phillips, Low, Bradish, Scott, Bellamy and Quelch.

Low was a desperate pirate from Boston. His visit to the Shoals was long remembered because he captured three fishermen and condemned them to death, allowing them to go free only if they would jump up and down and curse the name of Reverend Cotton Mather three times. Mather was detested by all pirates because he was so fond of preaching long funeral sermons to condemned pirates as they were about to be hanged.

In behalf of Shoalers generally we should add that no Shoaler was ever seriously accused of piracy, and only one, the maligned Philip Babb, was ever mentioned as friendly to pirates. There is no evidence whatever that Old Babb had any dealings with pirates, but many of our most reliable Shoals historians have perpetuated the tradition that he was one of Captain Kidd's men. Celia Thaxter said so in 1873, Drake confirmed it in 1875, Oscar Laighton elaborated on it in 1929, and the Portsmouth *Herald* repeated it in 1950. Babb's ghost has haunted the islands for almost three centuries.

Nathaniel Hawthorne in 1852 reported: "Old Babb, the ghost, has a ring around his neck, and is supposed either to have been hung or to have had his throat cut, but he steadfastly declines telling the mode of his death. There is a luminous appearance about him as he walks, and his face is pale and very dreadful."

Drake says: "They have still the ghost of a pirate on Appledore, one of Kidd's men. There has consequently been much seeking after treasure . . . I shrewdly suspect 'Old Babb' to be in the pay of the Laightons."

There is no mistaking Celia Thaxter's vivid description:

"There is a superstition among the islanders that Philip Babb, or some evil-minded descendant of his, still haunts Appledore; and no consideration would induce the more timid to walk alone after dark over a certain shingly beach on that island, at the top of the cove bearing Babb's name — for there the uneasy spirit is oftenest seen. He is supposed to have been so desperately wicked when alive that there is no rest for him in his grave. His dress is a coarse, striped butcher's frock, with a leather belt, to which is attached a sheath

31

ISLES OF SHOALS

containing a ghostly knife, sharp and glittering, which it is his delight to brandish in the face of terrified humanity. One of the Shoalers is perfectly certain that he and Babb have met, and he shudders with real horror, recalling the meeting. This is his story. It was after sunset (of course), and he was coming around the corner of a work-shop, when he saw a wild and dreadful figure advancing toward him; his first thought was that someone wished to make him the victim of a practical joke, and he called out something to the effect that he 'wasn't afraid'; but the thing came near with a ghastly face and hollow eyes, and assuming a fiendish expression, took out the knife from its belt and flourished it in the face of the Shoaler, who fled to the house and entered breathless, calling for the person who he supposed had tried to frighten him. That person was quietly eating his supper; and when the poor fellow saw him he was so much agitated that he nearly fainted, and his belief in Babb was fixed more firmly than ever.

"One spring night some one was sitting on the broad piazza at sunset; it was calm and mild; the sea murmured a little; birds twittered softly; there was hardly a waft of wind in the still atmosphere. Glancing toward Babb's Cove, he saw a figure slowly crossing the shingle to the path which led to the house. After watching it a moment he called to it, but there was no reply; again he called, still no answer; but the dark figure came slowly on; and then he reflected that he heard no step on the loose shingle that was wont to give back every foot-fall, and, somewhat puzzled, he slowly descended the steps of the piazza and went to meet it. It was not so dark but that he could see the face and recognize the butcher's frock and belt of Babb, but he was not prepared for the devilish expression of malice in that hollow face, and, spite of his prosaic turn of mind, he was chilled to the marrow at the sight. The white stripes in the frock gleamed like phosphorescent light, so did the awful eyes. Again he called aloud, 'Who are you? What do you want?' and still advanced, when suddenly the shape grew indistinct, first thick and cloudy, then thin, dissolving quite away, and, much amazed, he turned and went back to the house, perplexed and thoroughly dissatisfied. These tales I tell as they were told to me."

Oscar Laighton crowns the story with his own fertile wit:

"Appledore House stood in the valley between the north and

ISLES OF SHOALS

south hills of the island. The valley terminates on the east in Broad Cove, on the west in Babb's Cove, named for Philip Babb, who was a leading man here before the Revolution. Babb's house was on the south hillside near his cove. When we first came to Appledore there was a large excavation at the head of the cove, where Babb had dug for treasure. There has always been a story that Captain Kidd buried money over these islands, as Sam Haley's find of the silver on Smuttynose would seem to prove. Babb made a big effort to dig up something. The pit he made was thirty feet across and ten feet deep, as I remember it. The place was filled up level in the great storm of 1851. Father told Judge Whittle that Babb at last discovered a big iron chest at the bottom of the pit, and, with his friend Ambrose Gibbon tried to lift it out, but it was too heavy, and with a hammer and a cold chisel they finally started the cover a little, when smoke, like burning sulphur, came from under the lid; that when at last they burst it open, red hot horseshoes flew out. Babb and his friend escaped, but the chest is still there. Just at dusk on pleasant evenings we would see Babb's ghost standing at the head of his cove near the pit he dug. It was very real and no Islander would venture near after nightfall. Babb's ghost persisted until the Coast Guard built their boathouse over his treasure, when it disappeared."

Now the vindictive iconoclast must insert the poison-tipped stiletto of fact. The truth is that Philip Babb died a natural death in 1671, whereas William Kidd was not commissioned as a privateer until 1696, and was executed in 1702. We conclude that it was Babb's ghost who joined Kidd's crew.

The three authentic pirates known to have visited the Shoals were Blackbeard, Scott, and Quelch. There is so much romancing about each of these that it is not always easy to see where fact dovetails into fiction. For instance, it is said that Blackbeard had fourteen wives on Ocracoke Island off the Carolina coast. It is also said that he had forty children there, and that he attempted to kidnap the daughter of the Carolina governor, Eden. We have no way of checking the number of wives and children, but Governor Eden's daughter was not born until some time after Blackbeard was captured and beheaded. Was the girl kidnapped by a ghost?

However, historians accept as true the documented story that Blackbeard took his last (was it his fifteenth?) bride to the Isles of Shoals for their honeymoon and left her on Smuttynose Island to

33

ISLES OF SHOALS

guard his treasure. That must have been around 1720 while the second meetinghouse on Star Island was under construction "from the timbers of a Spanish ship," and the Reverend Joshua Moody was presiding over the spiritual destinies of the islands. It is true that Blackbeard's honeymoon was interrupted by the appearance of a strong British fleet on the eastern horizon. Blackbeard made his escape, but left his bride and never returned. She became a lonely Shoaler and died there, according to tradition, in 1735.

During the long years since, a ghost has appeared on various islands — "fair as a lily, and as still." She is always looking toward the far horizon, never seems aware of any one nearby, and says over and over again with mournful voice, "He will come again, he will come again." Was this Blackbeard's widow, or her companion in sorrow, the widow of one Captain Scott, who was left in similar fashion to guard another cache of pirate treasure?

The story of this ghost — or these ghosts — is so beautifully told by Celia Thaxter that we must include it here as a chapter in our anthology of ghosts.

"I have before me a weird, romantic legend of these islands, in a time-stained, battered newspaper of forty years ago. I regret that it is too long to be given entire, for the unknown writer tells his story well. He came to the Shoals for the benefit of his failing health, and remained there late into the autumn of 1826, 'in the family of a worthy fisherman.' He dilates upon the pleasure he found in the loneliness of the place, 'the vast solitude of the sea; no one who has not known it can imbibe the faintest idea of it.' 'From the hour I learned the truth,' he says, 'that all which lives must die, the thought of dissolution has haunted me; — the falling of a leaf, a gray hair, or a faded cheek, has power to chill me. But here in the recesses of these eternal rocks, with only a cloudless sky above and an ocean before me, for the first time in my life have I shaken off the fear of death and believed myself immortal.'

"He tells his strange story in this way: 'It was one of those awfully still mornings which cloud-gazers will remember as characterizing the autumn months. There was not a single vapor-wreath to dim the intense blue of the sky, or a breath to ruffle the almost motionless repose of the great deep; even the sunlight fell seemingly with a stiller brightness on the surface of it.' He stood on a low, long point fronting the east, with the cliffs behind him, gazing out upon the calm, when suddenly he became aware of a figure

ISLES OF SHOALS

standing near him. It was a woman wrapped closely in a dark sea-cloak, with a profusion of light hair flowing loosely over her shoulders. Fair as a lily and as still, she stood with her eyes fixed on the far distance, without a motion, without a sound. 'Thinking her one of the inhabitants of a neighboring island who was watching for the return of a fishing-boat, or perhaps a lover, I did not immediately address her; but seeing no appearance of any vessel, at length accosted her with "Well, my pretty maiden, do you see anything of him?" She turned instantly, and fixing on me the largest and most melancholy blue eyes I ever beheld, said quietly, "He *will* come again." Then, she disappeared around a jutting rock and left him marvelling, and though he had come to the island, (which was evidently Appledore) for a forenoon's stroll, he was desirous to get back again to Star and his own quarters after this interruption. Fairly at home again, he was inclined to look upon his adventure as a dream, a mere delusion arising from his illness, but concluded to seek in his surroundings something to substantiate, or remove the idea. Finding nothing, — no woman on the island resembling the one he had met, — and 'hearing of no circumstance which might corroborate the unaccountable impression,' he resolved to go again to the same spot. This time it blew half a gale; the fishermen in vain endeavored to dissuade him. He was so intensely anxious to be assured of the truth or fiction of the impression of the day before, that he could not refrain, and launched his boat, 'which sprang strongly upon the whitened waters,' and, unfurling his one sail, he rounded a point and was soon safely sheltered in a small cove on the leeward side of the island, probably Babb's Cove.

"Then he leaped the chasms and made his way to the scene of his bewilderment. The sea was rolling over the low point; the spot where he had stood the day before, 'was a chaos of tumult yet even then I could have sworn that I heard with the same deep distinctness, the quiet words of the maiden, "He *will* come again," and then a low, remotely-ringing laughter. All the latent superstition of my nature rose up over me, overwhelming as the waves upon the rocks.' After that, day after day, when the weather would permit, he visited the desolate place, to find the golden-haired ghost, and often she stood beside him, 'silent as when I first saw her, except to say, as then, "He *will* come again," and these words came upon the mind rather than upon the ear. I was conscious of them rather than heard them, — it was all like a dream, a mysterious intuition. I

ISLES OF SHOALS

observed that the shells never crashed beneath her footsteps, nor did her garments rustle. In the bright, awful calm of noon and in the rush of the storm there was the same heavy stillness over her. When the winds were so furious that I could scarcely stand in their sweep, the light hair lay upon the forehead of the maiden without lifting a fibre. Her great blue eyeballs never moved in their sockets, and always shone with the same fixed, unearthly gleam. The motion of her person was imperceptible; I knew that she was here, and that she was gone.'

"So sweet a ghost was hardly a salutary influence in the life of our invalid. She 'held him with her glittering eye' till he grew quite beside himself. This is so good a description I cannot choose but quote it: 'The last time I stood with her was just at the evening of a tranquil day. It was a lovely sunset. A few gold-edged clouds crowned the hills of the distant continent, and the sun had gone down behind them. The ocean lay blushing beneath the blushes of the sky, and even the ancient rocks seemed smiling in the glance of the departing sky. Peace, deep peace was the pervading power. The waters, lapsing among the caverns, spoke of it, and it was visible in the silent motion of the small boats, which, loosening their white sails in the cove of Star Island, passed slowly out, one by one, to the night-fishing.' In the glow of sunset he fancied the ghost grew rosy and human. In the mellow light her cold eyes seemed to soften. But he became suddenly so overpowered with terror that 'kneeling in shuddering fearfulness,' he swore never more to look upon that spot, and never did again.

"Going back to Star he met his old fisherman, who without noticing his agitation, told him quietly that he knew where he had been and what he had seen; that he himself had seen her, and proceeded to furnish him with the following facts. At the time of the first settlement, the islands were infested by pirates, — the bold Captain Teach, called Blackbeard, being one of the most notorious. One of Teach's comrades, a Captain Scott, brought this lovely lady hither. They buried immense treasure on the islands; that of Scott was buried on an island apart from the rest. Before they departed on a voyage, 'to plunder, slash, and slay,' (in which by the way, they were involved in one awful doom by the blowing up of a powder magazine), the maiden was carried to the island where her pirate lover's treasure was hidden, and made to swear with horrible rites that until his return, if it were not till the day of judgment,

36

ISLES OF SHOALS

she would guard it from the search of all mortals. So there she paces still, according to our story-teller. Would I had met this lily-fair ghost! Is it she, I wonder, who laments like a Banshee before the tempests, wailing through the gorges at Appledore, 'He will *not* come again'? Perhaps it was she who frightened a merry party of people at Duck Island, whither they had betaken themselves for a day's pleasure a few summers ago. In the centre of the low island stood a deserted shanty which some strange fishermen had built there several years before, and left empty, tenanted only by the mournful winds. It was blown down the September following. It was a rude hut with two rough rooms and one square window, or rather opening for a window, for sash or glass there was none. One of our party proposed going to look after the boats, as the breeze freshened and blew directly upon the cove where we had landed. We were gathered on the eastern end of the island when he returned, and, kneeling on the withered grass where we were grouped, he said suddenly, 'Do you know what I have seen? Coming back from the boats, I faced the fish-house, and as I neared it I saw some one watching me from the window. Of course I thought it was one of you, but when I was near enough to have recognized it, I perceived it to be the strange countenance of a woman, wan as death; a face young, yet with a look in it of infinite age. Old! it was older than the Sphinx in the desert! It looked as if it had been watching and waiting for me since the beginning of time. I walked straight into the hut. There wasn't a vestige of a human being there; it was absolutely empty.' All the warmth and brightness of the summer day could hardly prevent a chill from creeping into our veins as we listened to this calmly delivered statement, and we actually sent a boat back to Appledore for a large yacht to take us home, for the wind rose fast and 'gurly grew the sea,' and we half expected the wan woman would come and carry our companion off bodily before our eyes."

Captain Quelch, our third authentic pirate, seems not to have been so colorful a person. He left no widow, but in 1950 *Life Magazine* carried a brief note that in 1702 Captain Quelch is known to have buried $100,000 at the Isles of Shoals, half of which has never been recovered. Mr. F. L. Coffman in his recent book *1001 Lost, Buried or Sunken Treasures* says that the Isles of Shoals are famous for treasure hidden by such notorious pirates as Kidd, Teach, Quelch, Bonnet, Davis, and others. He says Quelch buried

ISLES OF SHOALS

loot in several places on White Island, and $275,000 on Star. He quotes no authority.

Captain John Quelch was a privateer commissioned from Boston to sail with Captain Plowman of the brig *Charles* in pursuit of pirates who were devastating the shipping along the Atlantic seaboard. Plowman soon died, leaving young Quelch in command. The crew was made up largely of hardened seamen who persuaded Quelch that piracy was more profitable than privateering. They followed a pattern closely parallel to that of Captain Kidd, except that when captured, the whole crew — twenty men — were sentenced to die. Six, including Quelch, were hanged on the Boston side of the Charles River on June 30th, 1704. The record does not show what happened to the other fourteen, or to the treasure hidden at the Isles of Shoals.

8

THE CHURCH AND THE GOSPEL

WHEN the brick church was built on Smuttynose Island is not known. It was there in 1640, and we surmise that it was erected by the Islanders to entice clergymen to come out and conduct services. The first of these was the Reverend William Tompson, who came from England and was settled at Accominticus (York) for two years. His pastoral duties included occasional services at the Shoals.

Reverend Joseph Hull followed Tompson. Hull was a man of exceptional ability who came with his family to the Bay Colony and settled at Wissagusset (Weymouth). There he gathered a church and served as pastor until his liberal views were known. He hoped to bridge the gap between Anglicans and Puritans, but was dismissed by the congregation he had gathered and after some wandering went to the Isles of Shoals, where he served around the year 1640. In 1643 he accepted a call to York, but he had become so much attached to the islands that he went back often to conduct services. About 1650 he was granted a living at St. Burian in Cornwall ,where he stayed about twelve years. He came back to the old friends at Oyster River (Dover, N.H.) and the Isles of Shoals, where he died in 1665, leaving an estate of £52, 5s. 5d., which included a claim against the Shoals for £20 for pastoral services.

In 1640-42 the Reverend Robert Jordan of Richmond's Island officiated at the Shoals, evidently sharing the pulpit with Mr. Hull.

The Reverend Richard Gibson was the last Anglican assigned to the Shoals. The Massachusetts Historical Collection says of him:

"Indeed, the parson himself, who resided at the Islands during 1641-1642, was a married man, and, we may presume, carried out his wife in his company. Mr. Gibson had, about 1637, while settled at Richmond's Island, married Mary, daughter of Mr. Thomas Lewis, of Saco, and his life with her seems not to have been one of unruffled confidence and repose. In January 1638, he wrote to Gov. Winthrop, in a distracted state of mind how that 'some troublous spirits, out of misaffection, and others, as is supposed for hire, have cast an aspersion upon her, and generally that she so behaved

ISLES OF SHOALS

herself in the shipp, which brought her from England hither some two years agoe, that the block was reaved at the mayne yard to have duckt her, and that she was kept close in the ship's cabin 48 hours for shelter and rescue,' and he therefore prays the Governor to take the testimony of several passengers in Boston, who came over in the ship with his Mary, and 'give a testimony of these Exacons.' "

This appeal to Winthrop was in vain, as he might have known it would be. He went to Boston intending to sail for England but was arraigned by the magistrate. Winthrop wrote in his journal that "he, being wholly addicted to the hierarchy and discipline of England, did exercise a ministerial function in the same way, and did marry and baptize at the Isles of Shoals which was now found to be within our jurisdiction." We hear no more about Mr. Gibson.

What the Shoalers did with their new brick church for eight long years following Mr. Gibson's unhappy departure in 1642 is not found in the records. We know only that in 1650 the Massachusetts authorities sent the Reverend John Brock, first of a long line of Congregationalists, to settle among them. Here was a difficult assignment, but the new minister was well chosen, and soon won the respect, admiration, and devotion of the fishermen. Many stories about him have become traditional in Island lore. Cotton Mather in his *Magnalia,* said of him:

"He dwelt as near heaven as any man on earth. I scarce ever knew any man so familiar with the great God, as his dear servant Brock."

To illustrate and demonstrate his power of prayer, Dr. Mather relates the following incidents:

"A child of one Arnold, about six years old, lay sick, so near dead, that they judg'd it really dead. Mr. Brock, perceiving some life in it, goes to prayer; and in his prayer used this expression: 'Lord, wilt thou not grant some sign, before we leave prayer, that thou wilt spare and heal this child? We cannot leave thee till we have it!' The child sneez'd immediately."

At another time Mr. Mather relates, Mr. Brock "brought the people into an agreement that, besides the Lord's day, they would spend one day every month together in the worship of our Lord Jesus Christ. On a certain day, which by their agreement belong'd unto the exercises of religion, being arrived, the fishermen came to Mr. Brock, and asked him that they might put by their meeting

ISLES OF SHOALS

and go a fishing, because they had lost many days by the foulness of the weather. He, seeing that without and against his consent they resolved upon doing what they asked of him, replied, 'If you will go away, I say unto you, catch fish if you can! But as for you that will tarry, and worship the Lord Jesus Christ this day, I will pray unto Him for you, that you may take fish till you are weary.' Thirty men went away from the meeting, and Five tarried .... the thirty which went away from the meeting, with all their skill, could catch but *four* fishes; the five which tarried, went forth afterwards, and they took five hundred. The fishermen after this readily attended whatever meetings Mr. Brock appointed them."

And again: "A fisherman, who had with his boat been very helpful to carry people over a river for the worship of God, on the Lord's days in the Isle of Sholes, lost his boat in a storm. The poor man laments his loss to Mr. Brock; who tells him, 'Go home, honest man; I'll mention the matter to the Lord; you'll have your boat again to-morrow.' Mr. Brock now considering of what a consequence this matter, that seem'd so small otherwise, might be among the untractable fishermen, made the boat an article of his prayers; and, behold, on the morrow, the poor man comes rejoicing to him, that his boat was found, the anchor of another vessel, that was undesignedly cast upon it, having strangely brought it up from the unknown bottom where it had been sunk."

With stories of this kind going about, it is understandable that while Mr. Hull's friends remained loyal and devoted to him, they cherished an equal if not greater affection for Mr. Brock. From this time on the Congregational ministers were welcomed to the islands.

Reverend Mr. Belcher, who followed Mr. Brock, spent thirty years in the Shoals pulpit, retired in 1692, and died in Newbury, Massachusetts, in 1716 at the age of seventy-four. He was followed by the Reverend Samuel Moody, who was settled at New Castle from 1694 to 1703 and rendered pastoral services at the Shoals during that period.

In 1702 Reverend Samuel Eburne took the Shoals pulpit for two or three summers. In 1705 the Massachusetts General Assembly granted 14 pounds and the New Hampshire Assembly 6 pounds toward the support of the Reverend Daniel Greenleafe for one year. Then came the Reverend Joshua Moody (1707-1730) (no relation to Samuel his predecessor) who seems not to have had the fine sense

ISLES OF SHOALS

of appropriateness which had distinguished John Brock. Cotton Mather described him as "a man of parts and a pathetic and useful preacher."

Reverend Jedediah Morse preserves an anecdote in sharp contrast to the stories about Mr. Brock. He says:

"During the ministry of Mr. Moody at the Shoals, one of the fishing shallops, with all hands aboard, was lost in a North East storm in Ipswitch Bay. Mr. Moody, anxious to improve this melancholy event, for the awakening of those of his hearers who were exposed to the like disaster, addressed them in the following language, adapted to their occupation and understanding. 'Supposing, my brethren, that any of you should be taken short in the bay, in a N. E. storm, your hearts trembling with fear, and nothing but death before you, whither would your thoughts turn? what would you do?' 'What would I do?' replied one of these hardy sons of Neptune, 'Why I should immediately hoist the foresail and scud away for Squam!' "

9

ERA OF JOHN TUCKE

DURING the last years of Parson Moody's pastorate, conditions reached a low ebb. Observing this, a young minister, Reverend John Tucke, born at Hampton, New Hampshire (August 23, 1702), declined a larger parish with higher salary to accept a call to Gosport. He must have gone to the islands in the summer of 1731, and inspired the town fathers for the first time in Shoals history to keep records.

In these records we find that on December 11th, 1731, it was voted "to give and allow the Reverend Mr. Tooke annually for his support and maintenance one hundred and ten pounds money or bills of Credit, so long as it shall please God to continue him among us in the work of the ministry." Another vote granted him 50 pounds by the last of May next to build him a house on a plot of ground of his own choosing.

There was no immediate reply to this call and we learn later that the delay was occasioned by the death of Mr. Tucke's infant son. On April 28th, 1732, the call was accepted and he was ordained in the historic meetinghouse on the hill on July twenty-sixth of that year.

The new minister began at once a lifelong campaign to lift the community to a higher level. His first move was to have the Islanders hold regular town meetings, keep records, and observe a few proprieties.

In 1852 Nathaniel Hawthorne while visiting the Shoals found the church book in Parson Tucke's handwriting and copied what seemed to him the more significant entries into his *American Note-Books*. He comments:

"No entries are so numerous as those like the following:

"'At a church meeting, 28th of April, 1733. This day the Brethren of the church met at the house of the Pastor, as they did at the foregoing church meet'g, 31 March, 1733, and Mr. Samuel Emery appeared before the church, and acknowledged his fault in drinking to excess; whereupon the church voted his restoration to communion, and that his confession should be read publicly tomor-

43

ISLES OF SHOALS

row, just before the sacrament of the Lord's supper is administered, and absolution from all church-censure pronounced.'

" 'March 4th, 1753. Upon my mentioning of ye Great Outward Straits that ye widow Anna Muchemore, a member of ye church, is at present under, ye church voted that Eight pounds of ye money in ye church-stock be given to her.'

" 'Aug. 9, 1747. Joseph, Son of Joseph White and Abigail his wife, was baptized.' [Murdered more than four score years afterwards in Salem.]

" 'Sept. 25, 1774. Jacob ye son of Amos Caswell and Rebecca his wife, was baptized.' This is the last baptism on record; the whole number, between Aug. 6, 1732 and the above date, 704 — whereof ten were adult."

The Gosport Town Records were meticulously copied by Dr. Joseph W. Warren of Bryn Mawr, Pennsylvania, and printed in the *New England Historical and Genealogical* Register during the years 1913-1914. He notes that the last entry was inserted some time after the event. This doubtless accounts for the error in date of Parson Tucke's death, which should have been early in September, not August twelfth.

Mary Dole Tucke died on May 24, 1773, a few weeks before her husband. Their life at the islands would have been rugged at best, but it was saddened by the early death of their children, as noted by Clifford K. Shipton in his biography of John Tucke for his *Biographical Sketches of those who attended Harvard College, 1722-1725.* He says that "only two or three of his eleven children survived him."

Following the ministry of John Tucke the Gosport pulpit was filled by the Reverend Jeremiah Shaw, who was called by the town on January 24, 1774. "It was also voted to give Mr. Shaw seven pounds lawfull money per month the full Term of Eight months." He completed this mission, but failing health and the impending hostilities compelled him to retire.

The tragic era of John Tucke closed in the twilight of the fishing village. Fort Star was dismantled and the nine four-pounders taken to Newburyport where they still are. The population of the islands was reduced from 284 to 44 or less.

In the early years of the Revolution all Shoalers were ordered to leave the islands, partly for their own protection, partly because each party to the conflict was afraid Shoalers might give aid and

ISLES OF SHOALS

comfort to the other. It is remembered that John Wentworth, last royal governor of New Hampshire, exiled from home and office, fled to the Isles of Shoals where he prorogued his assembly (September 1775) and sailed for England never to return.

Many families from the Shoals went to Ipswich and Newburyport in Massachusetts and York in Maine. Four took their houses apart, floated them as rafts, and assembled them in York. One was the parsonage, built by John Tucke, and after his death occupied by a son-in-law, Mark Walton. Three of the houses thus transported are still standing and inhabited, one by descendants of the original owners. This migration was between 1778 and 1780.

An episode long remembered was the fate of Mrs. Pusley's cows. Widow Pusley lived on Smuttynose Island and kept two cows. In summer when the grass was high she would cut half a ton of hay with a *knife* and store it for winter. The British officers butchered the cows for their own use and gave the widow fair compensation but could not heal her broken heart. When hostilities were over she returned to Smuttynose and died there about 1795, aged 90.

After the war Shoalers began to wander back to the remnants of their deserted homes, but the fishing industry was not to be renewed. Only a few small boats nosed the stages where dunfish had been proudly made. The doors of the meetinghouse swung on rusty hinges, and the voice of preaching was seldom heard. In 1790 the meeting house was burned and no hand was lifted to restore its walls. A later minister said it had been wantonly destroyed by drunken sailors, but a more authentic account is given by a correspondent who signs himself M.F.B. After visiting the islands, he wrote:

"But there is one thing I hope I will not see if I ever go again. Over the door is a sign, 'First built in 1680 (second church in 1720) burned by the Islanders.' I think this is a mistake, as my mother who was born there about a hundred years ago, told me a quarterly meeting was held there and some coming from the mainland went down to the old parsonage house for dinner. The church took fire from an overheated stove, and I think this is correct."

45

10

THE HALEY DYNASTY

SAMUEL HALEY, known to the Islanders and to history as Captain Haley, arrived at Smuttynose shortly before the Revolution and set about to restore the great tradition so well established by the Seeley brothers a century earlier. The islands had been washed clean of their work, but their names and achievements were well recorded in the lore of the Shoals.

Whether Captain Haley returned to the main during the war years we do not know, but shortly after the Stars and Stripes had replaced the cross of St. George, Islanders who drifted back found him shifting the center of gravity from Star to Smuttynose. He began by throwing a loose stone sea-wall across the narrow gut to Malaga, greatly improving his boat landing. Before many seasons he had imported upper and nether stones for a grist mill, lined out a ropewalk 270 feet long, set up a windmill, salt-works, bakery, brewery, distillery, blacksmith's shop, and cooper's shop, and planted a cherry orchard. This was the most successful venture with trees in Shoals history, but not a sprouting twig is left to mark the grounds.

While gathering stones for his sea-wall, Captain Haley uncovered four bars of pirate silver and used the proceeds, about $4,000, to lay up a landing pier for his snug little harbor. Both are still throwing back the proud waves and have been praised for a century and a half as forming the best harbor among the islands for small boats. Unfortunately the harbor is navigable at high tide only.

Captain Haley soon became the leading figure at the Shoals and was long known as "King of the Islands." He had two sons who shared his labors and inherited both his reputation and his island home. They and their families were the sole inhabitants of Smuttynose when Dudley A. Tyng came out at the turn of the century to restore Star Island.

Celia Thaxter gives an account of her residence on Haley's Island in the years 1841-43. She says: "The old square house which he built upon his island, and which still stands, had, long ago, a

46

ISLES OF SHOALS

broad balcony running the whole length of the house beneath the second-story windows. This being in a ruinous condition, I never dared venture out upon it; but a large, square lookout, with a stout railing, which he built on the top of the house, remained till within a few years; and I found it a charming place to linger in on still days, and watch the sky and the sea and the vessels, and the play of color over the bright face of the world."

It was from an upper window of this house that Captain Haley sent a candle beam out to guide ships "in distress of weather," a half century before the lighthouse was built on White Island. This was the candle made famous by the narration in the Gosport Town Records, dated January 14, 1813 — a record which has given historians much difficulty since: "Ship Sagunto Strand'd on Smotinose Isle Jany 14th 1813 Jany 15th one man found; 16th Jany 6 men found, 21 — 7 the Number of men yet found Belonging to said Ship twelve."

Based on this seemingly official entry writers from that day to this have said it was the *Sagunto* that came to grief on the north coast of Smuttynose that stormy night. But Samuel Adams Drake, writing in 1873, said that he had seen a news item to the effect that the *Sagunto* was safe in harbor at Newport on that fateful night. Again in 1913, Dr. Joseph W. Warren added a footnote to the Gosport Town Records, giving a bit of information which should be noted by all writers:

"In a petition of 12 Jan. 1818 to the General Court of Massachusetts, Samuel Haley, the son of the first Samuel, whose death is recorded above, gives a different story of this wreck. The vessel was a Spanish ship, which he calls the '*Conception* from Cadiz.' The captain was 'don Juan Coxara' (?). One man was found 15 Jan.; 6 men on 17 Jan.; 21 Jan. 5 more were found, one of them 'grap pled up in Hog Is. passage'; 27 Jan. 1 man 'grappled up in Hog Is. passage'; 8 Aug. 'picked up 1 man.' The wreck occurred at night in a violent snow storm. Nothing was known of it until the next day, and all were lost. According to the Boston *Gazette,* 18 Jan. 1813, it was a vessel of from 300 to 400 tons. A later account says that she was old and rotten but built of mahogany and cedar, and supposed to be laden with salt. She went entirely to pieces in a very short time. The first fragments came ashore Thursday morning, 14 Jan. There really was a Spanish ship *Sagunto* which arrived at Newport from Cadiz a couple of days before the wreck at Smutty-

ISLES OF SHOALS

nose. No explanation of this confusion of names has been given. Both accounts agree that the number of men found was fourteen. These bodies were buried on Smuttynose. The graves are still barely discernible and are marked by small stones."

Celia Thaxter was deeply moved by the story of this wreck. She was only six years old when her family moved over from White Island in 1841, so the sad fate of the nameless Spanish sailors was deep in her childhood memories. Many years later she wrote the poem so often quoted which closes with the lines:

Dear dark-eyed sisters, you remember yet
Those you have lost, but you can never know
One stands at their bleak graves whose eyes are wet
With thinking of your woe!

Again in her chief prose work, *Among the Isles of Shoals,* Celia gives her own version of the story with such beauty of expression and depth of feeling that it is akin to sacrilege to question any part of it. However, she is puzzled by a seeming contradiction more easily resolved than she thought. She says: "There is much uncertainty with regard to dates and records of those old times. Mr. Haley is said to have died in 1811, but I have always heard that he was living when the Sagunto was wrecked upon his island." The answer, is of course, that she and many others failed often to distinguish between senior and junior. The second Samuel Haley inherited his father's name, property, and tradition, and was known as Captain Haley until his death in 1839. He had kept the candle burning in the upper window, and was first to discover the wreck. Little wonder the Shoalers of that era lost the name of Smuttynose and called it Haley's Island — a name still in frequent use.

In 1816 Captain Haley took title to Hog Island under a grant from Massachusetts. Following is a transcript:

"On petition of Samuel Haley of the Isles of Shoals praying for a grant of land of said Island called 'Hog Island'

"Resolved that there be and hereby is granted to said Samuel Haley and his heirs, the northerly island of said Isles of Shoals, commonly called Hog Island; to be holden in fee simple by the said Haley and his heirs free from any claim of the Commonwealth to the same. *Provided* that the said Haley his heirs or assigns shall within four years after the passing of this resolve erect a sufficient sea-wall around the dock where the said Haley now

48

ISLES OF SHOALS

lives; and shall at all times hereafter keep the same in repair for the accommodation of open fishing boats, belonging to the citizens of this Commonwealth free from expense of dockage.

"And if said Haley or his heirs or assigns shall neglect to keep in sufficient repair said dock for the space of two years at one time, then said island so granted as aforesaid, and the title to the same shall revert to said Commonwealth, on such neglect being ascertained by process in the Supreme Judicial Court."

This grant, it will be noted, was made only four years before the Province of Maine was removed from Massachusetts jurisdiction and admitted to the Union as a state. At that time (1820), as previously noted, the boundary line through Gosport Harbor was reaffirmed and so remains.

Captain Haley seems not to have developed Hog Island, but in 1828 sold it to Benjamin Haley for $200.

In March and April of 1839, Thomas B. Laighton and his brother-in-law, Joseph Cheever, came into possession of the four habitable islands north of the boundary line. These are the transactions which crossed the twilight zone between the Haley dynasty and the Laighton era.

Still standing in the little family cemetery on Smuttynose is the stone bearing the inscription which is as appropriate for Samuel Junior as for his illustrious father.

In memory of Mr. Samuel Haley
Who died in the year 1811
Aged 84
He was a man of great Ingenuity
Industry, Honor and Honesty, true to his
Country & A man who did A great
Publik good in Building A
Dock & Receiving into his
Enclosure many a poor
Distressed Seaman & Fisherman
In distress of Weather

11

BUILDING THE STONE MEETINGHOUSE

M R. DUDLEY A. TYNG went out to the islands on September 3rd, 1799, and found that Reverend Jacob Emerson, who had been sent by the *Society for Propagating the Gospel Among the Indians and Others in North America* to investigate, had arrived the same day. They were well received and made a favorable report to the S.P.G.

The following summer Dr. Jedediah Morse went to the islands, laden with a small reading library of religious books, and spent five days among the villagers. He found on Smuttynose three families — all Haleys; Samuel Sr., his two sons Samuel Jr. and John, and their children, 20 in all. On Star were fifteen families, 92 in all, making a total of 112. Morse returned to the mainland (August 10) and began at once to call upon the clergy of Portsmouth, Exeter, and Newburyport, to help restore the islands, suggesting that a new church be erected to replace the frame building destroyed by fire in 1790.

On October twentieth, the schooner *Lucy* sailed with fourteen carpenters and materials. Mr. Tyng also went, and later wrote:

"On Wednesday the 29th we all returned to Newburyport having completed the Meetinghouse and repaired several Dwelling houses inhabited by the poorest of the people. I distributed some articles of Clothing and Bedding amongst them and some wood. About three cords of wood I stored for the use of the school this winter. Having accidentally discovered the Rev. Mr. Tucke's grave, I caused a decent Monument of stone laid in Mortar to be erected over it and intend to send a Top Stone with a suitable inscription.

"On Friday the 14th Dr. Morse took Mr. John Low to the Islands and introduced him as their new minister. Together they dedicated the new meetinghouse, Dr. Morse delivering the sermon, and returned home."

By January of 1801, Mr. Low's health gave out, and in the spring Reverend Josiah Stevens took his place. Romance was in the air, as it is written in the Gosport Town Records:

ISLES OF SHOALS

"Gosport, May 27, 1801. This day Mr. Josiah Stevens was married to Miss Susanna Haley of the Isles of Shoals, having been published as the law directs so far as the situation of things here admit, by William Pidgin V.D.M."

Mr. Stevens had gone to live with the Haleys on Smuttynose early that spring and must have fallen in love with the place. Susanna was the daughter of Samuel Haley Sr. This was too much for the Star Islanders, who lost no time in building a parsonage on the bleaching foundations abandoned by the Tucke descendants. The new parsonage was destroyed by fire in 1905.

The happy home was soon broken by the death of Mr. Stevens, and his beloved wife soon followed him. They lie buried a few yards south of the Tucke monument. Their inscriptions read:

In Memory of
The Rev. Josiah Stephens
A faithful Instructor of Youth, and pious
Minister of Jesus Christ.
Supported on this Island by the
Society for Propagating the Gospel,
who died July 2, 1804
Age 64 years.

Likewise of
Mrs. Susanna Stephens
his beloved Wife
who died Dec. 7, 1810
Aged 54 years.

For twenty long and dreary years after the death of Mr. Stevens the Village of Gosport was without a settled minister and welcomed only four missionaries, each of whom tarried only one halcyon summer. They were Reverend Daniel Lovejoy (1806), Reverend Enoch Whipple (1807), Reverend John Dutton (1817), and Reverend Reuben Moody (1822).

Reverend Mr. Moody stayed only a few months, and seems to have been rather cynical. He kept a journal in which were found many comments too personal too quote. Reverend T. B. Fox of Newburyport copied out the following:

"April 1. Mr. —— came into my room and asked when I intended to open my school? I answered, I could not before I had

ISLES OF SHOALS

wood; and that I was not authorized to purchase any; but if the people were willing to purchase it, and find me a room, I was ready to commence it any day. After about three hours he sent a message to me, to come and view a room. I found he had provided wood and seats in a small but convenient room. He said, 'This is all I can do; here is the key and you may open your school as soon as you please'. He afterwards gave me his reason for it: *that his children made such a disturbance at home, he could not sleep in the day time.* . . . My school presents a singular appearance in the morning. As soon as they see me with my brand of fire and key, they all leave their plays and run; and when I am building the fire they flock around me and squat down on the hearth like *pappooses.* Some with their books, some with their Indian bread, and some with none."

Mr. Moody tells also of an old man who lived alone and drank forty gallons of rum in twelve months. "The person with whom I board" he writes, "informs me that since I have been here, he has drawn out two barrels of rum; and he has but two hired men, his wife, and a child thirteen months old, who with himself compose his family. Since the first of April, his brother has drawn out seven barrels of rum. Admitting the other persons, four in number, who sell rum, to have retailed as much, in less than three months more than six hundred gallons of rum have been drunk here. The Island contains 65 inhabitants; of these 24 are under the age of twelve, 10 are females, who have not drank a gallon since I have been here; subtracting these, there remain 31; to these add 16 hired men, making 47 men, whose average allowance has been 12 gallons and 3 quarts to a person . . . " Mr. Moody gave up.

The Reverend Samuel Sewall came next and stayed two years, 1824-1826. We have no other word in regard to him. From this date to 1830 there was no minister. In 1834 three young theological students from Andover Seminary spent a few days on the islands with telling effect. They wrote in the *Town Records:*

"Gosport, Aug. 18, 1834. At the solicitation of some benevolent individuals of Newburyport, S. Pratt, C. F. Muzzy and P. S. Cleland, members of the Theo. Seminary, Andover came to this Island on the 15th inst. to spend a short time in visiting and preaching to the inhabitants. We were very cordially received and entertained."

ISLES OF SHOALS

In the meantime the *Society for Promoting Religious Instruction at the Isles of Shoals,* was organized in Newburyport, and in 1824, the Vice Pres., Reverend F. L. Dimmick, reported that Miss Hannah Peabody had been engaged to teach domestic arts, beginning September 30, 1823. She had opened her school at Star Island on October third with twenty pupils. He said: "As soon as Miss Peabody had commenced the school seven of the poorer female children were taken to lodge in the Parsonage House . . . . This measure was adopted to preserve them, as much as possible, from the influence of an evil example, which they were almost continually compelled to witness in their parents."

At the close of the year Miss Peabody reported that her pupils had made:

138 yards of cloth, of different kinds
416 skeins of yarn
33 skeins of twine
118 yards of netting, mostly fish nets
10 or 12 hats.

Mr. Dimmick announced that Mr. J. Ely had been engaged by the people of Newburyport as a permanent teacher, wages $200.00, and the Reverend Samuel Sewall as minister at $300.00. Mrs. Sewall or a daughter would teach in the school. While this report was being read in Newburyport the interior of the stone meetinghouse at Star Island was being gutted by fire.

The seventh annual report (1828) says the Islanders were anxious to have their building restored, and with aid from the outside had almost completed the work. This invites us back to *Gosport Town Records,* where we find a long entry:

"The Society at Newburyport visited the Islands in September, 1830, and dedicated the new meetinghouse. The Rev. Leonard Withington preached the dedication sermon from Genesis 28:17, 'How dreadful is this place! This is none other but the house of God, and this is the gate of Heaven!'

"The Society then invited Clementina B. Peirce of Portsmouth to instruct the school on Star Island, under their patronage. She had previously engaged to keep the school 3 months for Miss Peabody, who had been employed by the Portsmouth Society.

"She accepted their invitation, and instructed the school for

ISLES OF SHOALS

them 9 months. She left her charge the middle of Oct. 1831 on account of her health, and returned to Portsmouth."

Following the visit of the three young missionaries, the Reverend Origin Smith was sent to Gosport in 1835 (the year Celia Thaxter was born). After two years he accepted a call, brought over his wife and children, and settled down for a pastorate of ten years more. The "preaching mission" followed by his strong leadership transformed the village. In his report of 1840 to the Reverend Dr. Parkman, then a leading figure of the S.P.G., he says:

"The people of my charge seem to be willing to do what they can for my support, yet they are able to do but little. For the past year they have raised forty dollars for my salary, and about ten dollars to procure fuel for the School and Sabbath . . . .

"The cause of temperance is slowly advancing. About forty belong to the Temperance Society, which excludes all intoxicating liquors. The person who sold spirits the past year, has abandoned the sale, joined our Society, delivered an excellent address to the people, and pledged his future influence on the side of temperance. There is one man here who keeps spirits to sell to strangers and water parties; but he does not sell to the inhabitants on the Islands. There are four or five drunkards on all the Islands, and four who call themselves moderate drinkers. There are five men and five women who never attend public worship — three of the men, however, will frequently come and sit on the steps of the meetinghouse and listen to what is said; but we cannot prevail upon them to enter the sanctuary."

Mr. Smith was supported chiefly by the S.P.G., which had engaged the Reverend Andrew P. Peabody, minister of the Unitarian church in Portsmouth, to supervise their work at the Shoals. Dr. Peabody took a personal interest in the work and solicited funds from his own parish to help support Mr. Smith. He was assisted in his pastoral duties for four months in 1842 by Edwin Ritson, who was not ordained. In the spring of 1844 the Reverend Abner Hall gave him another respite, and later the same year the Reverend Mr. Plumer was invited to assume the duties of the pastorate. In 1847 Mr. Smith felt obliged to resign because of failing health.

12

ISLAND CULTURE

THE manners, customs, habits, dialect, and general culture pattern of these Islanders need study and evaluation. Unfortunately the source material is too fragmentary and scattered for any consistent review, but it opens tantalizing glimpses of a unique culture in the making. Modern psychology is much interested in a state of uninhibited freedom. The Islanders were never completely free nor uninhibited, but were so long in possession of their own little kingdom, with a minimum of outside influence or molestation, that they came near developing a unique culture.

Island dialect grew slowly and never reached any kind of maturity. Nevertheless we can see it in process. There is little written record of island speech, other than appears in various petitions, until the beginning of the *Gosport Town Records* in 1731. In these pages we find the extreme contrast of paragraphs written by educated, competent hands and those by uneducated, almost illiterate fishermen. These latter would reveal the process of falling into a local dialect. They would spell phonetically, thus giving some hint as to unusual pronunciation. English ancestry might be reflected in "clark" for "clerk" and the tendency toward long *i* in many words. A conspicuous example is "paist" for passed — "a voote was paist" occurs frequently.

Try reading the following phonetically, and see if a charming dialect does not emerge.

"If any person that have any hogs if they doe any damg from they do the damg to shall keep the hog for sattesfaxn."

"By a legol Ton meating of the freeholders and inhabetents of the ton of gosport Duly quallified to vot. Gospored Apirel 13, 1785."

"This is a Leagel vote by the town mating that if any presson or pressons shall leave their Cowks out after the fivftenth day of may and they do any Dameg they shall be taken up and the oner of the kow shall pay teen shillings old tener to the kow Constable

ISLES OF SHOALS

and one half he shall have and tother shall give to the pour of the place."

"A general free vot paist amongt the inhabetents of gosport fer ye Rev'd mr John Tuck sallery to payd in weanter fish Each man one Quen'll."

A few words used repeatedly with the same spelling would indicate general use of that form, suggesting an appropriate pronunciation. For example:

"counstable" for "constable"
"saillary" or "sairley" for "salary"
"weanter" for "winter"
"tiding mean" for "tithing men"
"paist" for "passed"
"cus" for "choose"
"ton offorsures" for "town officers"
"voot" for "vote"
"merchenable" for "merchantable"
"pressen" for "person"
"laist" for "last"
"taik" for "take"
"salarly for histing flig" for "salary for hoisting flag"
"pettishon to bill pear" for "petition to build pier"

Celia Thaxter, writing a century later (1873), devotes a few paragraphs to the Shoaler's dialect of her time.

"The local pronunciation of the Shoalers is very peculiar, and a shrewd sense of humor is one of their leading characteristics. Could De Quincy have lived among them, I think he might have been tempted to write an essay on swearing as a fine art, for it has reached a pitch hardly short of sublimity in this favored spot. They seemed to have a genius for it, and some of them really devoted their best powers to its cultivation. The language was taxed to furnish them with prodigious forms of speech wherewith to express the slightest emotion of pain, anger or amusement; and though the blood of the listener was sometimes chilled in his veins, overhearing their unhesitating profanity, the prevailing sentiment was likely to be one of amazement mingled with intense amusement, — the whole thing was so grotesque and monstrous, and their choice of words so comical, and generally so very much to the point.

ISLES OF SHOALS

"The real Shoals phraseology existing in past years was something not to be described; it is impossible by any process known to science to convey an idea of the intonations of their speech, quite different from Yankee drawl or sailor-talk, and perfectly unique in itself. Why they should have called a swallow a 'swallick' and a sparrow a 'sparrick' I never could understand; or what they mean by calling a great gale or tempest a 'Tan toaster.' Anything that ends in *y* or *e* they still pronounce *ay* with great breadth; for instance, 'Benny' is Bennaye; 'Billy' Billay, and so on. A man by the name of 'Beebe, the modern missionary,' was always spoken of as Beebay, when he was not called by a less respectful title. Their sense of fun showed itself in the nicknames with which they designated any person possessing the slightest peculiarity. For instance, twenty years ago a minister of the Methodist persuasion came to live among them; his wife was unreasonbly tall and thin. With the utmost promptitude and decision the irreverent christened her 'Legs' and never spoke of her by any other name. 'Laigs has gone to Portsmouth,' or 'Laigs has got a new gown,' etc. . .

"Grandparents are addressed as 'Grans' and 'Gwammay' ".

The folkways of the Islanders can hardly be appreciated without living at the Shoals through the four seasons. Summers are more delightful and exhilarating than Florida or California, but winters are difficult. The temperature is not so cold as on mainland, but the treeless terrain offers no protection from the howling winds. The population was driven indoors many weeks in winter.

Houses were very similar in size and design, usually about 15 x 30 feet on the foundation, with two rooms divided by a small entry and stairway on the first floor and two corresponding rooms above. In the early days, until the Franklin stove came into use, the only heat was from small fireplaces. Sometimes a large family would have an entire house with four rooms — rarely more. Sometimes a family would live in one room. It grew to be a universal practice to seal up the windows and doors as tight as possible for the winter. Celia offers a description of the stifling results:

"It would seem strange that, while they live in so healthy a place, where the atmosphere is absolutely perfect in its purity, they should have suffered so much from ill health, and that so many should have died of consumption — the very disease for the cure of which physicians send invalids hither. The reasons are soon

ISLES OF SHOALS

told. The first and most important is this; that, as nearly as they could, they have in past years hermetically sealed their houses, so that the air of heaven should not penetrate within. An open window, especially at night, they would have looked upon as madness, — a temptation of Providence; and during the winter they have deliberately poisoned themselves with every breath, like two thirds of the rest of the world. I have seen a little room containing a whole family, fishing-boots and all, bed, furniture, cooking-stove in full blast, and an oil lamp with a wick so high that the deadly smoke rose steadily, filling the air with what Browning might call 'filthiest gloom,' and mingling with the incense of ancient tobacco-pipes smoked by both sexes (for nearly all the old women used to smoke); every crack and cranny was stopped . . . Shut in that deadly air, a part of the family slept, sometimes all."

It is unfortunate that we have so little sampling of the better sort. We would like to know how the more intelligent Islanders lived. Being less spectacular, it was not so well recorded. We have seen enough, however, to show that life at the Shoals was most unusual in some respects!

PART II

THE LAIGHTON SAGA

1

THE ADVENT OF THOMAS B. LAIGHTON

THE LAIGHTON saga begins with the rediscovery of the islands by Thomas B. Laighton, who came to the throne vacated by the Haleys and in due course became "King of the Islands" in his own right. Thomas belonged to one of the oldest and best families in Portsmouth and was destined to a brilliant career, but no one guessed it would lead to the Isles of Shoals. In his early youth he cruised around the islands with his sea-roving family or alone under his own sail, dreaming of ships and whaling and adventures to far-off shores. Lying at anchor in Gosport Harbor was like visiting a foreign port, for the Islanders in the two and a quarter centuries since the landing of John Smith had fallen into strange customs and developed a local jargon as picturesque as their quaint island villages.

The Laighton family had long been prominent in Portsmouth business circles. Their ships cruised the coastal waters from Nova Scotia to the West Indies with cargoes of lumber, molasses, rum, fish, and general merchandise. They were known as exporters and importers, both wholesale and retail. The father of the family, Mark Laighton, was honored among seamen as inventor of the roller block which lightened the toil of every sailor who worked the rigging.

Thomas, the third of ten children, was born on February 2nd, 1805. While in high school he had the reputation of being "one of the best mathematicians in town," but like his contemporary Nathaniel Bowditch, he was denied the privilege of a college education. At the age of thirteen he had a severe attack of typhus fever, which left him lame. Much of his later success was undoubtedly the result of a determined effort to compensate this handicap. He mapped his own course of self-education, and as his fortunes prospered he organized a workingmen's reading club, assuming for some years the responsibility of selecting books. He was elected to the school committee and appointed to study and report on equipment and needs of the high school. Members of his

ISLES OF SHOALS

family and others included him as a business partner. In 1832 he and his friends Samuel Tuckerman, Samuel Cleaves, and Ichabod Goodwin organized The Portsmouth Whaling Co., with a capital stock of $25,000, later increased to $100,000. In 1833 he was appointed assistant postmaster under Abner Greenleaf, and later served in the Custom House. In 1836 he and Abner Greenleaf, Jr. were joint editors of the *New Hampshire Gazette.*

During this period, on June 23, 1831, he and Eliza Rymes were married. Their union was said to be ideal and so it proved. Their first child, Helen, died in infancy. Celia was born on June 29th, 1835, and Oscar on June 30th, 1839.

Thomas had resigned as co-editor of the *Gazette,* but continued his political career and became secretary of his party for District No. 1.

Known now as a public-spirited citizen, and "the most eloquent orator in the district," he found the doors of politics open to him. In 1837 he was elected to the State Senate on the "Democratic Republican" ticket. Although he was defeated the next year by Samuel Cleaves, he was re-electd a year later, and by a singular coincidence, on the very day his second victory at the polls was announced, he was signing the papers for the purchase of four islands — Hog, Smuttynose, Malaga, and Cedar. He was not, as some have said, defeated for governor by John Page. On the contrary, he helped to nominate Page and worked zealously for his election. There is nothing to show that Thomas ever ran or was even mentioned for governor.

Thomas had a long-standing agreement with Postmaster Abner Greenleaf that on his retirement Thomas should take his place. Thus matters stood in the summer of 1839, when the position of lightkeeper at White Island came open, and Thomas gladly accepted the appointment as an interim occupation pending Greenleaf's resignation. It would be an ideal base of operation for his long-cherished plan to revive the fishing industry at the islands. Only a few of his closest friends were aware of these secret hopes and commitments.

The Portsmouth waterfront — the whole city for that matter — had much to gossip about in late September of 1839 when it was noised about that the Honorable Thomas B. Leighton had engaged Captain Falls to take him out to the Isles of Shoals — to

ISLES OF SHOALS

live! Here was a young man with a more promising career than any of his contemporaries suddenly accepting the insignificant appointment as Keeper of White Island Light, next door to oblivion! Moreover, he was taking their beloved Eliza and the babies out to live on that desolate rock. There was at the time — and continues to this day — endless speculation as to the underlying motive for this melodramatic action.

Thomas went out first, on September twenty-ninth, to take over the lighthouse and ready-up the keeper's cottage for Eliza and the children. He hoped they would love it. The term was only two years, a mere vacation. Celia's description of the voyage, written thirty years after the event, and published in her classic *Among the Isles of Shoals*, reveals a loving and accurate memory:

"It was at sunset in autumn that we were set ashore on that loneliest, lovely rock, where the lighthouse looked down on us like some tall, black-capped giant, and filled me with awe and wonder. At its base a few goats were grouped on the rock, standing out dark against the red sky as I looked up at them. The stars were beginning to twinkle; the wind blew cold, charged with the sea's sweetness; the sound of many waters, half bewildered me. Some one began to light the lamps in the tower. Rich red and golden, they swung round in mid-air; everything was strange and fascinating and new. We entered the quaint little old stone cottage that was for six years our home."

Shortly before their first Christmas, a terrific northeaster struck the islands. Thomas reported it in his journal as of December fifteenth. In later years Celia described it is an experience of early childhood and wrote it into one of her favorite poems, "The Wreck of the Pocahontas." Her description lets us know what the little family in the keeper's cottage had to endure.

"During a storm in 1839, while living at White Island, we were startled by the heavy booming of guns through the roar of the tempest, — a sound that drew nearer and nearer, till at last, through a sudden break in the mist and spray, we saw the heavily rolling hull of a large vessel driving by, to her sure destruction, toward the coast. It was as if the wind had torn the vapor apart on purpose to show us the piteous sight; and I well remember the hand on my shoulder which held me firmly, shuddering child that I was, and forced me to look in spite of myself. What a day of pain it was!

ISLES OF SHOALS

how dreadful the sound of those signal-guns, and how much more dreadful the certainty when they ceased, that all was over! We learned afterward that it was the brig Pocahontas, homeward bound from Spain, and that the vessel and all her crew were lost."

No hint is given in any writings by Celia, Oscar, or even Thomas that this ship "homeward bound from Spain" might have been the whaling ship which had been the pride of the Portsmouth Whaling Co. Thomas had recorded in his journal that the *Pocahontas* sailed Sunday, September 23, 1832, and that on Thursday July 11 (1833) Mark Laighton, his brother, had gone to Sagamore Harbor for the purpose of shipping on a whaling voyage.

In William G. Saltonstall's *Ports of Piscataqua* we are told that the *Pocahontas* made the two whaling voyages, neither successful, and was advertised for sale in 1838 by Ichabod Goodwin and S. E. Coues. Since it is a tradition of the sea that a vessel once named retains her identity, we surmise that it was the same ship whose signal-guns boomed into silence past White Island. Were Thomas and Eliza so stunned by the premonition that Mark had gone down with their own *Pocahontas* that they could not mention it to the children? Oscar recalled many years later that R. H. Dana had said in one of his sea stories, "No danger on the ship with Mark Laighton at the wheel," and added his own comment, "That was the last word that ever reached us about Uncle Mark."

Thomas and Eliza were agreed in one vital particular — that the new home on White Island should bring to the children only the best from the mainland and leave the worst behind. The children while here must have regular instruction and whatever else lay within the power of devoted parents to give. It could never have occurred to either that they were leading these children through fairyland into an island kingdom where Celia would reign as queen.

Eliza was the guardian angel during those first months and years of uncertainty. It was in her nature to fill the little home with sunshine. She surrounded her babies with a protecting love and care which would mean more to them than all the lessons they would ever learn from books. Nothing is said in regard to the physical energy and moral courage required for this unusual responsibility. She left no diary or correspondence to speak in after years of the loneliness, the dark forebodings when the seas

ISLES OF SHOALS

were wild, or the need for help and companionship while Thomas was on his inland journeys. All sense of personal danger or feeling of personal neglect, if such ever entered her mind, was so deeply buried that no one thought to look for it or suggest it might be there. On the contrary, visitors spoke fervently of her cheerful hospitality, radiant spirit, and genial disposition; her wifely devotion and motherly care of the children; her competence, courage and unaffected simplicity; and her wonderful cooking — especially her wonderful cooking! So strong were these impressions that her guests paid high tribute to her character and ability but seldom commented on her appearance, yet she was known in her youth and long remembered as "exceptionally beautiful." Her crowning glory unconsciously achieved was an aura of loveliness above all physical charm. This her children absorbed and reflected in their several ways later in life.

Nothing finer has fallen from Celia's pen than her memories of childhood in the shadow of the lighthouse. There on that "lovely lonely rock" she was not lonely because she was intimate with the dancing waves, the laughing sky, the rising sun, the soaring gulls, and every living thing. The abundance of her own life, the keenness of all her perceptions, the full response of her nature to the greatness of Nature around her made every object glow as if possessed of some inner illumination. Wild morning-glories, so common to most of us, were radiant in the morning sun, reaching up to her in gladness from clefts in the rocks — rocks that are dull gray to us but glowing as opals to her sensitive eye. She identified herself with the struggle of a blade of grass to reach its freedom in the sea-scented breeze, or with the wild rapture of gulls battling against the savage fury of a storm. It was all so much a part of her that she must "*speak* these things that made life so sweet . . . speak the wind, the cloud, the bird's flight, the sea's murmur . . . in storm or calm, by day or night, the manifold aspects of Nature held me and swayed all my thoughts until it was impossible to be silent any longer, and I was fain to mingle my voice with her myriad voices, only aspiring to be in accord with the Infinite harmony, however feeble and broken the notes might be . . . I felt so much a part of the Lord's universe, I was no more afraid of the dark than the waves or winds."

ISLES OF SHOALS

She tells of a sunset after a storm: "this solemn gray lid was lifted at its western edge, and an insufferable splendor streamed across the world from the sinking sun. The whole heaven was in a blaze of scarlet, across which sprang a rainbow unbroken to the topmost clouds . . . the sea answered the sky's rich blush, and the gray rocks drowned in melancholy purple. I hid my face from the glory — it was too much to bear."

Eliza went to Portsmouth for the birth of her fourth child, Cedric, on September 4th, 1840. Celia and Oscar were delighted with the new brother, who soon took his place among them in their childhood adventures.

2

SHATTERED HOPES AND A NEW VENTURE

I T IS NOT surprising that Oscar should gain the impression in later life that his father had renounced the mainland and taken up residence at the Shoals under a vow never to return. Evidence has recently come to light, however, unfolding an entirely different story. In brief we do not find that Thomas ever made a "vow of renunciation."

During the first four years of the eight-year period from 1839 to 1847, he made frequent trips to Portsmouth, continued many of his business interests there, was twice elected to serve in the State Legislature (for the years 1841-42), was elected to the Board of Selectmen for Portsmouth, took part in political conventions, and for many months hoped for some lucrative post in Portsmouth. But his plans were wrecked by a letter from Abner Greenleaf telling him the Post Office was going to his rival Samuel Cushman.

The year 1846 has been ignored and virtually forgotten in Shoals history, but the discovery of Mr. Laighton's journal covering the years 1846-1848 has led to a complete reappraisal. His daily entries, though fragmentary and often enigmatic, not only give a maturer view of life at the islands but help to evaluate the childhood memories of Oscar and Celia. While they were dancing in glee over the rocks, he was reconstructing his life. We might reasonably suppose he would commit his thoughts, hopes, and plans to these pages, but we find nothing subjective from first to last. The entries are brief, factual, and impersonal. Imagine for example the background of interest and activity suggested by these four entries:

March 12 — Canary set
April 15 — Canaries hatched
April 25 — Canaries forsook their young
August 31 — Gave Weiss and G. a pair of canaries each

Thomas loved canaries. Judge Shaw says, "he seems to have been a man with the energy and activity of the average two men"; nevertheless he loved canaries, and this may serve as a token of

ISLES OF SHOALS

his care for the islands and his family. Everything under his hand was always shipshape, not that he ruled as an exacting despot as some have imagined, but because he took a personal interest in all that was going on and put his own hands into the work, even the drudgery. He would trim lamps, repair machinery, whitewash the out-buildings, paint the interiors of cottage and tower, and on occasion help in the garden so far as his lameness would permit. His journal says that baby Cedric was sick February fifteenth, and was given Lobelia. On January thirty-first and February twenty-fourth he vaccinated the children. March 13; "vaccinated Ben Whaling," March 14; "vaccinated self and wife."

To relieve Eliza he engaged Nancy Newton from Star Island for housework, and had Louisa and Eliza Randal brought over once a week to do the family washing.

The journal records frequent excursions around the islands, taking Eliza and the children for a sail, and visiting with his neighbors. The following entry is typical of his care for the fishermen and their families:

"Feb. 28, Sat. Gave Bunker 2 pr. Pantaloons, cap and gave John B. Downs clothing, and N. Berry large bundle clothing, socks, shoes etc. — John B. Downs brought 3 fish and N. Berry 2 coots."

While work on Smuttynose and Appledore was under the hands of Williams Rymes and Fabius Becker, the journal says, "June 17, commenced shearing sheep," on Hog, and two days later, "finished shearing sheep, 40 old sheep, 15 lambs."

The crowning event of the season was a wedding on Star Island, noted thus in the journal: "Fabius Becker married at Star Island, (Aug. 23). Family went to wedding — Went to Smuttynose in P.M. and brought back family."

At home on winter evenings he read to the children, and in later years Celia, commenting on her own lack of schooling said, "My father taught me all he knew." Oscar and Cedric and Celia unite in saying that the home on White Island was a remarkable instance of domestic felicity. They *all* loved canaries!

Ominous silence broods over the years 1841 to 1846, so far as Thomas is concerned. No entry appears in his journal between these dates. From other fragmentary sources we trace his move-

ISLES OF SHOALS

ments, learn of his mainland activities, which continued on to his last recorded act as selectman in Portsmouth, on March 14th, 1843. From Celia we learn that they lived for a time on Smuttynose, and from R. H. Dana, that Thomas was at home there on August 18th, 1843. There is nothing to indicate what was going on in his mind, why he did not run for office after that date, why he went over to Smuttynose Island instead of Portsmouth when Cheever displaced him at White Island, why he neglected his journal for five years, or what dim hopes he still held for the future. Nor is there anything to suggest that Thomas was purposely cutting himself off from the mainland. It seems rather that he was reconstructing his life. His brother Joseph and Eliza's brother William were helping him develop the fishing industry. Together they were building two dwelling houses, fish-houses and workshops on Hog. The islands offered a large freedom greatly to his liking. He was losing his taste for politics and was deeply hurt by the chicanery within his own party. Old friends and associates were paying him the tribute of an occasional visit. Levi Woodbury and Caleb Cushing were among the notables. So the family settled at Smuttynose — and when the political tides turned, they were doubtless overjoyed to kindle the fires once more on White Island.

The first entry in the journal after five years of silence has no particular significance until we see it as a key to later events. "1846, Jan. 1 Fabius brought Mr. Rymes over — gave Rymes letters to mail in Portsmouth."

Immediately we wonder what was in those letters, and how often a boat went to the mainland. In the writings of Celia and Oscar we are reminded that during winter months there would be no communication with "the main" for weeks on end. Was this January an exeption? From the journal entries we gather that the whole winter and spring of this year must have been very exceptional. Boats were plying from Portsmouth to the Shoals several times a week.

Thomas was making the hotel at Smuttynose a major enterprise. He sailed over to the island nearly every day, sometimes twice. He took out a partition to enlarge the dining room, put down carpet, papered, painted, shingled, installed new furniture, beds, silverware — planted a garden — set out trees. By May

69

ISLES OF SHOALS

first, guests began to arrive, Mr. Williams first among them. By June eighth the bowling alley was set up. By July fifteenth he had netted $100 from the hotel, and on August nineteenth, noted another $100.

In the meantime, Becker made the first haul of mackerel (18 barrels, June 24), and the Shoals venture was beginning to pay dividends.

It is now reasonably clear as to what Thomas had in mind when he gave William Rymes that packet of letters to mail on New Year's Day, and then removed five years of dust from his neglected journal. Was it a New Year's Resolution?

But the journal reveals no least premonition in the mind of Thomas or anyone else that the long winter months had been spent in preparation for one single event, very slight in itself, which would change the whole course of life at the islands and give them a new importance in American history. That event was the arrival of Levi Lincoln Thaxter at the hotel on Smuttynose on July 24th, 1846.

3

THE LAIGHTON-THAXTER PARTNERSHIP

WHEN Thomas looked out from his White Island window and spied a familiar sail making for Smuttynose that sunny afternoon in July, he wondered what new guests might be stopping at his hotel. That night he wrote in his journal: "July 24 Goodwin came out and brought to hotel wife and children, Mr. Thaxter. Went over in evening."

Thomas and Levi struck up an acquaintance on the spot. Thomas invited Levi over to White Island for tea, and three days later Levi was installed as a boarder with the Laighton family at the lighthouse. Young John Weiss, Levi's intimate friend, minister of the Unitarian Church at Watertown, came out to see him there. The discovery of the Laighton family was a rare event for both.

On Sunday August ninth, Thomas took his usual sail around the islands, with Levi, Weiss, and a friend named Reynolds as passengers. Weiss and Reynolds stopped off at Star to attend church in the old stone meetinghouse. Thomas and Levi sailed on across the harbor and out through Malaga Gut into the open sea.

Here were two dreamers in the long wake of Captain John Smith, lulled by the sound of flapping sail and ripple of waves on the bow. Levi could see that the skipper was no ordinary lightkeeper, but he was not prepared for the revelations soon to follow. Passing Duck Island they saw a whale stranded on the surf-bound rocks. It reminded Thomas of his own unhappy venture in whaling, and he therewith began a long conversation whose words drifted off with the breeze but whose content — made evident in later action — became one of the most significant items in Shoals history. Thomas laid bare his plans for reviving the fishing industry, once the pride of these waters, and developing the islands as a summer resort. Already, his old cronies who used to visit him at White Island were putting up at the Mid-Ocean House. Among them such notables as Levi Woodbury, Franklin Pierce, U.S. Senator from New Hampshire; Nathaniel Hawthorne, the

ISLES OF SHOALS

young writer and classmate of Pierce, at Bowdoin; Richard Henry Dana, who had just written *Two Years Before the Mast;* Abner Greenleaf and his son, owners and editors of the *New Hampshire Gazette;* Governor John Page, Caleb Cushing, and a dozen others. The Shoals had been good medicine for them all.

Levi responded in kind. His father was a well-to-do banker, real estate broker, and business man in Watertown, Massachusetts, who was determined that his eldest son should be a lawyer. Perhaps one day he would be governor, like his relative Levi Lincoln for whom he was named. His father was an ancestor worshipper immensely proud of the fact that the first five Thaxters to be graduated from Harvard were lineal descendants of Thomas Thaxter who settled in Hingham in 1638. The Lincolns had come over in 1635.

Levi said that all his life he had been chased up family trees like a Manx monkey — plenty of branches but nothing to hold on with. To help decorate his father's family orchard he had taken his A.B. and LL.B. from Harvard, but law was not for him! He was interested in dramatic arts and had persuaded his father to send him to New York to study elocution with Charles Kean, the famous actor from London who had opened a studio there. Elocution would be an ornament for any lawyer!

The experience was not all he had hoped and he came home convinced that he could not — or would not become a professional actor. He had arrived a "nervous wreck," had a row with his father, and turned to his old friend and Harvard schoolmate, Thomas Wentworth Higginson for advice. Higginson, known to his intimates as Wentworth, had sent him out to the Shoals to rusticate, get his feet on the ground, and make up his mind what to do next.

Thomas and Levi had discovered each other. Levi had never thought of the islands as a base of operations. The idea appealed to his imagination. If Thomas could entice politicians, businessmen and writers, why not others? Levi had friends, too. "The Brothers and Sisters" would love this.

Who were the "Brothers and Sisters?" Thomas wanted to know. They were a group of young people of college age, or recent graduates, who gathered now and then on Sunday evenings to discuss anything and everything. Emerson called them a little wild because they were always getting excited about some reform or

ISLES OF SHOALS

other. They called themselves Brothers and Sisters because so many were related in that way. They read Emerson, Browning, Tennyson, Longfellow, Carlyle, as fast as they were published. The oldest members were James Russell Lowell and Levi's cousin Maria White. Lowell had just written a rather long poem, *The Vision of Sir Launfal*. James and Maria were called the "King and Queen" because they were the natural leaders of the group. The blue-bloods of Boston were among them — Edward Everett Hale, Leverett Saltonstall, the Tuckermans, the Kings of Salem, the Higginsons, Fays, Storeys, Sam Longfellow, brother of the poet, all from Cambridge, the Whites, Thaxters, and John Weiss of Watertown, and sometimes Henry David Thoreau of Concord, although he seldom came to the discussions. These young people were just beginning their careers. Now if they were to discover the Isles of Shoals it would be the making of them — and of the islands!

Thomas and Levi sailed back past Smuttynose, told Bunker about the dead whale on Duck Island, picked up Weiss and Reynolds at Star, and scudded for White Island.

Finally on the nineteenth, after a stay of twenty-six days, Levi and Weiss returned to Watertown, and the first round was done. It had been exhilarating but no actual plans had been laid for the future. Levi, still battling his own problems, paid Kean a second visit in New York and then in April went back to the Shoals, where he stayed four weeks. After this second visit, he wrote to Thomas:

"And often I think of the lighthouse islands, and those who dwell there; and then come musings and wonderings about the future, and with them what seems conviction that the mutations of life will sometime bring me to those favorite rocks as a central and lasting abiding place. Some of my friends wonder at my excessive affection for the Shoals, and I am myself surprised to find how much they occupy me."

In the meantime Thomas was vigorously promoting a dream of his own. A newspaper clipping of later date says:

"An English gentleman named Frank Williams was sent out to Thomas B. Laighton at White Island for his health. He was a wealthy invalid. Mr. Williams passed several summers at White Island, and it is said it was he who first suggested to Mr. Laighton the idea of putting up a hotel on Hog Island rather as a sanatorium

ISLES OF SHOALS

than a mere pleasure resort, and was an annual visitor there until his decease." Acting on Mr. Williams' suggestion, Thomas had drawn plans for a summer hotel on Hog Island and had begun work there when he received Levi's nostalgic letter.

Late in the summer Thomas decided to invite Levi to come in as a partner, and "propositioned him." His journal says, "Sept. 10, Friday, Remmick and Henry came over, brought letters from Thaxter in which he agrees to my proposition to join in business at Hog Island." A week later Levi went out for one day only and to our amazement we discover that on September first, Levi's father had sent $2,500 to Thomas for "one undivided half of Hog Island." Evidently Levi had been so successful in persuading his father that this was the one business opportunity of a lifetime that he had bought a half interest in the island sight unseen! On September thirtieth, Levi brought his parents out for a four-day visit, and it was settled that the Thaxters should have the use of North Cottage, one of the two houses built some years earlier on Hog Island by Tom's brother Joseph and Eliza's brother William. At this time the Laightons gave the name Appledore to Hog Island.

Wentworth Higginson was first to see Utopia emerging from the combined dreams of Thomas, Levi, and Williams. He wrote to his mother:

"Levi popped in on his way to the Shoals. He and Mr. Laighton have bought the most beautiful of the islands and are going to bring it under cultivation, have a boarding house for invalids and aesthetic visitors and do something to civilize the inhabitants of the other islands. It is really quite the 'Locksley Hall' idea, 'to burst the links of habit,' etc., etc. He is in high spirits with the plan."

Levi went back with his parents to Watertown on October third and returned to the Shoals on October fourteenth determined to stay the rest of his life.

Turmoil now reigned at the islands. The journal says: "Tuesday, packing articles; Wednesday, packing; Thursday, the 16th, wind west, light. Moved from White Island to Hog Island. Mr. Becker moved to W. Island and took charge of Lighthouse for me. John Randall moved to Smuttynose."

From this date on, the journal is silent for a full year. We have only Oscar's narrative in his *Ninety Years*. He says:

"Father had built two good sized dwellings. In one of them Uncle William Rymes was taking care of the workmen; the other

74

ISLES OF SHOALS

we occupied. The first night we children slept in the southeast chamber, with beds made up on the floor, and the next morning we were up betimes, eager to investigate this new field of delightful adventure. We saw from our window a flock of sheep feeding on the side of the south hill, and gulls flying by, pink with sunrise. Mother and Nancy had a struggle to get the breakfast, for everything was in confusion. . . .

"We were finding Appledore delightful as the fall advanced. Great flocks of the now extinct wild pigeons would visit us, and every kind of bird on their southern flight. As late as November golden-rod was blooming and the Quaker lady's darling blossom still fringing the ledges. With sister we would ramble over our island until we were familiar with every spot of it. The North Valley we called fairyland. Here, with stones and dritfwood, we built a little house, and sister would tell us wonderful fairy stories, which a fiery-winged blackbird, swaying on a reed nearby, would try to verify with all his might. Far off we heard the fascinating call of the loon. The ocean, deep blue, was sparkling in the radiant sunlight! Perfect stillness save the murmur of the water about the shore, or the continued conversation of our little friend, the red-winged blackbird!

"At last on the fifteenth of June, in the year 1848, the doors of the Appledore House were open to the public. Father had advertized in a Boston, a Newburyport and a Manchester paper, and we awaited the arrival of the 'Springbird,' Captain Thurlow, from Newburyport, with strange feelings of great excitement. The immaculate hotel register lay on the counter, with only one name, that of the Reverend John Weiss, a friend and classmate of Mr. Thaxter, he having arrived the day before in the pilot boat 'Spy,' Captain Jim Goodwin. Mr. Weiss was a medium sized man, with dark hair and beard and splendid brown eyes, but what impressed me most about him was his irresistible spirit of fun."

The first year proved to be a "fair success" for the firm of Laighton and Thaxter, although Levi had decided that the hotel business was not his calling. No explanation is offered, but on October 7th, 1848, just a year from his last previous entry, (October 16, 1847) Thomas turned again to his journal:

"Since the above entry, being in business with Levi L. Thaxter of Watertown to erect a public House on Hog Island, and having erected the same and opened for the reception of company with

75

ISLES OF SHOALS

some success, but mutual misunderstandings having arisen, which resulted in an agreement to dissolve, and accordingly on "Saturday, October 7, 1848 we agreed to dissolve and divide the Island equally between us, Mr. Thaxter to retain the northerly house and I to have the public house with all buildings erected since our connexion in business."

What led Levi to dissolve the partnership is indicated in the Higginson correspondence. At the end of the first season his wife Mary wrote:

"Mr. Laighton, Levi's partner, is extremely unpleasing . . . . and Levi did not appear happy and satisfied. He feels great responsibility and anxiety — it is an awful life for a young man of refinement and cultivation . . . I pitied him very much. Mr. Laighton is lame so that Levi appears to do much more than his share — and while it was crowded he did a great deal of work — cleaning knives, etc . . . , this sort of thing can hardly be agreeable to him . . . Weiss had been exceptionally gay — so they said — but unfortunately his spirits left him and the day we arrived he was very quiet and silent."

Near the end of the first season, Star Island witnessed one of its most pathetic tragedies. Miss Nancy J. Underhill of Chester, N.H., who was teaching the Gosport school, wandered through the village pasture on a quiet afternoon (September 11) to her favorite seat at the brow of a cliff on the southeastern shore overlooking the lower ledges, the restless waves, and the far horizon. No one observed the huge wave that broke higher than the rest and swept her off. Helpless in the surging backwash she was carried into deep waters beyond rescue, nor seen again until a week later when her body was found on the sands of York Beach on the Maine coast.

The shelving ledge where she was last seen is known to this day as "Miss Underhill's Chair," and those who visit the place are warned to beware of tidal waves when the surf is high.

4

THE LONG ENGAGEMENT

IMMEDIATELY after the dissolution between Levi and Thomas, an interesting exchange of minor properties began. Levi was not minded to live with the Laightons but settled into bachelor's quarters in the North Cottage. On October twenty-third, he borrowed Thomas's crowbar and hoe, then sailed to Rye and returned with a gallon jug of port wine. November first, he sailed to Portsmouth on errands. A week later, 618 feet of hemlock plank and 1,000 laths came out. Thomas let him have three window sashes, the forequarter of a pig, a plane, carpet stretcher, parlor stove, brass fire dogs, and finally a watch.

The most surprising entry in the journal is for November 22, '48 "Levi handed me what he called a plan of the lot he wished to take—had some unpleasant words with him." This stands out as the only occasion in all the pages of the journal where Thomas makes reference to personal feeling. Presumably these unpleasant words were provoked by Levi's plans, but there may have been another reason.

Levi had grown to be so much a part of the Laighton family that he was taken for granted — as an older brother, friend and teacher to the children, a junior partner to Thomas, a son to Eliza — but Thomas was not ready for the suggestion which Levi proposed. A news clipping dated Aug. 27, 1894 states: "He [Levi] proposed for Celia's hand in due form to her father who flew into a rage (fancying his daughter to be a mere child) and ordered him off the Island."

Levi's answer, according to tradition, was that he would build himself a hut and live on the island until Celia was old enough to speak for herself. She was then thirteen.

Were these the "words" which Thomas had with Levi that cold November day? The circumstantial evidence points that way. Thomas notes in his journal that Levi went home to Watertown two days later and was sick, and that he himself was sick for several days. It was a week before he felt well enough to leave his room, "and then went out and killed a turkey."

ISLES OF SHOALS

Levi returned to the islands on December ninth, and the two men seem to have declared a truce. Levi took Christmas dinner with Thomas and family, continued to borrow what he needed for his bachelor quarters, went back home to see his brother Jonas off to the Golden West, and finally, on February second, Thomas's birthday, details of the dissolution of the partnership were signed in due form. This done they went out to divide the stock. Thomas took the tan and red cow, Levi took Long-legs and heifer. The heifer without calf they agreed to kill and divide.

The summer of 1849 came and went. The hotel closed for the season, and the Laightons found themselves more lonely than ever they had been at the lighthouse, for all the Thaxters had returned to Watertown and Celia had enrolled in the Mt. Washington Female Seminary in South Boston, conducted by Mrs. Maria Burrill. Levi was minded to spend the winter at home in Watertown, since Thomas had reluctantly consented to the wedding if Levi and Celia would wait twelve months. Eliza was pleased, Oscar and Cedric were delighted, but in Watertown the news of Levi's engagement must have echoed through every parlor and kitchen. Levi Thaxter, the eligible young bachelor with two degrees from Harvard and a year with the great English actor in New York, with generations of culture behind him, engaged to a mere child of no education, the daughter of a lighthouse keeper! Levi Sr. had seen it coming and was bitterly opposed to it, but reconciled himself even as Thomas had done. There is pathetic humor in the comment of Levi's sister Lucy that in her family only father had objected and he was so proud of himself to find that his prediction had come true that he seemed reconciled to the fact. This we learn from a letter by Higginson written on June 2nd, 1850. In it he quotes Lucy as saying that Celia had made a very favorable impression on her new acquaintances in Watertown and that her school mistress thought highly of her. What an ordeal for Celia!

In the summer of 1850 Samuel Longfellow made his first visit to the Shoals and wrote to his mother:

"He [Levi] is not married, but betrothed to Celia Laighton, the daughter of him who once kept the lighthouse and now keeps the hotel — a simple, frank and pleasing girl of fifteen, who has grown up on the Islands, the flower of the rocks; for the last year planted in the Boarding School garden or greenhouse of Mrs. Burrill at South Boston."

ISLES OF SHOALS

Mother Nature opened the season of 1851 at Appledore with a majestic and terrifying display of hidden powers. April 17 it was, and Oscar gives a vivid account of it. On that day, he says, "the fiercest northeast storm in a hundred years swept the New England coast. The sea went clear across both valleys of Appledore, making it look like three islands." It was in this storm that Minot's Ledge Light went down and the keepers drowned. Fortunately, a hundred years later, we are able to say that there has not been a storm to equal it since. No one living has seen the flood of green water washing through the valleys of Appledore as Oscar described it.

Within a few days the seas were calm again and the island was readied for the new season, which turned out to be, in Oscar's words "a whirlwind of activity."

In all the published volumes about the Shoals, in all the treasured documents and scattered correspondence, we have searched for some clue as to what went on that summer between Celia and Levi, but all are silent. We know from inference that it must have been the happiest of their lives.

Levi was radiant, his exuberance equal almost to that of Weiss, the perpetual clown. Celia was drinking in the sunshine of her new and illustrious friends, dreaming of life on the mainland. But no date was set for the wedding and no preparations made for it. Celia had written to Jennie that it would be "sometime in the fall." No invitations were sent out, no special assemblage of guests planned in advance, but suddenly on the morning of September thirtieth, Levi and Celia decided that this would be the day. Higginson says it was decided upon, the minister sent for, the ceremony performed, in one day. Oscar has only this brief comment: "In all the world there never was such a wedding cake as mother made for sister's wedding. Celia was married to Mr. Thaxter by the Reverend John Weiss in the south parlor at Appledore, before a distinguished gathering of friends and guests of the hotel. That was seventy-five years ago, yet I remember perfectly how magnificent the couple looked, standing up to be married before the dignified John Weiss. At the wedding-dinner, Weiss and Thaxter were doing their best to make mother laugh, for she seemed near tears. These young men were as fond of her as they would have been were she their own mother."

Wentworth was accepting a new pastorate in Worcester and did not happen to be at Appledore at the time of the wedding. Levi

ISLES OF SHOALS

wrote him the fullest account we have, and he repeated the substance of it to his mother, saying to her:

'...You do not fully appreciate this strange and impracticable but chivalrous and noble person whose immediate future it is hard and even sad to predict; whose past has been wayward and perhaps useless, but aspiring and stainless.... Levi writes a funny account of the quiet little Kittery Point minister, Rev. Seth Somebody, his survival of the voyage more easily than of Jonas' witticisms, Jonas [Thaxter] the joker, on whose every wink and word the Reverend Seth hung in ecstasy; then his palpitations at the explosion of champagne corks and the feats of his moustached colleague (little Weiss). There were present all the Appledore Islanders, including Captain Fabius Becker from Smuttynose; all the Weisses (the baby's cradle being kept in the room adjoining), and Jonas and Lucy Thaxter ... 'We had a merry time,' " closes Levi in his letter, "and then I took my dear wife home in the beautiful night, bright and clear with stars and a growing moon."

5

THE NOMADS

CELIA and Levi were nomads for five years following the wedding. Their honeymoon was in the North Cottage at Appledore. From there they went flitting to Artichoke Mills in Newburyport, to Watertown, back to Appledore, to Star Island, to Newton, and back to the Shoals again. The first son, Karl, was born at Appledore July 24, 1852, exactly six years from Levi's first arrival at the Shoals. Karl was said to be the first child born on Appledore in more than a century.

While Celia, Levi, and baby Karl were still in the North Cottage, two distinguished guests came to the hotel — Nathaniel Hawthorne and Franklin Pierce.

Hawthorne had risen suddenly to literary eminence as the author of *The Scarlet Letter*, published in 1850. Since then he had turned his brief experience at Brook Farm into *The Blithedale Romance* and had just finished *The House of Seven Gables*. He was now exhausted and burdened with a new and irksome obligation. He had come to the Isles of Shoals in rendezvous with his Bowdoin classmate of 1824, Franklin Pierce, who had been nominated as Democratic candidate for the Presidency at the June convention. Pierce insisted that Hawthorne should write his campaign biography. This assignment was entirely out of character for Hawthorne, but it was accepted out of loyalty to a personal friend. The book, the whole experience, was so distasteful to him that he tried in every way to erase the memory of it and would never list the slender biography among his writings.

However, the meeting of Pierce and Hawthorne at Appledore has favored the Shoals with a choice chapter of history. Hawthorne arrived August thirtieth. He spent the greater part of his time exploring the islands, visiting the natives, and finally copying entire the *Gosport Church Records* which he found in the hands of the town clerk. It is from his *American Note-Books* that we gain the one authentic glimpse into the lives of Celia and Levi as they lived in the North Cottage that summer. Hawthorne wrote:

"*Saturday, September 4th.* In the afternoon I walked round

81

ISLES OF SHOALS

a portion of the island that I had not previously visited, and in the evening went with Mr. Titcomb to Mr. Thaxter's to drink apple-toddy. We found Mrs. Thaxter sitting in a neat little parlor, very simply furnished, but in good taste. She is not now, I believe, more than eighteen years old, very pretty, and with the manners of a lady — not prim and precise, but with enough of freedom and ease. The books on the table were 'Pre-Raphaelitism,' a tract on spiritual mediums, etc. There were several shelves of books on one side of the room, and engravings on the walls. Mr. Weiss was there, and I do not know but he is an intimate of Mr. Thaxter's. By and by came in Mr. Thaxter's brother, with a young lady whose position I do not know — either a sister or the brother's wife. Anon, too, came in the apple-toddy, a very rich and spicy compound; after which we had some glees and negro melodies, in which Mr. Thaxter sang a noble bass, and Mrs. Thaxter sang like a bird, and Mr. Weiss sang, I suppose, tenor, and the brother took some other part, and all were very mirthful and jolly. At about ten o'clock Mr. Titcomb and myself took leave, and emerging into the open air, out of that room of song, and pretty youthfulness of woman, and gay young men, there was the sky, and the three-quarters waning moon, and the old sea moaning all around about the island."

In the spring of '53 came an appointment from the Reverend Andrew P .Peabody, minister of the Unitarian Church in Portsmouth, who was acting as agent for the *Society for Propagating the Gospel Among the Indians and Others in North America*. Dr. Peabody was asking a young minister, Reverend John Mason, and Mr. Levi Thaxter to serve as missionaries to the fishing village on Star Island. Levi had long been interested. In 1851 he had given the Reverend Oliver Eastman eighteen spellers and six arithmetics for the Gosport school. He and Celia went to live in the parsonage hardly a stone's throw from the meetinghouse on the hill. Oscar says: "my sister always said that those were the happiest days of her married life."

In the spring of '54 we find the little family back at Artichoke Mills, where the second son, John, was born (November 29, 1854). A wonderful Christmas was spent here, with boxes sent from Watertown and Appledore, and long letters filled with chatter about the children. Oscar hopes the new baby will be a "comfort critter" like Karly.

After another summer at Appledore the family returned to

ISLES OF SHOALS

the Mills, and seem to have settled down for a longer stay there, for Celia now writes to Oscar and Cedric telling them that since she will be away for a long time she thinks best to write to only one of the home folks and has decided on Cedric, because he is Mufti, and Oscar though older will understand. Hence it is that correspondence is chiefly between Celia and Cedric during the long years that followed.

For sparkling fun, vivid description, and revelation of daily life there is nothing similar to this long and happy correspondence, yet it remains unpublished. They tell us that in December Celia sent a lock of Karly's hair to be treasured at Appledore, and Cedric in his reply says that he is trying to kill a Fawn Gull for her, and we are soon to learn that Celia wants gull wings to decorate the hats of her friends! Celia in later years repented this, joined the Audubon Society and lent all her influence to persuade women against murdering birds for their own adornment.

During the summer Levi's father found a small house for him in Newtonville—a temporary residence until something better should turn up. The young family moved in September but quiet seclusion was not their portion. Thomas was not well. Eliza was in need of rest. On October second, Celia wrote to her: "Levi joins me in begging you to come as soon as you can." A few days later Celia and her mother exchanged places, and Celia wrote from her father's bedside at Appledore to Eliza in Watertown: "Father gets along very well. I fixed the big bandage on his back. The new chair is too hard ... Ask Christie to drive you over to Newtonville to see if they still live."

Soon after this Eliza returned to Appledore and Celia with Levi began to move into the larger house on California Street overlooking an open field and the Charles River. This was the modest mansion which Levi Sr. had bought of Mr. Alfred Hou and which was to be their permanent home.

Levi's father suffered a stroke in 1857, and both families were filled with anxiety. Celia and Levi had spent the summer at Appledore but returned in early autumn. Thomas, Oscar, and Cedric sent sympathy and hope for an early recovery, but the hand of time was heavy upon him and his long life closed with the waning year. His will bestowed all goods and chattels on his wife Lucy, to hold and administer during her life, then to be distributed. Levi L. was to receive $25,000 outright and "the use and improvement

ISLES OF SHOALS

of the estate where he now resides which I purchased of Alfred Hou; also use, rent, improvement and profits of store on Commercial Street, Boston," and other parcels of real estate. The home on California was made secure.

6

SUDDENLY A NEW CAREER

IN NEWTONVILLE Celia was a "fairy princess" in exile. At the islands she had known the wild joyous freedom of winds and waves and singing birds, she had been idolized by fond parents and adoring brothers, and been recognized by discerning visitors. Had not Nathaniel Hawthorne mentioned her as "the Miranda of the Island?" Had not Levi Thaxter bestowed all his talents upon her and led her out and away from her little islands to a beautiful home on that very mainland which she had pictured in her childhood dreams? Was he not her fairy prince and this new home her castle and these little boys her precious jewels?

But now in Levi's home at the edge of the wilderness she began to see herself as "a steady old drudge," burdened forever with housework, more servant than hostess to her husband's many friends. At his fireside while he read his beloved Browning she must be busy with patchwork—and she hated patchwork! Her glorious freedom was gone, and dear little Karly had to be spanked!

Now and then her active mind would revert to childhood memories and the song of birds echoing from Appledore. She would wipe her hands on the wilted towel and sit down to write a little poem which had drifted into her mind as a soaring obligato to the clatter of pots and pans. In the early winter of 1860 she had received a letter from Cedric: "Everything reminds me of you today," her dear brother was saying. "Norwegian Cove, Fairyland, Neptune's Hall. The little house you built so many years ago." She reached for her writing pad and sent a few lines back to fairyland. Cedric acknowledged it. "I am perfectly delighted with the little poem you so kindly sent me, and I shall keep it so long as I live." (May 27, 1860).

How this poem found its way into the pages of the *Atlantic* remains a mystery. Annie Fields said in her biographical sketch of Celia:

"Her introduction to the world of letters was by means of her first poem 'Land-Locked,' which, by the hand of a friend, was

ISLES OF SHOALS

brought to the notice of James Russell Lowell, at that time editor of the *Atlantic*. He printed it at once, without exchanging a word with the author. She knew nothing about it until the magazine was laid before her."

There is a persistent tradition that the "friend" was Levi, but there is another tradition that Levi knew nothing of it until he saw it in the *Atlantic*.

Celia nowhere mentions Levi in connection with "Land-Locked," but consistently says that it reached Mr. Lowell "by the hand of a friend." Lowell did not, as Annie Fields says, print it at once but mentioned it in a letter to Higginson in 1860, and left it in the files for his successor, James T. Fields. It appeared in the issue of March 1861, almost a year after she had sent it to Cedric for the family at the Shoals.

In her long letter to the family at Appledore dated February 25th to 28th, 1861, Celia says:

" . . . Then I had to go to Mrs. Bigelow's and then to Barbara's. Barbara I found highly excited on the subject of the little poem, Land-Locked. She said she considered herself the God-mother—and she was very kind and jolly . . .

"Levi went to Boston before he came out yesterday but I found all the chicks well and happy when I got here. I found a most delightful letter from Mr. Folsom waiting for me . . . and also one directed to Mrs. Celia Thaxter in an unfamiliar man's hand—What can this be thought I opening it. I unfolded and read the following extraordinary document. Feb. 26th—C. T. Watertown, Mass. We enclose our c'k for $10 in payment for the poem 'Land-Locked' in the Atlantic Monthly for the ensuing month. Yours respectfully, Ticknor and Fields, per J. S. Clark! I burst into a shout of laughter and for a minute felt somewhat as I did when Miss Revere last summer said she supposed I wouldn't be paid for making a necklace of shells. When L. came home, I showed it to him (the first mention of the existence of the 'pome' which we have made to each other) 'Well' said he, 'didn't you expect it?' 'It never occurred to me,' I replied—and that was all, but he called to me after I had gone into the bedroom to say that a lady had congratulated him on the subject that day. I know very well what he would say if I asked him if he liked it. Yet I think he is pleased. I would rather so much that he would like it than anybody else. But if nothing else prevented, the fact of his Land-Locking me himself would prevent.

ISLES OF SHOALS

He wouldn't go to Susy's party. It is funny—he feels as if often he were invited because I am a sort of 'appendage' — such an absurd idea! The other day I brought him several messages from different people when I came out of Boston—'Oh', he said, 'I'm getting quite into notice.' "

Soon she received a letter from Cedric which had crossed hers in passage:

"Just after breakfast, while Bocky and I were out by the barn, Mr. Folsom came rushing out with Mr. Manley's *Atlantic* Magazine for March, and pointed triumphantly to a poem. I recognized it in an instant as I have a duplicate in my desk. It seems better than ever in print, and the title is very appropriate. . . "

LAND-LOCKED

Black lie the hills; swiftly doth daylight flee;
 And, catching gleams of sunset's dying smile,
 Through the dusk land for many a changing mile
The river runneth softly to the sea.

O happy river, could I follow thee!
 O yearning heart, that never can be still!
 O wistful eyes, that watch the steadfast hill,
Longing for level line of solemn sea !

Have patience; here are flowers and song of birds,
 Beauty and fragrance, wealth of sound and sight,
 All summer's glory thine from morn till night,
And life too full of joy for uttered words.

Neither am I ungrateful; but I dream
 Deliciously how twilight falls tonight
 Over the glimmering water, how the light
Dies blissfully away, until I seem

To feel the wind, sea-scented on my cheek,
 To catch the sound of dusky, flapping sail
 And dip of oars, and voices on the gale
Afar off, calling low—my name they speak!*

O Earth; thy summer song of joy may soar
 Ringing to heaven in triumph I but crave

ISLES OF SHOALS

> The sad, caressing murmur of the wave
> That breaks in tender music on the shore.

*In the first publication in the *Atlantic* (March 1861), this line reads:
> "Afar off, calling softly, low and sweet."

When the poem appeared in the *Atlantic Monthly*, unsigned as the custom was, many readers, Whittier chief among them, were pleased to welcome a new voice in American letters. Nevertheless, only a select few would ever know what it cost Celia to write it, and these remained compassionately silent, allowing romance and and tradition to work their will upon it. Eliza was delighted with the poem, and its sheer beauty was enough to open the floodgates, but she cried because it revealed the stark beauty of a broken heart. Cedric, a youth of nineteen, could not understand the tears. Whittier knew by the power of his own intuition and was drawn to the author, whoever it might turn out to be. He visited Appledore that summer and was disappointed to find that Celia had just left. Thomas knew. He had premonitions. Folsom knew and would wonder how it would set with Levi.

Perhaps they all wondered how Levi would feel now that Celia had said to the world that regardless of all he could offer she did

> "but crave
> The sad, caressing murmur of the wave
> That breaks in tender music on the shore."

Those who undertsood joined in a chorus of joy that Celia had come to her own and was being recognized as an authoress. By the close of that summer her poems had appeared in various magazines, and Cedric wrote (September 30): "Glad to hear of the success of your poems," and on October twenty-second, "the new poem is splendid, but in my poor opinion 'Land-Locked' is better. I discover new beauties in 'Land-Locked' every day. Bockey says that people used to come to him last summer and say, 'Your sister writes for the magazines doesn't she?' "

It was as if Celia had spent all her twenty-five years behind a closed door wistfully hoping it might be opened yet with no assurance that it ever would, and suddenly her own furtive touch had turned the key. A new world lay before her. She was ushered

ISLES OF SHOALS

into as select a circle of authors as New England ever produced. What young mother could be expected to receive such recognition without a burst of pride or a shudder of stage fright? There is no evidence of either. She remained "self poised and independent still." If she wrote any letter of ecstatic joy, or triumph, or boding fear of ability to cope with the new situation, it was not saved. She seems never in her entire life to have taken pride in her own writing and rarely mentioned it in her correspondence, except to ask advice or instruct her editors. She said of her babies, "I always thought small of my own goslings." The one exception was her outbursts over the discovery that she could paint. She wrote to Feroline Fox (September 22, 1874):

"Did Carry tell you I have taken to painting, 'wrestling with art,' I call it, in the wildest manner? This woodbine leaf at the top of the first page of this note I copied from nature. Of course it isn't very good, but it shows hope of better things, don't you think so ? Do say you do! I can scarcely think of anything else. I want to paint everything I see; every leaf, stem, seed vessel, grass blade, rush, reed and flower stem has new charms, and I thought I knew them all before. Such a new world opens, for I feel it in me; I know I can do it! and I am going to do it. What a resource for the weary days to come! I know you will be glad for me."

In similar words she wrote to John Weiss, and soon was illuminating pages in her little book of poems for friends. In a short time guests at the hotel would order gift copies, and Celia found herself at times overburdened with orders. The flower and bird designs, as clear and vivid today as when first dry from her brush, are the most perfectly drawn of any we know since Audubon; in some respects even more accurate. Little black seeds on a ripe red strawberry can be counted. The veins on a leaf are as nature traced them; the ribs on a bird's feather, silk strands of a spider web, are photographic.

Celia next took up china painting with equal zest, and for some years took orders for plates, jugs, vases, and tea sets, using fundamentally the same technique but with floral designs better adapted to china. Her visual memory was so clear cut and accurate that she could sit at her desk in a crowded parlor with some gifted musician at the piano and paint china or illuminate a book without a specimen before her. These pieces would bring from fifty

ISLES OF SHOALS

to one hundred dollars each, and from this income she was able to do more than the family budget would otherwise permit.

Yet with all this remarkable output of art and literature she rarely mentions any of it in her correspondence, and never with pride of authorship. On the contrary at one period, shortly before the death of her mother, she became despondent, and wrote an amazing letter to Annie Fields (March 14, 1876).

"I'm growing old and decrepit fast. I have been painting Kim Kirby's copy of my poems all day and found it insufferably tedious. I hate the pictures and I hate the poems and I hate myself for perpetuating either. I've had this copy years and haven't done it; now I'm going to finish and send it to her or die in the attempt. . .

"It seems to me every thing I do is feeble and futile and fatuous and quite unnecessary and uncalled for, and if it wasn't for very hard cash I would cease rude Boreas once for all, and no longer force my stupidities upon the attention of my suffering race. I detest all I do with a hearty and unmitigated venom."

Celia was a brilliant hostess, with friendly outgoing personality and gracious hospitality learned from her mother. Levi was shy and retiring. He must have relied on Celia to make his guests feel at home in his parlor. She had a dignity as well as a charm far beyond her years, and withal an excellent taste in dress. No one would believe that she designed and made her own gowns, for she was always known as one of the best costumed women of her time—she who hated patchwork! After she had become well known in literary circles C. T. Young wrote of her:

"Celia Thaxter was, I sometimes think, the most beautiful woman I ever saw, not the most splendid nor the most regular in feature, but the most graceful, the most easy, the most complete,—with the suggestion of perfect physical adequacy and mental health in every look and motion. She abounded in life, it was like breathing a new life to look at her."

These words help us of a later day to understand why she was so quickly accepted by the cultured people of Boston. She was at first a bit untutored, and was given to loud laughter among people of more subdued cultural background, but her abounding vitality, self-assurance, and infectious good humor always won the day. Elizabeth Stuart Phelps could truly say of her:

"She was one of the brightest figures in literary Boston, for many years—the most fearless, the most independent of beings.

ISLES OF SHOALS

It mattered little to her what other people did or thought—at least on secondary subjects. She was never afraid of herself. To certain modulations of manner she never consented . . . She was the incarnation of good spirits. Vigorous physique had much to do with this."

There was however one modulation taught her by her parrot. Celia became aware one day that the bird's raucous laughter was an imitation of her own. Her friends observed that in later life her laughter was more subdued.

Levi and Celia were invited to the most select gatherings of the literary elite, to the banquet given to Charles Dickens, to the Saturday Club, from which one cold night Levi walked home with Henry Wadsworth Longfellow. Celia was a guest of James and Annie Fields that night. They attended concerts, lectures, the theater, and were welcomed to many parlors. Levi would be invited now and then to give a Browning reading, and soon became known as the leading Browning scholar in America. The London publishers were curious to know why Browning was selling better in America than at home, and discovered it was because Levi Thaxter was able to interpret him. In 1880 when Celia went abroad she was invited to visit Browning, and received his thanks for Levi's generous tribute.

Celia counted among her closest friends some of the leading writers of her time: Whittier, James and Annie Fields, Sarah Orne Jewett, Elizabeth Stuart Phelps, Lucy Larcom, and a host of artists and musicians who counted it a privilege to enter her parlor at Appledore. It was evident then as now that Celia was recognized not only for her literary gifts, but even more because of her character and personality.

91

7

CELIA'S PROBLEMS

CELIA'S public life was free from all reference to her domestic problems. Only intimate friends knew the weight of her burdens, and they in love and loyalty formed a conspiracy of silence. They did not know that the veiled mystery would be grossly misinterpreted. We read our own distorted imaginations into any obscure event. Such is human nature.

Shortly after Celia died (1894) her son Roland with two of her closest friends, Annie Fields and Rose Lamb, published a volume of her letters. Annie Fields had written a biographical essay for the *Atlantic Monthly*—itself a classic—and Thomas Wentworth Higginson (in 1898) wrote her a letter of congratulation in which he said:

"I think that on the whole you handle the difficult subject of the relation between the two with great delicacy and substantial truth . . . . The more she plunged with eagerness into the novelty of social attention, the more he shrank from it; and, moreover devoted himself to a motherly care of the eldest boy . . . But in youth he was a master of the revels, full of fun and frolic; and his great desire was to be an actor,"

The passage by Annie Fields which drew Higginson's praise reads:

"The exuberant joy of her unformed maidenhood, with its power of self direction, attracted the shy, intellectual student nature of Mr. Thaxter. He could not dream that this careless, happy creature possessed the strength and sweep of wing which belonged to her own sea gull . . . Their natures were strongly contrasted, but perhaps not too strongly to complement each other, if he had fallen in love with her as a woman, and not as a child. His retiring, scholarly nature and habits drew him away from the world; her overflowing, sun-loving being, like a solar system in itself, reached out on every side, rejoicing in all created things."

Bliss Carman was outspoken against the silences. In his review of the volume he said:

ISLES OF SHOALS

"The letters read as if the heart of them had been edited away too much.

"She was in no sense a citizen of the world. Hers was a hearthstone life, though of the rarest and best. . .

"Her editors, I should imagine, have suppressed too much. Reason,—Mrs. Thaxter's life does not belong to the public; it still belongs to the family and friends . . . The editors have carefully refrained from publishing anything of an intimate character.

"A. W. E." (Mrs. Annie Weld Edson Macy), whose tribute to Celia appears in the *Heavenly Guest,* echoed Bliss Carman's feeling in a letter some forty years later (August 11, 1939):

"I am not sure that I blame the Thaxters and Laightons for sealing up the record, in the light of some of the cruel debunking of great literary lights. But the trouble is that a lot of cheap imaginative interpretation creeps in, to assuage curiosity."

Now that Celia has been gone for more than half a century her grand-daughter, Rosamond, has done us the favor of drawing back the veil. With great charm and frankness she tells the story without reserve as she found it in many sources not hitherto available. We cannot fail to appreciate her willingness to open the door with gracious and sympathetic hand.

According to tradition there was a "rift" between Celia and Levi, beginning early in their married life and widening to a virtual "separation." To dispel this myth it will be necessary to examine the entire situation. We regret the use of the words "rift" and "separation," for as we see it there was no real rift or separation in the sense implied. Celia and Levi lived much apart by force of circumstance. The conditions which were theirs to meet challenged them with a maze of conflicting interests and loyalties. The wonder is not that they were compelled to live so much apart, but that they held together to the end, preserving the integrity of the family, meeting their separate obligations, and fulfilling their separate destinies.

Reference is often made to the disparity in their ages and temperaments. Levi was eleven years her senior, but that is of little consequence. Of more importance, but still not the determining factor, was the difference in character and disposition. They were extreme opposites in temperament, background, and interests, nevertheless they were loyal and sympathetic toward each

ISLES OF SHOALS

other and indulged in no greater outbursts of temper than is expected in ordinary family life.

Levi was a well-educated gentleman of leisure. In character he was aesthetic, sensitive, reserved, and intellectual — a scholar and a nature lover. His personality was negative and indecisive — he was an extreme introvert. He rejected law as a career, could not bind himself to the discipline of the stage, recoiled against the restrictions of partnership with Thomas, and could not settle himself into any profession or calling. Yet he moved in the best circles of Boston and Cambridge, and found his chief satisfactions in Browning's poetry and in nature rambles. His abilities were above average, but his nature was restless. He felt his responsibilities but could not face them, which led to morbid introspection. He derived little or no income from his own skill or abilities until late in life. It was only four years prior to his death that he began seriously to give Browning readings on a professional basis, receiving from fifteen dollars for a parlor reading to three hundred for a public performance. If he had conserved his inheritance and made the interpretation of poetry his career, he could have become a man of wealth and distinction. His peculiar instability defeated him.

Celia grew up on a desolate island with almost no associates of her own age and with so little schooling that in later life she forgot that she had ever attended any school outside her own home. Her comment was "Of course I never went to school. My father taught me all he knew." From both parents she learned to be skilled and industrious, energetic and responsible. She belonged to a family of close-knit loyalties and loving devotion. In contrast to Levi, Celia was an extrovert, positive, cheerful, outgoing. She was not a naturalist and cared nothing for specimens to be hoarded in musems, but loved nature for its own sake in all its forms. From early childhood she identified herself with birds, flowers, sea, and sky. Perhaps her greatest gift was the power of appreciation. She had sympathetic understanding to an unusual degree. In every instance on record where she was compelled to choose between her own interests or comfort and the welfare of other members of her family, she invariably decided against herself.

To what extent these personal characteristics may have entered into the difficulties which beset Celia and Levi will not be considered here. We are concerned with various incidents and con-

ISLES OF SHOALS

ditions which made it necessary for them to live so much apart. Out of innumerable contributory causes four stand out: Karl's mental status; Levi's failing health; the final illnesses of Thomas and Eliza, and finally, Celia's literary career.

Poor Little Spud

It was Karl, "poor little spud!" as Celia called him, who unwittingly compelled his parents to follow divergent trails so many long years. Karl was the apple of many eyes during his infancy, but as he grew into childhood his congenital lameness and his retarded mentality became more evident. The lameness was never serious, but made him appear a bit awkward. When he was only five, Thomas wrote to Celia asking, "What's the matter with little Karl: thought he was cured," and Celia wrote to Elizabeth Hoxie, "Karly, I think is getting less nervous than he was. I try very hard to let him alone, but he is so mischievous that I can't help visiting him with small thunder occasionally, also spanks. Poor little spud! He is very loving and sometimes very sweet and gentle."

Cedric comments briefly, "Glad you have seen Dr. Bowditch," and again, chiding Celia, "You should not say Karly is disagreeable."

As the years passed, and Roland was born, "poor little spud" did not improve. When he was nine and Roland only three, Celia wrote to Elizabeth Hoxie (July 10, 1861): "Karl and John do nothing but fight; they live on it all the time. They roared in chorus, all three, under the windows at supper time tonight, and on going out I found Karl (9) and Roland (3) beating each other with barrel staves."

As soon as the boys could carry guns, Levi took them on long rambles, but Karl was sometimes left at home with Celia. Vague anxieties grew into unhappy premonitions as Celia and Levi saw that Karl could not keep pace with his younger brothers physically or mentally. During these early years Levi was gentle, even motherly in his care of Karl as Higginson says, but when it became evident that the child was mentally backward and would require special care it was Celia who became companion to Karl while Levi fathered the two younger brothers. The boys were sent to a private school conducted by Mr. Prentice Allen. In 1866 Mr. Allen died and Levi undertook the education of John and Roland himself, while sending Karl to the New Church school in Cambridge

ISLES OF SHOALS

with a new member of the family mentioned by Celia in a letter to Mary Lawson:

"I have an addition to my family in the shape of a young Hungarian by the name of Ignatius Grossman, about fifteen years old. We have taken him for good."

Karl was seventeen when the forebodings of many years came to a crisis. The exact date is unknown, but the prolonged emotional agitation of both Levi and Celia, together with other indications, point to the spring of 1868 as the time when physician and schoolmaster must have pronounced the solemn verdict — Karl should no longer attend school. He had the mentality of a child. He would never grow up. Levi could not admit to himself that he was the father of a mentally deficient boy. Celia for her part accepted, and kept Karl at her side the rest of her life, for it was now evident that no one else would befriend him. Levi was in poor health, and in January of '69 was stricken with a fever, and ordered to a warmer climate. From this hour on Karl made it inevitable that his parents should walk in separate paths.

Levi's Failing Health

Levi's minor illnesses had increased steadily. Never rugged in childhood nor athletic in youth he had developed a negative reaction to any prolonged or consistent effort. His chief recreation—evidently an escape from reality—was tramping through the woods collecting specimens which were later given to the Harvard Museum. Celia wrote to Elizabeth Hoxie (April 24, 1865), "The boys and Levi have guns and go murdering round the country in the name of science till my heart is broken to shreds. They are horribly learned but that doesn't compensate for one little life destroyed, in my woman's way of viewing it."

Three years later she wrote to Anson Hoxie, (June 17, '68) "Mr. Thaxter and Lony (Roland) have been gone three days and I milk the cow and she is tied to an apple tree." When writing this she had no thought of a more serious turn of events, but within a year she was writing to her friends that Levi had suffered a severe illness, and they must leave New England in search of a better climate.

To Elizabeth Hoxie she wrote from Appledore (March 7, 1869):

"Did you know Karl and I are moored here for seven months?

96

ISLES OF SHOALS

Such is the remarkable fact, and Levi, Lony and John are gone down to Jacksonville, or rather to the State of Florida, generally and promiscuously, with powder and shot by the ton, and arsenic and plaster ditto, and camp-kettle and frying pan and coffee-pot and provisions and rubber blankets and a tent, and a boat and three guns, and a darkey to be obtained upon arriving at Jacksonville, and heaven knows what besides . . . and then return sometime in May and stop here for a while to examine the windfall of birds killed by the lighthouse in the spring, and then they are to pursue their way up north, to Nova Scotia or the coast of Labrador, still to pursue the unwary sea fowl and cure the skin thereof and bring it as a tribute to the feet of Science. Meantime Karl and I remain here, moored for seven months. Our house is let and we are houseless and homeless."

Roland was taken with malaria while in Florida, and the excursion was terminated as soon as he was able to travel. There is no further comment on the proposed journey to Nova Scotia, or Levi's health during the summer and autumn, but Celia wrote to Mary Lawson from Appledore (March 11, 1870):

"What a busy year I have had, and now the last part of it has been entirely engrossed with sickness and breaking up housekeeping, and heaven knows what not.

"Mr. Thaxter is now in St. Augustine, Fla. with Lony and is better in health than he was. He was so ill with rheumatism, which struck the stomach in January and February that I really feared he would die. Lony has been quite sick too, with chills and fever, and all winter long we had sickness—at the last I had my turn with the mumps.

"Ignatius Grossman, also with us, had chills and fever for a month. I do not know whether we shall go back to Newton or not. I shall feel dreadfully to give up my pleasant home,—I am keeping house for Oscar,—my mother and Cedric are in Portsmouth—Karl with me. John is staying in Dedham with our friends the Folsoms."

Levi had begun to keep a journal in 1869, and in it after a long account of the first excursion to Florida there is a despairing note under date of August 26th, 1870:

"Let me collect myself. When did we leave here? Lony and I started in search of health in Florida. After the rheumatic fever and the chills and all that. The house has been going to wreck

97

ISLES OF SHOALS

since then, and the grounds have had their own way—Of the south I will say naught—of the interim at Watertown naught. Only the Shoals I have to deal with now, to jot some account of my visit there, record a little of its external aspect in this year of grace, and what Lony and I found there."

The journal here is blank for twelve pages evidently left for the account of the Shoals visit. Then follows a passage of profound self-negation — pathetic beyond belief:

"Newtonville, Sept. 2nd (1870)

"Somehow things went askew this morning. We had all gone to bed early last evening, the boys with valorous intentions of rising early and shooting blackbirds—and I for virtues sake—because, to pay for past neglect, my poor body needs all the rest it can get.

> Early to bed and early to rise
> Is the way to be healthy, wealthy and wise.

Well said, and true enough for the growing subject,—but for the being in decline,—looking beyond, far on his inevitable path, has a glimpse already of a future with a level horizon line as of a sea — a sea of which his spirit cannot detect the element — what matter? Is not late to bed and late to rise as well for him. Health gone irredeemably, wealth not yet attained, so unattainable, wisdom, a poor store of it laid up at what a price!"

Then follows a brief description of the parched brown countryside at Newton, with only a green margin along the river banks. "Water lilies were tolerably plenty along the river's edge, graceful as ever and sweet, their pure white petals opened wide for the glad heart of gold within to meet and embrace the loving sun. All plants are individual to me and seem to contain a life that partakes of the human, or is intimately connected with it. Nymphen I fancy to be upborne by a hand and arm of human form—grace of all graces—hidden beneath the element in which they live. What is it Browning says? I have hunted it up in Paracelsus—my dear old yellowed copy with the brown paper binding.

> 'The peerless cup afloat
> Of the lake-lily is an urn, some nymph
> Swims bearing high above her head.' "

The journal ends here. The depth of feeling so perfectly expressed is more fully appreciated if we remember that on February

ISLES OF SHOALS

9 of that year, before undertaking his second journey to Florida, he had conveyed all his remaining property on Apledore to Oscar and Cedric and felt that he must dispose of the Newtonville home also.

On December fourth Celia wrote to Annie Fields:

"I have been going through an ordeal in the last fortnight, such as never fell to my lot before . . .

"Mr. Thaxter has been dangerously sick with rheumatism which settled in the stomach and about the heart. I hardly dare to think he is not out of danger yet. The physician's fiat is exile for us, as soon as Mr. T. is well enough he must flee for his life to a milder climate. The thought of leaving New England is desolate to me."

By Christmas the family was united in despair, and Celia wrote to Mary Lawson (December 21, '70):

"Levi's health is so precarious that it is very doubtful whether we shall be able to stay through the winter, — never seems to have a comfortable minute. We have advertized our house and mean to sell it,—in the spring. I shall hate to go away from here more than I can tell."

Levi seems to have recovered enough to continue his excursions and to become a recognized naturalist, but he was a semi-invalid during all his remaining years.

The Passing of Thomas and Eliza

"Father has been sick for a week," wrote Cedric to Celia in May of '61. A few days later he wrote in behalf of Eliza, "Mother has been rather unwell—neuralgia in her knee." They must have known that they could offer no greater persuasion to Celia and at the same time give her legitimate excuse for coming back to her "level line of solemn sea." They could not have known, however, that their failing health and their constant pleading were multiplying the weight of Celia's burden. No family was ever more closely knit emotionally than these five. They never lost the intimacy that had grown among them in the little stone cottage on White Island.

Celia recognized her own family in Newtonville as her first obligation, a husband and three boys dependent upon her beyond belief, with husband and first-born son demanding more and more of her strength, judgment and patience. Yet all the inclinations of her heart were toward the dear associations with Appledore.

ISLES OF SHOALS

There could be no keener anguish for Celia than to witness the slow disintegration of her Appledore home and withhold what comfort she might give. Cedric wrote in November '63, "Mother sick nearly a week.... Father sick lately. Expect lumber to build new house." (This house a little northwest of the hotel was built as a retreat for Thomas and Eliza where they might live out their sunset years in peace.) On December twenty-eighth, Cedric wrote: "Father has paralysis: or something of the kind."

Then, a few days later (January 4): "Dear Father was taken sick about ten days ago and since that time has hardly been able to move without assistance, and has not been able to move his right arm and leg. How I pity him. What a life of physical torture he has had to endure, and yet he has struggled manfully with the world, and his great misfortune; and has triumphed." In February, "Father longs for a change." Finally the new house, begun in September, was ready for its new tenants. Cedric's letter telling of the removal from the hotel to the new cottage is a classic—long, witty, and filled with tender solicitude. "Father was taken in his chair and Mother in a wheelbarrow."

From this time on, Thomas was helpless, and Eliza was constantly at his side. He would rally and fade from week to week, but after a few months Cedric wrote, "Father seldom laughs now." Eliza read many books at the bedside and Celia's verses as they came out. "Nov. 1, '65. Mother is reading 'The Little Sandpiper' and is crying over it. She says it is the most beautiful thing ever written." On November thirtieth Cedric notes, "Father indulged in a snatch of song." On May 6th, 1866, Cedric wrote: "Father rather worse today . . . Father doesn't seem to know anybody." Celia came down at once, and the family was together on May sixteenth as Thomas subsided into dreamless sleep.

It was as if a gallant ship, beaten by many gales and crippled in heavy seas, had sailed into home port. The "King of the Island Empire" handed the scepter to his valiant sons, but Celia would remember that as the noble ship came to anchorage the skipper had "indulged in snatches of song."

Thomas was laid to rest on the summit of a little hill where spring violets grew northeast of the hotel. Celia returned to Newtonville to set her own house in order, but had hardly entered the door when she was handed a letter from Cedric saying once more but with more emphasis, "Mother misses you very much." And

ISLES OF SHOALS

a little later, "Mother wants to see you dreadfully." These repeated appeals to Celia reveal the persistence and strength of Eliza's demands upon her. Was she unaware of Celia's obligations to her own family in Newton—or was she all too keenly aware of Celia's need to be at the islands?

Soon after Thomas had gone Eliza seemed for a time to recapture her early zest. Excursions were planned to the White Mountains and New York, with shorter visits to Portsmouth and Boston. In the late months of 1870, however, her strength began to fail, and she became even more insistent that Celia should visit the islands.

In November of '73 Celia wrote a despairing letter to Feroline Fox: "I am a fixture here for the winter. Mother so poorly I could not leave her. I miss my boys so much I can't bear to think of it."

From this day on, the story is of slow decline for Eliza. Celia lived with her almost continuously through five years of lingering illness, and until her death on November 14th, 1877. On the thirteenth, Celia wrote to Annie Fields:

"My eyes are stiff with weeping and watching, but I want to send you a word. My beautiful, dear mother is sinking away, and we are heartbroken beyond bearing. It seems as if I must go too; I cannot let her go alone. She lies looking like an angel, talking and babbling of green fields, and clinging to us, and whispering blessings, and smiling as no one else can smile for us in the world."

Then the next morning: "Dearest Annie, this morning, at half past seven, the sweetest Mother in the world went, God alone knows where, away from us!"

CELIA'S LITERARY CAREER

Somewhere in the journals and correspondence we should find a word or two about Levi's part in Celia's new career. He was well versed in the poetry of his time, and so competent a critic that we assume he was of great help to Celia in writing her poems. Nothing of this kind appears on the record! His chief act of appreciation was to have the first volume of collected poems published at his expense. He advanced five hundred dollars for this, and secured the copyright for her. The book appeared in 1872.

Celia's earnings from her writing during this ten-year period could not have been large, but they were steady, her reputation was established, her writing in demand, and her pen more pro-

ISLES OF SHOALS

ductive. In contrast, Levi had never earned a dollar from any creative effort of his own. Moreover, when "Land-Locked" first appeared he found that he and Celia had suddenly reversed status. It had seemed natural and right that all his friends should think of Celia as his young wife from the Islands, but now he was known as Celia's husband! That was hard to accept. Instead of being proud of her achievement, celebrating her successes, matching her work with his own, he went out hunting specimens with the boys. He turned in upon himself, brooded over his failures, and in silence concealed his wounded pride under a mantle of chronic illness.

Here then are the four compelling reasons for the divergent paths which Celia and Levi followed for so many years: Karl's mental status, the long, lingering illnesses of Thomas and Eliza, Levi's chronic ailments, and Celia's literary career.

Is it not amazing that the disparate family maintained its integrity against such overwhelming odds?

8

A BOOK, A HOTEL, AND A MURDER

THREE milestones mark the year 1873. First was the publication of Celia's book *Among the Isles of Shoals*. Celia had been urged by Whittier and others to tell the story of the islands in prose, and she had reluctantly written it out for the *Atlantic Monthly*, where it had appeared serially to the delight of many readers. Charles Dickens was impressed by the strength and vividness of her writing. The first volume of collected poems had come out in 1872, and was well received, but now it was conceded that her prose was superior to her verse. The book remains a classic in its field and is the crowning literary achievement of the islands.

Second was the building of the Oceanic Hotel on Star Island by John Poor, whose name is still perpetuated in the firm so well known as "Stickney and Poor's Spices." This young man of wealth had visited Appledore and felt that he could outdo the Laightons. Secretly he bought out most of the property owners on Star during the summer of 1872, and spent the winter putting up a sumptuous hotel and building a long pier where large boats could land passengers without the inconvenience of clambering into small boats. This added attraction was widely advertised with the deliberate intention of drawing patrons from Appledore. The Laightons took advantage of the publicity and built a similar pier in front of their own hotel. As the summer of 1873 opened, both Islands were swarming with guests.

The Oceanic burned to the ground at the close of its second season. Poor immediately began construction of the second Oceanic (still standing), but after one season sold the whole island to the Laightons, who continued to operate both for the next forty years.

The third milestone in 1873, was the tragedy at Smuttynose, the brutal murder of Anethe and Karen Christensen by Louis Wagner. Two years after the event Celia gave a full account to the *Atlantic*, where it was published as "A Memorable Murder." Both author and publisher were criticized at the time for desecrating

ISLES OF SHOALS

the pristine pages of the *Atlantic* with the vivid narration of this horrible crime, "using the real names of real people." On the other hand, no less a critic than Laurence Hutton said in his *Talks in a Library*, "I have seen her auditors literally moved to hysterics as she related the story of the 'Murder at Smuttynose' which I consider one of the strongest pieces of prose in the English language."

It was the most famous murder of its time, and has been retold more fully and more frequently than any other known to us. The best presentation after Celia's will be found in the book of famous murders, by Edmund Pearson, bearing the title *Murder at Smuttynose, and other Murders*.

At the time of the murder, there were no more than fifty people on all the islands together; six at the lighthouse on White Island, two families remaining of the old Gosport village on Star, and with them a crew of workmen building the Oceanic Hotel for John Poor. On Appledore were the Laighton brothers, their invalid mother, and their sister, and the usual winter employees at the hotel. There was also the Ingebretson family in one of the Laighton cottages on the south shore facing Malaga. On Smuttynose all buildings were empty except the red house, occupied by the Hontvets, a family of six. They, with their nearest neighbors across Malaga Gut on Appledore, were Norwegian fishermen, recently come to American waters. Celia says of them:

"The more I see of the natives of this far-off land, the more I admire the fine qualities which seem to characterize them as a race. Gentle, faithful, intelligent, God-fearing human beings, they daily use such courtesy toward each other and all who come in contact with them, as puts our ruder Yankee manners to shame. The men and women living on this island were like the sweet, honest, simple folk we read of in Bjornson's charming Norwegian stories, full of kindly thoughts and ways . . . . They rejoiced to find a home just such as they desired in this peaceful place; the women took such pleasure in the little house which they kept so neat and bright, in their flock of hens, in their little dog, Ringe, and all their humble belongings.

"From the little town of Laurvig, near Christiana, in Norway, came John and Maren Hontvet to this country, and five years ago took up their abode in this desolate spot, in one of the cottages facing the cove and Appledore . . . John making a comfortable living by fishing, and Maren, his wife, keeping as bright and tidy

104

ISLES OF SHOALS

and sweet a little home for him as man could desire. . . . In the month of May, 1871, came her sister Karen, who stayed only a short time with Maren, and then came to Appledore, where she lived at service two years, till within a fortnight of her death. The first time I saw Maren she brought her sister to us, and I was charmed with the little woman's beautiful behavior; she was so gentle, courteous, decorous, and left on my mind a most beautiful impression. Her face struck me as remarkably good and intelligent, and her gray eyes full of light.

"Karen was a rather sad looking woman, about thirty nine years old; she had lost a lover in Norway long since, and in her heart fretted and mourned for him continually. . . She had a pensive way of letting her head droop a little sideways as she spun, and while the low wheel hummed monotonously she would sit crooning sweet, sad old Norwegian airs by the hour together. . . .

"On the twelfth of October, 1872, in the second year of her stay with us, her brother, Ivan Christensen and his wife, Anethe, came over from their Norseland in an evil day, and joined Maren and John at their island, living in the same house with them.

"Ivan and Anethe had been married only since Christmas of the preceding year. Ivan was tall, light haired, rather quiet and grave. Anethe was young, fair and merry, with thick, bright sunny hair, which was so long it reached, when unbraided, nearly to her knees; blue eyed, with brilliant teeth, and clear fresh complexion, beautiful and beloved beyond expression by her young husband, Ivan. Matthew Hontvet, John's brother, had also joined the little circle a year before, and now Maren's happiness was complete."

These were the people of Gosport. All were friends and neighbors bound together by strong ties of mutual dependence. A sailor in distress was to be rescued, a stranger was to be welcomed. Thus it was that all unwittingly they accepted and befriended a lone fisherman who was soon to plot their destruction.

It was on the fifth of March that Louis Wagner made his desperate raid. The wind had been blowing half a gale since morning but sank with the sun to a westerly breeze as the silver half moon scattered diamond flashes over the crisp snow in the streets of Portsmouth, and on the Isles of Shoals. Celia had come to the islands with Karl just a week before, and was living in the great house on Appledore. She wandered out on her piazza, listening to the ripple of distant waves and later, remembering, wrote:

105

ISLES OF SHOALS

"It was so still, so bright! The hope of all the light and beauty a few weeks would bring forth stirred me to sudden joy. There should be spring again after the long winter weariness.

'Can trouble live in April days,
Or sadness in the summer moons?'

I thought as I watched the clear sky, grown less hard than it had been for some weeks, and sparkling with stars. But before another sunset it seemed to me that beauty had fled out of the world, and that goodness, innocence, mercy, gentleness, were a mockery of empty words."

The islands went to sleep that night with no premonition of the role they were to play in the gruesome train of events now beginning.

In the early light of a new day the three fishermen from Smuttynose set sail in the *Clara Bella* to draw their trawls, which they had set some miles to the northeast. The Ingebretsons from Appledore soon followed. The Hontvets were intending to be home again about noon, and then sail to Portsmouth to sell their catch and lay in a supply of bait, which would come on the four p.m. train from Boston. Karen was to go with them to do some shopping, and all would return that night. But a strong southwest breeze sprang up in the forenoon and the Hontvets knew that they could not beat their way home against it in time to go on to Portstmouth, and they must have new bait so they shouted across to Emil Ingebretson and asked him to stop at Smuttynose and tell the girls that they were going directly into Portsmouth, and would not be home until after dark. Emil delivered the message. The women prepared a hot dinner for the men, knowing well they would be famished since they had not taken their usual lunch. But as the sun went down and the wind came to rest, with no sail nor sound of oars, they knew the men would not be home that night. It would be the first time they had ever been left alone through the dark and silent hours, but they were not afraid. All the neighboring islands were friendly.

Near ten o'clock the three women thought they might as well clear up the kitchen and go to bed. The upstairs would be cold and lonely, so they brought down a mattress and spread it over the lounge and some chairs to make a bed for Karen in the kitchen. Maren and Anethe would sleep in the next room. They were so

ISLES OF SHOALS

confident of their isolated security that they neither drew the shades nor tried to fasten the door.

That night Louis rowed out from Portsmouth in a dory, with the evident intent of helping himself to whatever money he might find in the Hontvet home. He had met the boys John, Matthew, and Ivan at the dock in Portsmouth and satisfied himself that they would not be sailing home before morning, and that John had saved $600.00 toward buying a new schooner. He was mistaken in the amount, but his intent was unmistakable. He knew the islands well since he had been for a time a fisherman in the Hontvet crew on the *Clara Bella* and had lived with them in "the read house" on Smuttynose. With the men in Portsmouth it would be an easy matter to steal into the house and take the money without even waking the women. He thought he knew where to find it.

While rowing the twelve miles from the landing at the foot of Pickering Street out to Haley's Cove, he tried to think out every move. Maren and Anethe would be asleep in the southwest bedroom which opened off the kitchen. He could fasten that door by poking a slat from a lobster trap through the latch. The money would be in the kitchen. Karen would be with the Laightons on Appledore. He was not thinking of violence; he had no murder weapon, and seemingly little to fear.

At about eleven o'clock he sculled silently into Haley's Cove, saw no boats or signs of life, and rowed on around to the south shore of the island to shelving rocks where he could beach with less danger of discovery. The moon was brilliant on the unbroken blanket of snow. It would be down in three hours or less. He spent the better part of two hours skulking around the island, watching the windows darken on Appledore and Star as the sleepy fishermen and workmen went to bed. When all was dark he scurried through the snow with his lobster slat in hand, made directly for the southwest window, and could see dimly in the slanting rays of the moon that the two women were apparently asleep. The moonlight fell across their bedroom and through the open door into the kitchen. With the stealth of a stalking cat he went around to the front door and noticed an axe leaning against the house. He remembered the axe—it might come in handy! His entrance into the kitchen was noiseless. He drew the bedroom door shut and fastened it with his slat just as he had planned. But he was startled, frustrated, by the sudden barking of Maren's little dog. Fortunately the dog

107

ISLES OF SHOALS

was in the bedroom with the women. Louis was startled again by another unexpected sound. Someone in the kitchen had roused up. He heard a familiar voice from the dark shadows behind him calling out "John, is that you?"

With equal suddenness Maren's voice called from the bedroom, "What's the matter?"

Karen had not recognized Louis in the dark, and still thinking it was one of their own men coming home unexpectedly, answered "John scared me."

Louis had the presence of mind not to betray himself by answering. Now he could see the dim outline of Karen's white gown silhouetted against the window and lunged at her with a kitchen chair. His swinging blows knocked the clock from its shelf above the couch — it was stopped at seven minutes past one. Karen screamed in terror:

"John kills me—John kills me."

Louis swung the chair frantically in the darkness while Karen struggled through the barrage of blows to the bedroom door, fell against it, dislodging the slat that Louis had poked through the latch, and slid down under the kitchen table in an agonized stupor.

Louis not observing that the door was opening, groped to each of the two windows at opposite ends of the kitchen and drew the shades. Maren was screaming at Anethe to climb out through their bedroom window and shout for help. Clambering out and standing with her bare feet in the snow, Anethe was so paralyzed that she could not utter a sound. Maren meantime had opened the door in time to see the figure of a tall man silhouetted against a window as he drew a shade. There at her feet with a moonbean falling across her face was Karen groaning. Maren grabbed her around the waist, drug her into the bedroom, slammed the door and pushed the bed against it, all the while urging Anethe to run for help.

Louis rushed out and turning the corner saw Anethe standing mute and motionless outside the window, and remembered the axe. He rushed back for it and soon Maren heard Anethe screaming: "O Louis, Louis, Louis!" Through the open window she saw Louis Wagner striking Anethe down with the axe. "He was so close I could have touched his elbow," Maren later testified. She held her eyes on the sickening butchery as Louis hacked and chopped his helpless victim, crushing her skull and mutilating her face, neck and shoulders. Knowing that she and Karen would be next,

ISLES OF SHOALS

she urged the half-conscious Karen to help barricade the door, and shout for help, but heard only the feeble response. "I can't, I too tired."

Louis came back to the bedroom door and pushed his way in. Maren saw that they were doomed, and thought in her frenzy that someone must stay alive to identify this maniac. While Louis was pushing his way in she grabbed little Ringe, and a skirt, and clambered through the window, over the ghastly form of Anethe and out into the snow to find a hiding place. She went down to the dock thinking to find Wagner's boat, but it was not there. She then thought to hide in one of the empty houses or sheds, but was afraid Ringe would bark, and give her away. Her only hope was to stumble with bleeding feet over the snow and ice-covered rocks to the eastern end of the island where she could hide beneath a huge boulder. As she was passing the murder house she heard Karen scream, "so loud I thought she must be outdoors." At last she found her icy den and waited through six hours of agony with only the little dog to keep her from freezing.

There was no one to witness the next scene, but trailing evidence tells the story. While Maren was climbing through the window Louis struck at her with the axe, but missed and cut a deep gash in the window sill. He struck again, and this time brought the handle down on the sill snapping it in the middle. He ran around to recover the head with its stump of a handle, and seeing that Maren had escaped into the shadows, went back to quiet Karen. She had crawled from the bedroom through the kitchen out to the entry of the north apartment where Wagner had lived. He had overtaken her just as she was re-entering the house and began slashing, when Maren heard her screams. Louis dragged her into the house, into his own old room and mutilated her head, face and shoulders even as he had done to Anethe. Then in vicious and vengeful fury he had strangled her with a scarf, and kicked the quivering form under the bed.

It was his evident intention to burn the evidence, for his next move was to drag the limp form of Anethe into the kitchen where he left her in the middle of the floor while he found with fumbling bloody fingers a lantern and matches. It was time now for rest and refreshment. He rekindled the kitchen fire, brewed a pot of tea, ransacked the pantry and sat down at the table, evidently indifferent to the slaughter which had bloodied his hands, his face, his

ISLES OF SHOALS

shirt, his boots! He then searched the entire house to find the money, leaving traces of blood on linen in the bureau drawers, on chests, on shelves everywhere. He found only some loose change and a few bills in purses and pocketbooks totaling about $17.00. He dumped the contents of Karen's purse into his pocket without noticing what was in it, but here unwittingly he was filling his pocket with the evidence necessary for final conviction. His searching hand had nearly touched John's money, folded between sheets in a bureau drawer, but missed it, leaving stains of blood to mark his near approach.

Seemingly as an afterthought, he went to the well, drew water to wash the blood from his hands and shirt, left the pan and towel at the well, and started on a long hunt for Maren. The tracks of his huge boots were traced around all the buildings, down to the cove and everywhere on that end of the island, but in the darkness — the moon had hidden its face from the horror — he did not see Maren's tracks leading to the other end. He must have concluded that she was frozen to death. Soon the early rising fishermen on the southern slope of Appledore would be up. He decided not to burn the house, but he shoved off and rowed back to the mainland, beached his boat at a point near the site of the Wentworth Hotel, and after many minor episodes that helped to identify him as the criminal, took the nine o'clock train to Boston.

During the long hours from 1:30 until 7:30, Maren remained in the cold embrace of the rocks, holding close the faithful Ringe, her only warmth and comfort. The tide came creeping in, hour by hour, and if a southeast wind had sprung up it would have driven the cold surf into the narrow channel where she lay. She could only wait and hope in the terrifying dark, listening for the sound of a heavy foot crunching the snow.

Slowly the sky turned gray in the east. The sun took an eternity to rise. Even when it burst out of the shimmering waves she was still afraid to move from her hiding place. At last — it must have been seven o'clock—she heard the music of hammers drifting over the harbor from Star Island, where the carpenters were beginning their day's work on the new hotel. Slowly she crept out, hardly able to move at first, and stumbled her way back, skirting the south shore, until she came in sight of the red house. There was no sign of life! No life there, nor anywhere else on her island. She came to the western point and shouted across to the carpenters.

ISLES OF SHOALS

They looked up from their work. She waved her skirt; they saw, they heard, but made no response and turned again to their hammering. She went on around the shore until she crossed over the breakwater onto Malaga and saw the Ingebretson children playing in the morning sun. They heard her cries and ran into the house. Jorge, the father of the family, came out and in Celia's version:

"He sees the poor little figure waving her arms, takes his dory and paddles over, and with amazement recognizes Maren in her nightdress, with bare feet and streaming hair, with a cruel bruise upon her face, with wild eyes, distracted, half senseless with cold and terror. He cries, 'Maren, Maren, who has done this? what is it? who is it?' and her only answer is 'Louis, Louis, Louis!' as he takes her on board his boat and rows home with her as fast as he can. From her incoherent statement he learns what has happened. Leaving her in the care of his family, he comes over the hill to the great house on Appledore. As I sit at my desk I see him pass the window, and wonder why the old man comes so fast and anxiously through the heavy snow.

"Presently I see him going back again, accompanied by several of his own countrymen and other of our workmen, carrying guns . . . . I call downstairs. 'What has happened?' and am answered, 'Some trouble at Smuttynose; we hardly understand.' Probably a drunken brawl of the reckless fishermen who may have landed there,' I say to myself, and go on with my work. In another half hour I see the men returning, reinforced by others, coming fast, confusedly; and suddenly a wail of anguish comes up from the women below. I cannot believe it when I hear them crying, 'Karen is dead! Anethe is dead; Louis Wagner has murdered them both!' I run out into the servants' quarters; there are all the men assembled, an awe-stricken crowd. Old Ingebretson comes forward and tells me the bare facts, and how Maren lies at his house, half crazy, suffering with torn and frozen feet. Then the men are dispatched to search Appledore, to find if by any chance the murderer might still be concealed about the place, and I go over to Maren to see if I can do anything for her. I find the women and children with frightened faces at the little cottage; as I go into the room where Maren lies she catches my hands, crying, 'Oh, I so glad to see you! I so glad I save my life!' and with her dry lips she tells me all the story as I have told it here. Poor little creature, holding me with those wild, glittering, dilated eyes, she cannot tell me rapidly

111

ISLES OF SHOALS

enough the whole horrible tale. Upon her cheek is yet the blood stain from the blow he struck her with a chair, and she shows me two more upon her shoulder, and her torn feet. I go back for arnica with which to bathe them. What a mockery seems to me the 'jocund day' as I merge into the sunshine, and looking across the space of blue, sparkling water see the house wherein all that horror lies."

While Celia was gone the white sail of the *Clara Bella* rounded the point. Her story continues:

"From Appledore they are signalled to come ashore, and Ivan and Matthew, landing, hear a confused rumor of trouble from tongues that hardly can frame the words that must tell the dreadful truth. Ivan only understands that something is wrong. His one thought is for Anethe; he flies to Ingebretson's cottage, she may be there; he rushes in like a maniac, crying, 'Anethe, Anethe! Where is Anethe?' He does not wait for another word, but seizes the little boat and lands at the same time with John on Smuttynose; with headlong haste they reach the house, other men accompanying them; ah, there are blood stains all about the snow! Ivan is the first to burst open the door and enter. What words can tell it! There upon the floor, naked, stiff and stark, is the woman he idolizes, for whose dear feet he could not make life's ways smooth and pleasant enough—stone dead! Dead—horribly butchered; her bright hair stiff with blood, the fair head that had so often rested on his breast, crushed, cloven, mangled with the brutal axe. Their eyes are blasted by the terrible sight! Both John and Ivan stagger out and fall, senseless, in the snow. Poor Ivan! his wife a thousand times adored, the dear girl he had brought from Norway, the good, sweet girl who loved him so, whom he could not cherish tenderly enough. And he was not there to protect her! There was no one there to save her! . . . .

"When I reach the cottage with the arnica for Maren, they have returned to Smuttynose. John, her husband is there. He is a young man of the true Norse type, blue eyed, fair haired, tall and well made, with handsome teeth and bronzed beard. Perhaps he is a little quiet and undemonstrative generally, but at this moment he is superb, kindled from head to feet, a firebrand of woe and wrath, with eyes that flash and cheeks that burn. I speak a few words to him—what words can meet such an occasion as this!—and having given directions about the arnica for Maren, I go away, for

112

ISLES OF SHOALS

nothing more can be done for her, and every comfort she needs is hers. The outer room is full of men; they make way for me, and as I pass through I catch a glimpse of Ivan crouched with his arms thrown around his knees and his head bowed down between them, motionless, his attitude expressing such abandonment of despair as cannot be described."

In less than an hour every building, cave, and rocky gorge in the island had been explored. The only clue to Wagner's escape was the trampled snow where he had beached his dory. John sailed with a small crew to Portsmouth and alerted the police. Reporters for the evening papers began to feed ravenous presses with scraps of news about the "Terrible Tragedy at the Isles of Shoals."

"The men who came from the Shoals are so excited," says the Portsmouth *Evening Times,* "that it is impossible to get any particulars from them and this news reached us just as we go to press."

Louis was arrested in Boston a few hours after his arrival there, brought back to Alfred, Maine, for trial, convicted, and sentenced to be hanged. In the trial much was made of three or four trivial bits of evidence, bread crumbs, a white button, a mended buttonhole, a few bloodstains, and deeply worn thole pins in James Burke's dory.

The bread crumbs found on the kitchen table in the murder house were not from any bread made at the islands. They were "foreign", and must have been brought in by an outsider. It was Wagner's habit to carry a "hunk of bread" in his pocket, and these crumbs matched the bread from a bakery in Portsmouth where he often bought a loaf or a few rolls.

The white button was found in Louis's pocket when he was arrested in Boston. It was in Karen's purse when he dumped the contents into his pocket, and at the trial was identified as one she was to take to Portsmouth for matching.

The mended buttonhole identified the bloodstained shirt, which Louis had thrown into a privy vault in Portsmouth. Mary Johnston testified that she had done the mending "while it was on him," the day before the murder.

The bloodstain on this shirt was evidence that this garment too, was involved in some bloody incident.

The worn tholepins were proof enough that the man who borrowed James Burke's boat must have been a powerful oarsman,

113

ISLES OF SHOALS

and that he pulled hard during the night, since Burke had put in new hickory pins less than an hour before the boat was taken.

These items and all other evidence pointed to Wagner and no one else. His chief defense and alibi was that "Maren must have done it herself."

Pearson says, "The execution at Thomaston became a shocking spectacle; it is not surprising that it was the last ever held in Maine." This remark, though generally believed and often repeated, turns out not to be true. Mr. Allen L. Robbins, now warden of the Maine State Prison at Thomaston, has this to say:

"According to our records the last man to be executed at this institution was one Daniel Wilkinson on the twentieth of November, 1885, for the killing of a police officer in Sagadahoc County.

"The execution preceding was a double one: Carmen Santore and Raffaele Capone on the seventeenth of April 1885—murder in Androscoggin County.

"Louis H. F. Wagner and John T. Gordon were executed on the twenty-fifth of June, 1875."

Mr. Philip W. Wheeler, special investigator for the Attorney General of Maine, informs us that the death penalty was abolished in 1876, one year after the Wagner execution, restored in 1883, and revoked again in 1887.

The red house on Smuttynose went up in flames in 1885, and the other buildings have fallen in ruins, except the Haley house, which still keeps vigil over the lonely island. White gulls are nesting now near the rock where Maren hid, and the sea moans through the long night, and the gray light comes, and the sun rises again in all his ancient glory.

Leif Ericson discovers Vinland, about 1000 A.D.

Fish frames and stages, making dunfish

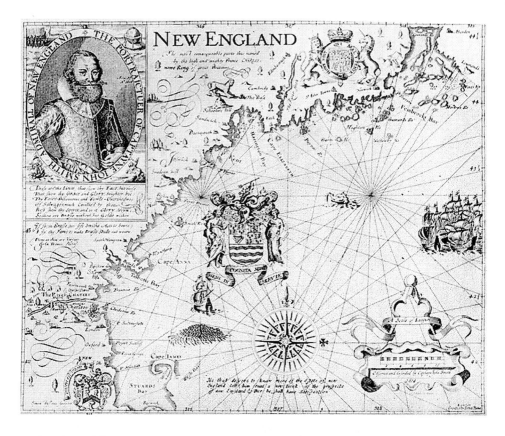

John Smith's map of New England, 1616

John Smith monument, erected 1814

The monument today, remodeled 1914

Gosport Village School

*The second parsonage,
built 1802, burned 1905*

Foundation of Tucke Parsonage

Gosport House

Atlantic House

Caswell Cemetery

Beebe Cemetery

The Samuel Haley House

The Mid Ocean House

Graves of the Spanish sailors

Haley burying ground

Maren's Rock

Louis Wagner

The graves of Anethe and Karen Christensen

The Hontvet House

Celia Thaxter in 1880

John Weiss

Levi Lincoln Thaxter

The Appledore Hotel in 1880

Celia Thaxter's cottage on Appledore

The Thaxter home on California St. in Newton, Mass.

Cedric Laighton

The Laighton cottage on Appledore, built for Cedric in 1882

Sketch by Oscar Laighton

Oscar Laighton at 97

Roland Thaxter

Karl Thaxter
John Thaxter

The Appledore Hotel burning in 1914, and after the fire

The Castle on Appledore

*The Gosport Meetinghouse,
built in 1800*

Sconce

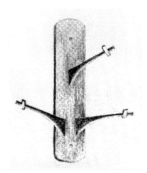

Candlelight procession

Mr. Elliott leading candelight service

Thomas H. Elliott at 90   *Lilla N. Elliott at the turnstile*

The five founders, From left, Mrs. Jessie E. Donahue, Oscar Laighton, Mrs. Thomas H. Elliott, Mr. Elliott, Mrs. William B. Nichols

Y.P.R.U. Shoalers. Standing, Carl Wetherell, Margaret Nichols, Charles S. Bolster, Ruey Packard and Ruth Twiss. Seated, Elizabeth Monroe Bolster and Sara Comins

Y.P.R.U. and Sprague Cottages

Gosport village today. From left to right, Vaughn Memorial, built 1960; the Meetinghouse, 1800; Parker Memorial, 1948; Newton Centre House, 1950; Tucke Parsonage, 1927

A conference group on the piazza of the Oceanic Hotel

Air view of Star Island

Let the Story Be Told —
author and children

St. Hilaire house on Appledore

View of Stone Village on Star Island

Foye cottages on Cedar Island

Sullivan cottage on Appledore

Miss Underhill's Chair

Entering Betty Moody's Cave

Illingworth rock garden

The New York Yacht Club in Gosport Harbor

The Viking

White Island Light

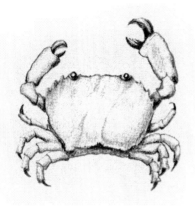

Old Man of the Sea

9

THE PASSING OF WILLIAM MORRIS HUNT
AND LEVI THAXTER

ONE OF the many bonds that drew Celia and Levi together in their later years was the devoted friendship of both for William Morris Hunt. He and Levi were classmates at Harvard, although he did not take his degree. A long and serious illness during his senior year prompted his widowed mother, herself an artist, to take her five children to the south of France, where William found art teachers greatly to his liking. On returning to Boston, he set up a studio and soon became "the most influential artist of his time." He renewed his friendship with Levi, and would listen to his reading of Browning by the Newton fireside. At the Shoals he became chief among artists in Celia's parlor. His sketches adorned her walls.

Hunt's life ambition was to create a mural wherein he could express his ideals on the enduring walls of some worthy hall or temple. In the early spring of 1879 his opportunity came. He was commissioned to do the large murals for the yet unfinished capitol of New York at Albany. The work must be ready for dedication in late summer. He took a corps of his best students as assistants and completed the assignment in time, but had driven himself to exhaustion. He set sail at once for the Isles of Shoals.

Celia wrote of his coming: "Just think of our having William Hunt here, just shuddered back from the dreadful verge, so attenuated, so pathetic! He and his sister and his brother, and his man Carter, are all housed beneath this cottage roof, and I hope and trust the air is going to do everything for him.

> 'Fold him to rest, O pitying clime!
> Give back his wasted strength again.'

Poor, dear fellow! There is nobody I pity so much. Mr. Thaxter is here, next door to his room; everybody is taking care of him, W. H. I mean . . . . I told him I wished he would consider my little den, my nook, my bower, this fresh and fragrant little parlor, as his own particular property, and he said, 'You dear child! you don't

115

ISLES OF SHOALS

know what a miserable, sick, weak, good-for-nothing I am, fit only for my bed! But he really is coming back to life and eats and sleeps again, and yesterday rowed a little in the children's boat on the pond, and takes an interest in things, in the charming music of the band, etc. He was suffocating in that hot Weathersfield. I'm so glad he could get here."

Ten days later (July 28), Celia wrote to Annie: "Hunt continues to improve. Mr. Thaxter still here and apparently enjoying it. We have music every day, piano and violin. Expect Appleton Brown tomorrow."

From her letters we gain the impression that this had been an unusually happy summer for Celia, shadowed only by her sympathy for Hunt.

On September first Celia wrote to Annie Fields: "For us it has been glorious, never, never, never was anything like it! Music from morning till night and dear charming people making a charmed circle through which it seemed for the moment impossible that pain and loss and grief could break — Mr. Thaxter was here two whole months, really enjoying it and having a happy time like other people—all my family at once—John doing a tremendous execution among the hearts of youthful compeers. He, poor fellow, never had such a beautiful time in his life, and after he had gone the young ladies came begging his picture of me—he is so extremely jolly that he won hearts . . . "

Then came the tragedy. Celia tells the story in a letter to Annie Fields:

"I found him. It was reserved for me, who loved him truly, that bitterness. All the island was seeking him. It was I who went to the brink of that lovely little lake, round which the wild roses have breathed and glowed all summer, and the little birds have come to drink and wash in the early morning light at its peaceful brim."

At first they all thought that Hunt had taken his own life, but the examining physician, reviewing his medical history, concluded that he must have been seized with an attack of vertigo while standing near the edge of the pool, and leaning heavily on his umbrella, fell as it broke under him. Celia's own matchless observation also offered a clue, for she had noted that "the wind stirred a fold of his long coat on the water." This could hardly have happened if he had plunged in. Later this opinion was confirmed, as one of the

116

ISLES OF SHOALS

boys found the broken staff of the umbrella on the opposite side of the pool.

Funeral services were held in the Unitarian church at Brattleboro, Vermont, on September eleventh. The interment was in the family lot in the village cemetery beside his father. Above him is a granite slab with the simple inscription, "William Morris Hunt, born March 31, 1824; died September 8, 1879."

With sadness of heart the Thaxter family returned from Hunt' funeral directly to the home on California Street, which Levi's father had given them twenty-three years before. They had put it up for sale when Levi was fighting his way back from oblivion, but now in the long absence of buyers, they had no other choice than to camp here another winter. Perhaps the old joys would return to the fireside where Hunt had read his "talks." The ceiling was still black with the smoke which Hunt humorously said had pickled so many pleasant evenings.

The dreary months of the winter went dragging on until the hope of a decade was suddenly fulfilled. A buyer knocked at the door.

Immediately Levi entered negotiations for a coveted farm at Kittery Point in Maine, and in the early spring the family took leave of Newtonville forever. Before they closed the door Celia wrote a brief note to Annie Fields about the new home:

"The name of the place in Kittery is really Dartington. Captain Francis Champernowne so called it after his family place in England, on the banks of the river Dart.

"Captain Francis was a nephew of Sir Ferdinando Gorges and came over here to look after his uncle's estates, settled there and called it Dartington; so we pick up the name and rechristen it, as we did Appledore. Rather a nice name, don't you think? Isn't it curious that the name Thaxter should appear in some of the old records of the Champernownes?"

They had waited ten years for this. To Levi it meant relief from the many anxieties and an ideal place for his taxidermy and botanical studies; for John, his long desired farm, for Roland, a wonderful new home where he would find his family together, at least on holidays; for Karl, a workshop and a new life; for Celia almost a re-creation of her childhood "fairyland." All this in anticipation. There was little sadness in the farewell to Newtonville!

117

ISLES OF SHOALS

In a letter to Mr. Blake (April 3, 1884), Celia gave an account of Levi's last illness:

"I am sorry to say Mr. Thaxter does not gain as I hoped, but lies day after day, not yet able to sit up a moment. It is twelve weeks now—a long time. But I trust the warmer weather will restore him. This is Fast Day, April 3rd, and it has been snowing two days and a night, and blowing a gale. Not much like Spring!"

Levi died on the thirty-first of May, and was buried in the seclusion of his own forest glade, Kittery Point cemetery at Champernowne. A few years later, Celia and Roland suggested to Robert Browning that an epitaph from his gifted pen would be most appropriate, and he responded with the cryptic lines now deeply carved on the great boulder that marks Levi's grave.

An undated newspaper clipping pays him generous tribute:

"The death of Levi Thaxter will be deeply felt by his circle of warm and devoted friends. By the more cultivated public of Boston and other cities, he was known and will be remembered as the accomplished reader of Browning, from whom he drew his profoundest inspiration, and of whom he was the most prominent interpreter of this century. Acquaintances will think of him as the courteous gentleman whose distinguished presence made him noticeable among all, while those who stood in closer relations towards him must regard him as one of the most exceptional persons whom it has been their privilege to meet. He was a man of singular simplicity, but a born enthusiast, a lover of beauty in all its forms; one of those true sons of nature who feel her loveliness like a poet, and know her secrets like a naturalist. No image of him would be complete which did not include the delight he took in flowers, especially wild flowers and the other tender growths of woods and fields. He possessed natural delicacy of taste and sentiment, combined with great strength of character and a wide and ready sympathy. He never stood mentally still, but was always progressing and advancing. Those of the younger generation never felt themselves misunderstood or mistaken by him; they knew that he was their friend and comrade, that he entered into and sympathized with the feelings and emotions which form changing atmosphere from year to year. But the qualities which most set apart and elevated him were his absolute genuineness, his constancy to his ideals, his courage, patience, and fortitude, his clear understanding of the real opportunities of existence, and his unrepining accept-

ISLES OF SHOALS

ance of the inevitable. In an age so largely characterized by display and pretentiousness, he was conspicuous as a hater of shams. There was no brilliancy about his external fortunes or position, but he had brought his inward life to a degree of fulfillment and completion but rarely attained. His life taught a lesson, not loud, but deep, which will live always, an abiding and sustaining force, in the hearts of those he leaves behind."

10

CELIA'S PARLOR AT APPLEDORE

GUESTS at the hotel found long rows of rocking chairs on the western piazza overlooking the tiny harbor with its fleet of small boats nosing the pier, and the *Pinafore* at the dock. Beyond was the broad expanse of sunlit waters with white drifting sails and the far horizon where the continent of North America was lost in summer haze. In such tranquil moments the world takes on a new aspect. The continent fades into unreality as if it were slipping over the edge of the ocean into oblivion, while these little islands lift their solid reality above the aggressive tides. Here at last is an observation point where life may be viewed in truer perspective.

Suddenly it occurred to an alert guest that people are never "lost in contemplation." The world is lost while the person is finding himself. That may be the secret of "Celia's Parlor."

Her cottage stood on a gentle rise of ground about two minutes' walk from the hotel. Strains of music usually drifted through the open windows.

Once through the gate the visitor would find himself in a new world of color. The garden was without formality except for the narrow paths that separated tiny beds, but even those were half hidden by spreading plants. It seems odd that so small a garden, only fifteen by fifty feet, should have had so great a variety of flowers. Mrs. Larz Anderson said she often "counted as many as one hundred and fifty different flowers, each carrying out its habit of growth in the manner and height of its arrangement." But Celia said, "I plant my garden to pick, not for show. They are just to supply my vases in this room." It was all so casual that the informality became impressive. Nothing seemed to have been premeditated, yet it was more effective than any formality could have made it.

If by chance William Mason was in Celia's parlor back of the wistaria vines, the Preludes of Chopin would mingle with the choir of birds, over the garden. The visitor might wonder if he had been suddenly transported to the gardens of the Hesperides, or some land of celestial dreams. But no! this was not fiction, or a

ISLES OF SHOALS

magic spell, or any premeditated artifice to capture the imagination. This was Celia's garden; this, if you wished to name it at all, was "Appledoria"—a moment of response to one's total environment. Some would call it a mystical experience. It was no more mystical than a slice of apple pie. It was simply life at its best.

Is this a legitimate part of history? It must be so considered since it is not only a record of what happened many times, but of the most significant factor in Shoals history. It is known to those who "see life steadily and see it whole." The only act of imagination is to see that poppy seeds and constellations are one fabric perfectly woven.

The visitor would be invited to enter Celia's parlor. It was understood that one did not usually speak to her on entering. She would be at her desk or work table in a far corner, and would come forward when she had reached a stopping place.

The first impression was of radiance. The sun streamed through south or west windows and shone through the delicate petals of innumerable flowers. (One of her visitors reported: "There were blue delphinium of all shades, red and yellow poppies [her favorites], white and pink phlox, hollyhocks of different colors, bachelor's buttons, and all the flowers in old-fashioned gardens. The effect she achieved . . . . cannot be described in words, for it was unlike any other flower arrangement I have ever seen." These were in vases. (Maud McDowell counted one hundred and ten one morning.) The vases, with their several varieties, were so placed around the room as to make a delightful color scheme, yet the ensemble seemed accidental rather than obvious. A large sea shell hung from the ceiling was filled with nasturtiums, pansies, and a variety of blue flowers.

The dominant tone of the room was green. There were half a dozen green scatter rugs on the hardwood floor. The walls, peeping from behind solid banks of pictures, were dull green. The pictures were an unorganized array of the sort usually found in parlors of that day. An interior view of the James T. Fields library in Boston was very much like Celia's, but with a little more wall space visible. On Celia's walls the culture of the world was represented—large reproductions of famous portraits; photographs of notable places and people; landscapes in oil and watercolor, some fresh from the easels of artists then summering at Appledore; one

121

ISLES OF SHOALS

—the most arresting—a large sketch of a torso, by William Morris Hunt.

The atmosphere of the parlor and Celia's informality are charmingly revealed in a brief article by Maud Appleton McDowell in *The Heavenly Guest*:

"It was my privilege as a young girl to be for several summers in the cottage of Celia Thaxter the poet, on Appledore . . . . I went first with my father and mother in 1890 to Hotel Appledore . . . but I was soon taken by our dear mutual friend, J. Appleton Brown, the painter, to Mrs. Thaxter's cottage where she held a sort of salon mornings and evenings.

"I shall never forget my feeling of awe when I first went into her room . . . Besides the 'Altar,' where all her flowers were mostly massed, there was the 'Throne,' as we called it, where she sat, or half reclined, for at that time she was not very strong . . . she was always in very light grey or white dresses, usually made simply and according to her own style, not changing with the prevailing fashions. She nearly always wore a soft white kerchief fastened with an old-fashioned brooch. Her hair was very white, her eyes very blue and her cheeks very pink; and she had an adorable smile which lighted up her whole face when she greeted you. I fell in love with her at once, of course, and nearly died of joy when, the second day after my meeting her, she said, 'Child, I like you! You may come and stay here in my cottage,—I believe there is one empty room left.' . . . .

"Each morning at eleven we would rush for the best seats on sofa or chairs facing the piano and listen to divine music. . .

"What concerts we had and how like boys they all were! Just enjoying their holidays and 'making music' when they wished and playing what they wanted. And in such an atmosphere of beauty! Something to appeal to the eye and ear and even the sense of smell, with the scent of honeysuckle coming in through the many windows.

Then in the evenings we had reading aloud or recitations by her or by some of the literary guests. The room was dim and mysterious, lighted only by a lamp on the piano or by her side. She would read us weird stories, or the adventures of the early settlers on the island." . . .

Annie Fields in her book, *Celia Thaxter and Whittier,* gives

ISLES OF SHOALS

an interesting view of Celia's parlor as Whittier saw it one idle Sunday.

"Occasionally he would pass whole days in Celia's parlor watching her at her painting in the window, and listening to the conversation around him.

"I remember one season in particular, when the idle talk of the idle people had been drifting in and out during the day, while he sat patiently in the corner of the pretty room. Mrs. Thaxter was steadily at work at her table, yet always hospitable, losing sight of no cloud or shadow or sudden gleam of glory in the landscape, and pointing the talk often with keen wit. Nevertheless the idleness of it all palled upon him. It was Sunday, too, and he longed for something which would move us to 'higher levels'. . . .Suddenly as if the idea had struck like an inspiration, he rose, and taking a volume of Emerson from the little library, he opened to one of the discourses, and handing it to Celia said, 'Read that aloud will thee? I think we should all like to hear it.'

"He continued after that with a discourse of his own on the subject of the essay."

We may wonder how important this parlor was to Celia since she makes so little mention of it. It is as if she were never aware of her own commanding position as the central figure in the circle of celebrities. Indeed she avoided all reference to her own literary career as such. I have read every available letter, every scrap of undated comment from her pen that I could lay my hands on, and I do not remember a single line to indicate that she thought of herself as a career woman, except in the form of resentment when friends or strangers called her "the queen of the islands," or addressed her as an important person. She dismissed all such flattery. Her parlor was simply her studio, and those who came were only friends and casual guests. It was all part of her life. She did not see it as history in the making.

The floods of music which echoed from this studio over the island and over the continent were woven into her deepest emotional experiences, associated with her love for flowers, birds, friends, and the islands themselves. On a summer evening when Julius Eichberg played, she wrote:

> Clear eyes brood upon the path of light
> The white moon makes . . .

ISLES OF SHOALS

Needs the enchantment of the summer night
    Another touch to make it perfect? Hark!
What sudden shaft of sound, like piercing light,
    Strikes on the ear athwart the moonlit dark?
Like some keen shock of joy is heard within
The wondrous music of the violin.

It is as if dumb Nature found a voice,
    And spoke with power, though in an
        unknown tongue.
What kinship has the music with the noise
    Of waves, or winds, or with the flowers,
        slow-swung
Like censers to and fro upon the air,
Or with the shadow, or the moolight fair?
But every head is bowed. We watch the sea
    With other eyes, as if some hint of bliss
Spoke to us, through the yearning melody.

Can anyone fail to see the effect these lines would have upon the violinist? No word of flattery, but an impersonal tribute, a mark of deep appreciation. Those who were invited to Celia's parlor could feel that here as nowhere else their finest talents were felt and understood. And so it was that Paine and Whiting and even Ole Bull would say that in Celia's parlor they felt a strange new power — that the presence of Celia there in one corner painting her china, or writing little verses, inspired them more than any cheering audience on the mainland. It was literally true that by her power of sympathetic understanding Celia had a profound influence on the most gifted artists of her time, and heard within her own parlor finer concerts than could be heard from any stage.

Harriet Prescott Spofford said of her, "In all our literature she is the most picturesque figure."

John Albee, who felt that Celia was much greater than all her works, said that she

"stood among the first women writers in the country, and it is through her published writings that she was known to her contemporaries . . . Not there, however, will we find the inward struggles, which, could they be known in all their completeness, would be of more worth than many volumes. We amuse ourselves with literature and miss the lessons of lives which create it."

ISLES OF SHOALS

Celia presided in her island parlor the better part of twenty-five summers, yet we hear of no formal reception ever held there. The nearest we come to it will be found in two or three quotations which betray the difficulty writers had in trying to describe the spontaneous outpouring of genius. They speak of "receptions" and the "salon," merely for lack of more accurate words. An unknown writer designated only as "A Visitor to the Blessed Isles" said, "It is a subject of satisfaction with Mrs. Thaxter's visitors at her morning and evening receptions that there has been a great deal of music in her parlor this season." Another said, "Since practical America has not too many salons for the cultivation of the higher things, it is pleasant to think of the longtime appreciation of poetry and art of Appledore." From these and from the necessity of her restricting the number of guests by extending invitations, we gain the impression that Celia had almost formalized these gatherings, but the regulations went no further than to state the hours in the morning and evening when guests would be welcome and to let it be understood that unless you had a personal invitation you might not find room even to sit on the floor. Moreover she usually welcomed guests who wished to come at other times. She was indifferent only to those who did not seem worthy —the idly curious, whom she quickly detected.

One of the most discriminating comments on Celia and her parlor comes from the pen of Laurence Hutton.

"Celia Thaxter's life and personality were absolutely unique. She was carried to her island home as a child, and for many years she knew nothing else. Her brothers were her only playmates, and her only playthings were the shells on the beach. The children were as wild and as unartificial as were the waves and the winds, the sea-birds and the ocean plants. She knew a fisherman or two, and a dun cow. It was a wonderful school for a poet of nature, but a poor school for a woman of society or of the world, — and this latter she never became. So long as she lived she went but little into the world, and almost the only world she knew was the small fraction of the world which came to her. Nature was her only teacher until she became a woman, and her intercourse with her fellow-beings, and her study of the literature of the ancients, or of her contemporaries, had but little influence upon her work. She was, as a writer, as unique as she was as an individual. And unique—that

125

ISLES OF SHOALS

hackneyed, much-abused, often misapplied word—is the only word which describes Celia Thaxter, the poet and the woman.

"I had spent some portion of the summers of ten years at the Isles of Shoals, and my wife had been going there for upwards of a quarter of a century. Naturally, we knew Mrs. Thaxter, and knew her well; although never intimately. We did not belong to the set, and did not altogether care for the set, of men and women who were frequenters of her daily and nightly levees. The atmosphere of the place, when she was not alone in it, seemed to us artificial . . . . The hostess was generally surrounded by a dozen young women of all ages who adored and worshipped her; and by commonplace droppers-in from the hotel. For all that, Mrs. Thaxter's guests were sometimes the most brilliant men and women of the day, and what was said there was often well worth listening to. Hawthorne, Lowell, Whittier, William Hunt, were among her intimate friends, drawn towards her by feelings of genuine respect and affection. She had a personal magnetism which was not to be resisted; and old and young, the ignorant and the educated, came under its influence.

"The strongest head in the world would have been turned, and the simplest nature spoiled, by the flattery and adulation so openly bestowed upon Celia Thaxter for so many years. And the occasional trace of artificiality of manner which sometimes repelled strangers, is not altogether to be wondered at. These affectations however, were reserved for the crowd, and for the crowd of a certain kind. When she was among natural persons, she was as natural as any of them, and then her full charm was apparent, and then the true Celia Thaxter appeared.

. . . .

Her greatest interest in life was her flowers. She was in her garden (not so large as the ordinary grass plot of a city back yard) at three or four o'clock every morning, watering, cherishing, petting and communing with her plants.

"Celia reigned not only in the little society of intelligent people she drew around her, but also in the hearts of the fisherfolk who inhabited the little group of islands known as the Shoals. Among them she was queen indeed; and as good and as great a queen as ever won and held the devotion and esteem of her subjects. They were a colony of simple, hard-working Swedes [Norwegians], to whom she was physician, patron, pastor, friend. She

ISLES OF SHOALS

nursed them when they were ill; named their babies; shared their joys and sorrows. And it is pleasant to think that two of these Swedish [Norwegian] girls, Mina and Niccolina whom she had almost immortalized in verse, were with her at the last and caught her in their arms as she died."

11

WHITTIER

IF WHITTIER had favorites among the young writers who held him in affectionate regard he kept his secret well. All looked upon him as a patriarch whose kindliness fell as a benediction impartially bestowed. Few if any were aware of his early romance, which was ended by mutual agreement with great sorrow of heart. Neither he nor his beloved could accept the views of the other nor give up his own. It was a matter of integrity and conscience. After the parting Whittier knew that he would never be so deeply moved again. He was not embittered or estranged, but more perfectly attuned to the finer qualities of friendship. It is fair presumption that certain lines in the prologue to his "Tent on the Beach" echo a long lingering heartache.

> And the dear
> Memory of one who might have turned my song
> To sweeter music by her delicate ear.

When these lines were composed in 1868, Whittier cherished the friendship of many women, any one of whom would readily agree that he must have been thinking of her. If he had any favorites among them, Lucy Larcom would have been one and Celia Thaxter another by common consent. Some said Lucy was jealous of Celia.

Whittier had known Lucy since 1844, and Celia only since 1863 (although there is a cherished tradition that Whittier visited the Laightons on Smuttynose in 1842, and later remembered Celia as a little island waif in a white frock stained down the left front with the royal blood of crushed blueberries). Whittier visited Appledore on July 7th, 1861, and persuaded Cedric to row him over to Star to attend services in the stone meetinghouse. Celia had returned to Newtonville the day before, and Whittier was disappointed not to meet the author of "Land-Locked."

Whittier revisited Appledore in the summer of '63, and Celia recalled the event many years later for Whittier's biographer, Samuel T. Pickard. She wrote: "Ever since he first came here to

ISLES OF SHOALS

the Shoals with his dear sister, thirty years ago, and fixed me with those brilliant eyes of his as he quietly asked me, 'Can thee tell me who wrote The Summer Day?' we have had the most delightful friendship, and I miss him out of the world more than any words can say."

So little is known by the general public about Whittier's love for the Isles of Shoals, and so much is available on the subject that a separate chapter should be devoted to it. Various writers have touched upon it, some with understanding, others with devastating ignorance.

Typical of the latter is the comment by Albert Mordell in his *Quaker Militant, John Greenleaf Whittier.* He says:

"There were other women writers who made a deep impression upon Whittier during the years he philandered with Lucy Larcom and Gail Hamilton. Celia Thaxter and Edna Dean Proctor stand out conspicuously among them, because their personal charms impressed him more favorably than did those of many of his other women friends and because their literary work attracted him more than that of other women contemporaries."

Careful reading of this quotation will reveal nothing in the least questionable. However, the author has introduced innuendoes which create a false impression of Whittier. He speaks of "the years he philandered with Lucy Larcom and Gail Hamilton." Whittier was not a philanderer!

Whittier's more acceptable biographer was Samuel T. Pickard, whose book, *John Greenleaf Whittier,* was published in 1894. The following excerpts bear ample testimony to Whittier's love for the Shoals and personal regard for Celia. They prompt us to say that instead of suggesting any questionable conduct, we ought to be deeply grateful that two people with the gifts and attainments of Whittier and Celia could be "so much in love — even romantically if you will—for so many years without losing their own dignity, or calling forth any serious criticism from their contemporaries."

"15th, 2nd mo., 1867. God has been very good to me. I sometimes think I am about the richest man in the world, not exactly in greenbacks and deeds of warranty, but in loves and friendships, and the dear sense of kind remembrances and wishes flowing in upon me, peopling loneliness with forms of beauty and displacing silence with sweet sounds. Would I forego all this for a name on

129

ISLES OF SHOALS

'Change?' By no means. I ought to be thankful to the dear Lord, and I trust I am. But it all seems so undeserved; the partial praise of my friends makes me feel like one whose credit outruns his capital, I don't want to obtain anything under false pretenses . . . I thought after it was too late that it would have been so nice to have thee stay till the next morning; and when the firelight flickered and danced on the walls in the evening twilight, I thought how pleasant it would be to have thee with us, warmed and glorified in the hearth-light . . . I will send thee a copy of my little book *The Tent on the Beach* in a few days. There are some things in it that I think thee will like. I wish thee would write out for the *Atlantic* some of the good things thee know of the Shoals and the Shoalers. I have never heard anything equal in dramatic effect to thy stories one evening in the parlor on Appledore.

"Aug. 8, 1867. It is to sheer kindness of heart, my dear friend, that I owe thy pleasant letter so vividly representing life at the Shoals. They are wonderfully hospitable letters—they give me the freedom of the islands. I sit by thy parlor fire in the stormy nights; I see the tossing boats in the little harbor; the island ringed round with foam; I feel thee telling stories to the young folks, and half fancy myself a boy among them, nestling close to thee, with 'not unpleasant horror' as the tragedy deepens. It's all very nice, but it puzzles me to know why I am favored in this way. There must be some mistake; I am getting what don't really belong to me. . . That Sunday night when thee was up aloft in the cupola, I was sitting until late on the piazza of our shanty at Salisbury beach, watching the revolving light of White Island, and telling my nieces of my pleasant day there. All the afternoon we saw the dim outline of the Shoals. At sunset the level sun flashed on the windows of Appledore, as if a sudden splendor had risen out of the ocean."

On his return from New York he wrote:

"June 10, 1870. I ought to have told thee before how welcome were thy letters but I have been in Babylon for some weeks. . . . I must tell thee that many people speak of thy Shoals paper in strong terms of admiration, poor Alice Cary—who is very ill—among them. One day when I sat by her bedside, Horace Greeley came in. He spoke of Boston writers and magazines, and then said in his slow Yankee drawl: 'Well, the best prose writing I have seen for a long time is Mrs. Thaxter's *Isles of Shoals* in the *Atlantic*. Her

ISLES OF SHOALS

pen pictures are wonderfully well done.' Now I call that praise worth having."

Pickard says:

"Mrs. Thaxter contributes to these pages this interesting note of reminiscence of her long and intimate friendship with Mr. Whittier:

"His sympathy and interest in all I did were invaluable to me. He never gave me any peace till I wrote the books about he Shoals. 'It is thy Kismet,' he said, 'Thee must do it.'

"Po Hill in Amesbury, where he lived so long, is the last hill of any importance that marks our coastline toward the southwest from the Shoals, and I never looked across without thinking of him there in the pleasant years that are gone, and greeting him silently as a near and dear neighbor.

" 'Po Hill sends Appledore good-morning' was a favorite way he had of beginning his letters. His very last letter to me, dated a year ago, said 'I want to go to the Shoals once more, if possible, this summer.' But when at last the crowd thinned toward autumn, and I wrote that a comfortable room was ready for him, he had gone out on an unknown sea upon a longer voyage, and I saw him no more. For the inestimable boon of his beautiful friendship I am profoundly grateful, as all must be to whom such a blessing was vouchsafed. Our correspondence continued from the first year of his coming here through the whole thirty years, and the sonnet which I enclose was written the second summer, on his way home to Amesbury, as he left the Shoals. Celia Thaxter."

Whittier had written in 1864: "When we were just losing sight of Appledore the sun was in clouds and the sea all around dark, but the island itself lay, far off, steeped in warmest sunshine. Having nothing better to do, I thought of some rhymes, which I venture to send thee, only wishing I had something more graceful and beautiful to offer:

> Under the shadow of a cloud, the light
> Died out upon the waters, like a smile
> Chased from a face of grief. Following the flight
> Of a lone bird, that scudding with the breeze,
> Dipped its crank wing in leaden-colored seas,
> I saw in sunshine lifted, clear and bright,
> On the horizon's rim the Fortunate Isle

ISLES OF SHOALS

That claims thee as its fair inhabitant,
And glad of heart I whispered, "Be to Her,
Bird of the summer sea, my messenger;
Tell her, if heaven a fervent prayer will grant,
This light that falls her island home above
Making its slopes of rock and greenness gay,
A partial glory 'midst surrounding gray,
Shall prove an earnest of our Father's love,
More and more shining to the perfect day."

J. G. W.

In her *Personal Recollections of John Greenleaf Whittier,* Mary E. Claflin wrote: "Not the Bay of Naples nor the Bosphorus could rival in his affections the North Shore, and the expanse of foam-crested waters about the Isles of Shoals."

12

FROM TURBULENCE TO CALM

THE YEARS immediately before Whittier's death were of increasing joy for Celia. The Boston residence where she had been spending her winters had its advantages. Whittier was a regular guest at the Winthrop House until his failing health induced him to take permanent rooms at Oak Knoll in Beverly. Celia found larger and sunnier rooms for herself and Karl at the Hotel Clifford on Cortes Street, and we find them there from the autumn of '85 to the spring of '88. "Karl and I have two rooms above my brother Cedric's flat," she wrote to Mrs. S. G. Ward on Christmas day in '85, "the brightest, sunniest rooms, where the sun pours in from his rising to his setting! It is wonderful. I never saw such breadth and plentiousness of radiance; it is delightful. And I have my little Ruth [Cedric's four-year-old daughter] all I wish . . . . I have a bay window full of ferns, so fresh and airy, and they grow so fast I don't know what to do with them."

In the spring of '86, Celia had become active in a crusade for the protection of birds. She wrote to Feroline Fox:

"I cannot express to you my distress at the destruction of the birds. You know how I love them; every other poem I have written has some bird for its subject, and I look at the ghastly horror of women's headgear with absolute suffering . . . I don't care to head a league, because I think I can do just as much good in other ways, and I hate to drag myself into public vices any more than I can possibly help. Have you not noticed how carefully I keep out of publicity?"

Nevertheless she agreed to join the Audubon Society, and be designated local secretary for Appledore. Soon she was soliciting signatures to pledges in behalf of bird protection. She implored Whittier to circulate cards "and if you *can* give me your beloved and honored name, and Phoebe's or any of the rest, I shall be glad."

The following June both John and Roland were married; John to Mary Gertrude Stoddard on the first, and Roland to Mabel Freeman on the fifteenth.

Celia's cup of joy was overflowing, but after another happy

133

ISLES OF SHOALS

winter in Boston, came the first severe illness she had known. It occurred during the summer, but we hear nothing of it until the Appledore is closed for the season. On October 11, '88 she wrote to Mrs. Ward: "I have had a sudden sharp attack of illness since I wrote last which makes me fear a little about being away from my physician through the tempestuous winter, and makes my brothers fear more than myself . . . for this attack is very nearly a repetition of last summer's."

A third attack came the following spring. Celia told Whittier (April 11, '89):

"Yes, I had a quiet, lovely winter in Portsmouth. I did more writing than for years and was well content until about three weeks ago, when I was suddenly very ill, as I have been twice before, for no reason that anybody appears to find out, except 'overwork' the doctors say, in years past. I say as little about it as possible.

"I do not mind the thought of death, it means only fuller life, but there is a pang in the thought of leaving Karl . . . Sometimes I wonder if it is wise or well to love any spot on this old earth as intensely as I do this!"

In May 1889 began a long and delightful correspondence with Bradford Torrey, the leading ornithologist of his time. Celia bargained with him to describe all strange birds that visited her sanctuary at Appledore if he in turn would name them. "I am always up at four," she told him, "and I hear everything every bird has to say on any subject whatever."

After this came the episode of the toads. Celia had made some uncomplimentary remarks about the slugs and other insect pests which might be good diet for toads, and her friends took it upon themselves to supply the island. "You would laugh," she wrote to Annie Fields, "to see the box of toads which came for me night before last! Ninety toads, all wired over in a box, and wondering what fate was in store for them, no doubt. Soon as the mowing was done, all the million slugs in the grass charged into my poor garden, and post haste I sent for more of my dusky little pets, my friends, my saviors! And I turned the ninety loose in the fat slugging grounds, and such a breakfast as they must have had! If there's one thing I adore, more than another, it's a toad! They eat every bug in the garden! In France it is quite an industry, catching toads and selling them to gardeners; did you know it? I have only just found it out."

134

ISLES OF SHOALS

The next year witnessed a relapse and increased feeling of uncertainty. "I have to be so careful of myself," Celia wrote to Anna Eichberg King "and this mysterious thing which seizes me is *so* mysterious, coming upon me with no reason and no warning, I never feel safe a moment, though I take every precaution in my power to circumvent the enemy. Oh, it is not death I fear and dread, but a long, suffering illness, dying a hundred deaths of pain before release, and making those who love me suffer involuntarily through my suffering . . . Last spring I was near that crumbling verge, and oh, what fiery torment I went through! I don't like this feeling of uncertainty and I am half afraid to go to the Shoals, much as I desire to do so, before boats run regularly."

In the meantime came the thought of giving up the Shoals altogether. The Laighton brothers had been under a heavy burden of debt since taking Star Island in 1875. They had obligated themselves with the encouragement of Portsmouth and Manchester banks for $100,000. Their cousin Christopher Rymes had come in as a partner, but now found it necessary to withdraw, leaving Oscar and Cedric to carry the entire load. Moreover the competition of new summer resort hotels throughout New England, the growing popularity of golf and "cycling," which could not be indulged on the rocky terrain of Appledore and Star, was steadily undermining the Shoals prosperity. The Laightons were minded to accept an offer from an English syndicate and expected to close the deal in the spring of 1891. Cedric and Celia agreed between themselves that in this extremity they would build cottages for themselves on the south slope of the hill on Appledore, where Levi had put up his little hermit's lodge nearly half a century before. But Baring Brothers made trouble, and the deal fell through.

Celia's health improved rapidly during the summer of '91, and she was pleased to tell Mrs. Ward that she had fought her way out of her environment of illness. "I have not been so well for four years as I am now." Roland was given a professorship at Harvard and built a house for himself in Norton's Woods, near Kirkland Street in Cambridge (about where the Andover building now stands). His wife and two children remained with Celia in Portsmouth until the new house was livable, and Celia said, "I never knew what it was to be happy, I think, till I became a grandmother!"

Could Celia know that these few months were the crowning jewel of her life? She was stirred with the deep emotions of being

135

ISLES OF SHOALS

a grandmother, seeing her youngest son elevated to a professorship in Harvard, indulging in fond reveries of her own childhood, spending long hours with her choicest friends at Appledore, and reveling in her garden, where it seemed to her in the sparkling of morning dew and the song of many birds that earth had renewed its "ancient rapture." Yet she lamented her own failing strength, and was dismayed when her friends insisted that she write a book about the garden. But this too was a victory, a late blossom, and a classic in its field.

In June of 1893, perhaps as a result of working so continuously on the garden book, she confessed to Elizabeth Hoxie, "Year after next I am going to be sixty, and I am conscious of every bone in my skeleton every time I weed my garden."

Three months later she wrote to Sarah Orne Jewett: "I am pegging away hard on the book, and I want to ask you lots of things . . . I have got the whole thing about done, the writing, but there is much copying and arranging of parts to make a proper unity. I have been so ill since the house closed, just about *dead* with the stress and bother of things and people, and feared to slip back to the hateful state of three years ago. The doctor said, 'You are going to have the whole thing over again if you are not *mighty* careful,' and mighty careful I have been and I am better."

With the publication of *An Island Garden* the year 1894 was ushered in, and Celia felt once more the darting pains so mysterious to her, so well known to the physician. Her last letters to her friends, Rose Lamb, Mina Berntsen, Mary Cowden Clark, Annie Fields, Sarah Orne Jewett, Ignatius Grossman, Elizabeth Hoxie, Feroline Fox, Sophie Eichberg, all retain the inner radiance, yet reveal a hidden premonition that she must leave them soon.

There were cherished memories, too, of those who had created her world for her, but would return no more to the kingdom of the Shoals: Lowell, Longfellow, Higginson, Weiss, Hawthorne, Franklin Pierce, William Morris Hunt, Ole Bull, Levi, James T. Fields, Julius Eichberg, Lucy Larcom, John Greenleaf Whittier, and her own beloved parents. Time was when she felt herself surrounded by their unseen presence as if by a "cloud of witnesses." Now she thought only of a glad reunion in a fairer land. To her newest friend, Bradford Torrey, whom she knew only by correspondence, she wrote on July twentieth:

"I scribble this little line flying, as it were, to beg you, when

ISLES OF SHOALS

the whirl of people passes and tranquility settles once more upon our little world, to steal a moment and slip down here and let us see and know you; will you not? Some of us may be slipping out of this mortal state, and we shall never know each other in this particular phase of existence, which would be a pity, I think."

Torrey made no visit to Celia's Island, but others whom she knew and loved were with her during these last summer months, and Sarah Orne Jewett wrote in her preface to Celia's collected poems published the next year:

"Those who have known through her writings alone the islands she loved so much, may care to know how, just before she died, she paid, as if with dim foreboding, a last visit to the old familiar places of the tiny world that was so dear to her. Day after day she called those who were with her to walk or sail; once to spend a long afternoon among the high cliffs of Star Island where we sat in the shade behind the old church, and she spoke of the year that she spent in the Gosport parsonage, and went there with us, to find old memories waiting to surprise her in the worn doorways, and ghosts and fancies of her youth tenanting all the ancient rooms."

Within a few days she was gone. "She had been listening to music, had been reading to her little company, had been delighting in one of Appleton Brown's new pictures, and then she laid her down to sleep for the last time, and flitted away from her mortality."

The next morning when a guest at the hotel asked Oscar about his sister, not knowing what had happened, he could only say, "Her mother came in the night and took her away."

To the eastward from Celia's cottage a grass-grown path led down the rugged slope of a narrow valley, past Childe Hassam's studio and on, hardly a stone's throw, to the summit of the "little hill" where Cedric had found the early violets blooming. Here was the family burying-ground, no larger than Celia's own parlor. Here Celia had come often before sunrise with flowers for the two graves where her father and mother had been long at rest.

"Celia's funeral," Oscar says, "was in August, when her garden was a perfect cyclone of blossoms. Every kind of beautiful flower was buried with her, and in her parlor William Mason was playing Beethoven's music that she loved so well . . . Annie Fields, Rose Lamb, Lucy Derby and all my sister's children were there. As I saw Celia lying there, the thought came to me that surely anyone so gifted and beloved could not be lost forever."

137

ISLES OF SHOALS

Annie Fields adds this note: "her parlor, in which the body lay, was again made radiant, after her own custom, with the flowers from her garden and a bed of sweet bay was prepared by her friends Appleton Brown and Childe Hassam, on which her form was laid.

William Mason once more played the music from Schumann which she chiefly loved and an old friend, James DeNormandie, paid a brief tribute of affection, spoken for all those who surrounded her."

From another source we learn that the little company of friends included Charlotte Dana, Charles E. Fuller, Mrs. E. G. Loring, Miss Margaret Sayward, Judge and Mrs. John Lowell (father of Ralph Lowell), Jacob Wendall, Mrs. Evans, Anna Eichberg King, Sarah Orne Jewett and her sister Alice Curtis, Dr. J. W. Warren, Laurence Hutton, Howard Van Sinderin and Dr. and Mrs. H. R. Stedman. Mrs. Stedman was a daughter of Reverend John Weiss. Hers too, was a Shoals romance. With them was their small daughter Mabel, now Mrs. Albert Hale, who remembers still the unusual ceremony.

Dr. William Warren, Childe Hassam, J. Appleton Brown, Ed. Caswell, Dr. Stedman, Laurence Hutton, Cedric and Oscar, carried Celia through the valley to the hilltop. Annie Fields continues: "The day was still and soft, and the veiled sun was declining as the solemn procession, bearing flowers, followed to the sacred place. At a respectful distance above stood a wide ring of interested observers, but only those who knew her and loved her best drew near. After all was done, and the body was at rest upon a bed prepared for it, the young flower-bearers brought their burdens to cover her. The bright, tear-stained faces of those who held up their arms full of flowers, to be heaped upon the spot until it became a mound of blossoms, allied the scene, in beauty and simplicity, to the solemn rites of antiquity.

"It was indeed a poet's burial, but it was far more than that: it was the celebration of the passing of a large and beneficent soul."

Those who had come with Celia to the summit of her little hill turned again to the waiting flowers, now to be tended by other hands, and to the silent parlor whose windows must remain open to the morning sunlight and the salt sea breeze. Oscar and Cedric and Julia would care for the garden with Celia's newly published book as their guide. Cedric and Julia would care for the parlor, keeping all its appointments as Celia had left them,

ISLES OF SHOALS

the vases freshly filled, the piano tuned for William Mason, or other
visiting musicians, and the door open for guests.

13

THE TWILIGHT OF APPLEDORE

IN 1888, while the islands were still the most widely known summer resort on the Atlantic seaboard, the Laighton Brothers introduced a new policy to make them more attractive to permanent summer guests. On September eleventh, they entered into an agreement with J. Ingersoll Bowditch, who had been a guest for more than thirty years, whereby he was to meet the cost of building a cottage for himself and family, while boarding at the hotel. The property would revert to the Laightons in twenty years, unless the time were extended by a new agreement. Three years later Mr. Bowditch died, and the cottage was assigned under his will to Clarence H. Clark, and the agreement extended twenty years from January 1, 1892.

Other cottages were built under similar arrangements for Dr. M. Emil Richter, J. Appleton Brown, Frank B. Mayes, Childe Hassam, Ross Turner, Larz Anderson, Eleanor Clark, and others. While this proved a great advantage in many ways, it was not enough to stem the tide which had set in against them. Income from all sources began to decline, while the upkeep of property on three islands steadily increased. In 1899 Cedric went to Florida hoping to establish himself in a winter resort there, but was stricken with typhus and cancer and died that summer, leaving Oscar to battle heavy seas in a disabled ship. Harry Marvin, who ran the Oceanic for the Laightons, said of Cedric: "He was taller than Oscar. He looked like a handsome Viking. He had a beautiful voice like a bell. He could have been anything. He was the center of conversation among the hotel guests. Surrounded by distinguished men, he dominated the whole group. He always was the life of the party. He made marvelous extemporaneous speeches. Cedric excelled in everything he did."

Oscar and Cedric together had mortgaged their Appledore holdings for $25,000. Empty rooms at Appledore were echoing for want of guests. The bank which held the mortgage foreclosed on December 7th, 1900. Oscar continued to manage Appledore, while Harry Marvin was still in charge of the Oceanic.

ISLES OF SHOALS

In 1905 Mr. A. J. Lane of Manchester, a realtor, was asked to assist Oscar in final disposition of the property. For the summer of 1906, Mr. Charles Ramsdell, who among other interests was managing the well known Randall Dining Hall at Harvard, was engaged to supervise Appledore. In a desperate effort to raise funds for maintenance and improvement, a corporation was formed to be known as "The Isles of Shoals Hotel Co.," with $85,000 capital to be divided into 850 shares at $100 each. Payment would not be binding unless the full amount were subscribed by December 31, 1906.

January 1, 1907, came and went with no sale of either real estate or shares in the new corporation. Pressure from creditors did not diminish. The property was mortgaged back to the bank. Mr. Lane died and the bank foreclosed. Then followed another mortgage and another foreclosure. Finally in October of 1908, the bank sold to the United States Government for a life saving station, a small tract of land—less than an acre—on the summit of Appledore hill near the John Smith cairn. At the same time, a small plot at the head of Babb's Cove was conveyed to the Government for a landing and boathouse.

In desperation the island was now surveyed and divided into small building lots — 585 of them — to be sold at prices ranging from $100 to $500 each; $25 down and $5 monthly. No interest and no taxes. The results of this campaign were negative. The Isles of Shoals Hotel Co. was dissolved, and the "Appledore Land and Building Co." was formed in 1909. The new company continued to dispose of the island by any and all means possible, but only 61 of the 585 lots were sold or given away.

Meanwhile Mr. Ramsdell continued to operate the Appledore Hotel, and summer guests knew little of the distress that the owners and Oscar and the Laighton relatives were compelled to endure. The end came in 1914, when a disastrous fire swept the hotel and many of the cottages from the island.

The last lingering summer guests had gone, leaving only Oscar on Star and the custodian on Appledore, when an explosion of acetylene gas set fire to the great hotel. A stiff breeze from the south meant that in the absence of any fire-fighting equipment or manpower the entire hotel and all cottages north of it must go. The Portsmouth Navy Yard was alerted by the Isles of Shoals Life Saving Station, and the naval tug *Penacook* with the Portsmouth

ISLES OF SHOALS

fire-fighting company, followed by the tug *Piscataqua* steamed out under forced draught. The hotel was in ruins before they reached the island, and the firemen could do no more than extinguish a few blown brands that were threatening Cedric's cottage to the northwest, and a half dozen cottages south of the hotel on the hillside. Accounts in the current press read like obituaries:

"As the smoke and flames from the burning Appledore House at the Isles of Shoals rose into the clear air and sunshine on Saturday afternoon, September 4, and signalled the destruction of one of America's most famous hostelries to thousands of people who lined the beaches and waterfront from York, Maine to Cape Ann miles away, there passed into history a building which has left undying influence on American letters and public life."

The Appledore Land and Building Company had no further success in disposing of lots, and as a final gesture voted on January 9th, 1922, to authorize Daniel S. Kimball to negotiate the sale of Appledore. On September twelfth of that year the Company sold to James A. Donovan of Lawrence, Massachusetts, "for $1.00 and other valuable consideration," (said to be $4000) Appledore, "meaning," the deed says, "to convey all our existing rights to said Island and divest ourselves of any and all rights of every name and description in said Island." Two years later, Mr. Donovan sold Appledore Hotel Reservation, its buildings now a wilderness of tumbled foundations, together with the Anderson, Stelwag, and Clark cottages, to the Star Island Corporation, and finally, in 1929, all his holdings on the island. This left only a few buildings and vacant lots in the hands of individual owners. These are as of 1965:

The ruins of the Cedric Laighton cottage, lot 175, now owned by Charles Currier.

The cottage on lot 253, still owned by Mr. Jesse Riley.

The Richter cottage on lot 222, owned by Miss Rosamond Thaxter.

The United States Coast Guard Reservation on the hill and at the head of Babb's Cove.

The Abbie W. Johnson property, consisting of the house on lots 569 and 570, together with vacant lots as previously listed, now owned by Ralph St. Hilaire.

The Brewster cottage on lots 574 and 575, now owned by Mr. Ray Burge.

ISLES OF SHOALS

The Athorne property, lots 505, 506, 581, 582, now owned by Mr. Harry Sullivan.

These seven parcels total 3.5 acres. Since the total area of the island is 95.85 acres it is evident that the Star Island Corporation owns 96.75 per cent of Appledore.

Water lilies, blueberries, and wild cranberries still grow on Appledore. White gulls nest among the rocks, and those who live on the south shore overlooking Gosport Harbor are heirs to the glory of an island kingdom.

PART III

THE CONFERENCE ERA

1

AS IT WAS IN THE BEGINNING

WHEN Mr. and Mrs. Thomas H. Elliott of Lowell, Massachusetts, appeared at Star Island in the summer of 1896 they had no premonition of the role they were to play in the destiny of the Shoals. Mr. Elliott, a devoted layman in his own church, was a missionary in spirit who felt that churches, ministers, and laity were greatly benefited by frequent conferences. He was president of the North Middlesex Conference of Unitarian churches which had its summer meetings at the Weirs on Lake Winnipesaukee in New Hampshire. What turned him to the Shoals is disclosed by Mr. Elliott in a conversation held in the parlor of the historic Tucke Parsonage on Star Island. He was saying:

"As it was in the beginning, there were two factors that entered into it very strongly, and which probably controlled it. One was the really definite control, my wife's health. I suppose the other was my great love for conferences. I had been only a little while in the Unitarian church when I was elected President of the North Middlesex Conference, which interested me at once. I enjoyed it and worked for it. It was next to my business and my family.

"How many of you hark back to the Weirs Meetings? We had the Conference there for a good many years and we had some very good conferences but it was intensely hot at the Weirs. I asked them if they ever thought of taking that conference to the shore. immediately there was a great objection, and it seemed afterwards that a number of the leaders had property interest in the Weirs. My wife and I had our trunks all packed and labelled to go to the Weirs and were chatting away when she said, 'Thomas, I almost wish we were going to the shore. The way I feel tonight it seems that I ought to go.'

" 'So you really feel that way'? said I.

" 'Yes,' she said, 'I believe it would be better for me.'

" 'All right, where shall we go?'

"She thought for a moment, and said, 'We have always heard

147

ISLES OF SHOALS

a lot of the Isles of Shoals, but we have never seen them. What would you say to going there?'

" 'All right, we'll go to the Shoals.'

"We changed the tags on our trunks, and next day we came down here. That was in 1896. Both hotels were running then, but with very little patronage. I think it was the very next day after dinner that I came out and sat down on the very settee that is there now. Soon Harry Marvin, who was running the hotel that year for the Laightons, came out and sat down beside me. It was a beautiful day. It was never more beautiful than it was those two days.

"Mr. Marvin said to me, 'How are you enjoying yourself, Mr. Elliott?'

"I said, 'Fine—this place suits me right after my own heart. There is only one thing that would improve it to my mind.'

" 'What's that?' he said.

" 'There are some meetings going on at the Weirs that I value very much. If we only had those here I should be as near heaven as possible.' "

The two men reached an agreement, and Mr. Elliott spent the following winter organizing the Isles of Shoals Summer Meetings Association which had its first conference at the islands in July of 1897.

By rare good fortune we have still a faded newspaper clipping from the *Lowell Courier-Citizen*. Their Billerica correspondent, Miss Abby Jaquith, tells the story of the first conferences. Was it mere coincidence that the boat which took them out was named the *Viking*? It seemed as if Leif Ericson had returned after a thousand years. The *Viking* was waiting at the dock when the Billerica delegation arrived in Portsmouth. The voyage down river was tranquil, but when the boat emerged into the open sea a brisk wind sprang up, and Miss Jaquith wrote: "deeper and deeper the *Viking* plunged; higher and higher it rose, and from side to side it rolled." The chilly breeze brought out the winter wraps. The first stop was Appledore, then a brief sail across the harbor to Star.

"To enter the broad, hospitable doors of the Oceanic was to give to and receive greeting from the gentlemanly manager, Mr. H. G. Marvin, and into the ledger enter our names. Being shown to our rooms, situated in the right wing of the house we began to catch the views from the windows. The ocean was everywhere .... All the lullabys of the ocean depths were being attuned

ISLES OF SHOALS

for us; sometimes in soft, murmuring cadences, and then in bold, rushing vehemence of impetuous sea."

The opening service for the next day was conducted by Reverend William E. Barton who "made a touching allusion to some of the facts connected with the Island, among them being the solitariness of the graves of three little children of one household, all of whom passed away within one year. In our wandering we came upon their burial place among the rocks. . . . .

"Evening came. On Appledore Island a memorial to Celia Thaxter was to be held. A dense fog rose from the sea, but a calm had settled upon it. The *Viking* filled with expectant listeners and an immense crowd assembled to hear the story of her life given by Mr. John Albee. Rev. Philip S. Moxom read several of her pathetic poems. A sweet singer also sang several of her pieces which had been attuned to music.

"We had been in her cottage, had seen the garden where she had cherished her flowers, and felt how the influence of one poetic but human mind could draw higher so intent an audience to hear and learn of her . . . . "

Conference delegates followed the pattern so familiar to Shoals historians—the pattern of Caliban who had taught them to say "This Island's mine." They took possession of the meetinghouse on the hill as if they had built it themselves and felt guilty of its neglect, for it had seen little use during the last quarter of a century.

The interior had fallen into ruinous decay. The wooden steps at the north entrance and the wooden floor had rotted until it was hardly safe to enter. The pews, still showing carved initials and boat designs done by schoolboys, rocked uneasily on the weakened floor. Plaster on the walls was dingy and broken. The opening which had been a door at the west end was left ragged and unplastered. The pulpit at the east end was holding its own with simple dignity—a forlorn symbol of a forgotten era, school no longer kept, town meetings no more assembled, sermons no longer preached. No one was left of the old tradition to restore the falling timbers or give new voice to the aging pulpit.

Conference leaders and guests began at once to restore the shrine. A fund of $800.00 was raised for the interior. The rotting floor was replaced with red brick to preserve the atmosphere of antiquity. Roger Greeley the architect found a small wooden bracket in a pile of rubbish and by matching it to the spot on the

ISLES OF SHOALS

wall where it had once been attached, discovered that it had been used by early villagers as a sconce for hanging a lighted lantern. There must have been a dozen or more. Each bracket had three branching arms, and each arm was in the form of a horizontal cross. This seemed to confirm an old tradition that in the early days while the Islanders were without benefit of clergy, they had made up a devotional device of their own. They were from varied religious backgrounds but remembered little of the worship which they had known in childhood. All that remained of their liturgy was a thought which they all agreed upon; that the three points of the cross represent Faith, Hope and Charity. They made these horizontal branching crosses that the lights from their lanterns might shine upward upon the three great words of their religion.

Without reference to the symbolism, or even a knowledge of the tradition, Mr. Greeley had replicas made and mounted on the inner walls, where they now remain.

Mr. Elliott's first thought was that the Shoals must be unhampered by denominational boundaries. He invited both Unitarians and Congregationalists to participate in the Conferences, and put no prejudicial word into the name of the organization formed in the autumn of 1896. He called it "The Isles of Shoals Summer Meetings Association."

After the first session (1897) came the question of continued interest. Would the first visitors return? The answer flows from the gifted pen of Emma E. Marean, who for fifteen years filled the columns of the *Boston Evening Transcript* and the *Christian Register* with illuminating accounts of the islands and the conferences. In the *Register* she says:

"The summer meetings at the Isles of Shoals have opened with promises of coming delight and profit. We are renewing the ancient rapture, and assuring ourselves that never in all the history of Unitarianism have there been meetings quite like these. It is good to arrive on the day before, and accustom our tired city eyes to these wide spaces of sea and sky. The day before is like the grace which Charles Lamb wished to say before opening a good book. It is like the first taste of cool water on eager lips. Even more, it is like the master's touch upon his musical instrument, to make sure that it is in perfect tune before he begins the sonata. That means that somehow the loveliness of the place has come to seem a part of

ISLES OF SHOALS

the summer meetings themselves, and to lend its own rare influence to the words that will be spoken here."

These early meetings soon proved to be the outflowering of the Appledore tradition and rich fulfillment of all that the islands had promised from the beginning. From 1850 to 1900, literary and artistic celebrities had come on their own initiative to this remote and self-contained "Kingdom in the Sea" as to a retreat whose climate and cultural atmosphere were conducive to creative work. Now with the advent of the Summer Meetings Association people of the same high rank came by invitation or were sent as delegates to take part in the varied programs offered by conference leaders. Thus it came about that as Appledore declined, Star Island developed into a cultural center of an even higher order. The new generation of Shoalers soon felt a proprietary interest in the islands themselves. They took possession by squatter's rights after the manner of the earliest fishermen, and entered the life of the islands. Hence it was that in 1902, the sixth year of their meetings, they were deeply affected by a tragedy which lingered long in their memories.

2

TRAGEDY OF THE WAITRESSES

ON THE gloomy afternoon of July 17, 1902, guests and delegates on both islands witnessed the most heartrending tragedy at the Shoals since the murder at Smuttynose. The headwaiter, his assistant, and twelve waitresses from the Oceanic Hotel were drowned by accident about 200 feet off the west coast of Appledore.

Captain Frederick Miles, a local fisherman, had been engaged many seasons to take out sailing parties at the Shoals. According to his own account, he had on this overcast day taken out a party which included Mr. Dingley, son of the late Governor Dingley of Maine, and on returning them to Appledore was handed a message that a party was waiting for him at Star.

Mr. William Roger Greeley, a conference delegate at the Oceanic, says in a recent letter that he was a member of the party which had just been out:

"We were sailing in a whale boat owned and operated by a local fisherman, when my uncle, Hon. George P. McLean, Governor of Connecticut, noticed a black cloud in the south and asked the 'captain' to make haste to the wharf to escape a squall. He said there was no danger, but my uncle insisted. As soon as we got out of the boat a party of fourteen or fifteen—the headwaiter, a fine young college student, and a dozen or more waitresses got in over my uncle's protests."

Mr. Greeley did not know, however, that five waitresses refused to go, much as they desired to join the party. Ella Adams, Helen Twombly, Nellie Collins, Nellie Raitt and Hattie Gilmore stayed on the pier and watched the others sail off in gay laughter.

Skipper Miles said, "I never sailed a jollier party than these young people . . . I said to them, 'Where do you want to go, girls?' and they told me just to sail around the islands and not to go too far out."

There was a brisk breeze from the southeast, so the skipper headed northwest, intending to keep within the lee of the islands, and as he came up the west coast of Appledore young Oliver Adams, brother of Ella who had stayed behind, and two other sisters who

152

ISLES OF SHOALS

were on the boat, shouted and waved them to turn back, but the party sailed on and cruised for nearly an hour to the north and east of Appledore.

The Reverend Charles E. Park watched the whole performance from the piazza of the Oceanic, and after more than fifty years revived his memory of it in a note for our "Living History."

He says:

"A young fisherman had offered to take them for a sail; and probably it was up north toward Boon Island. On their return they were surging merrily along, close-hauled on the port tack to a brisk southeast breeze. The girls were all ranged along the port gunwale to offset the list of the boat. . . . As they opened up the harbor between Appledore and Star, so they could see the steam-boat pier, there was the steamer just in, and bringing another batch of delegates. Very soon they had to go about on the starboard tack in order to shoot up into the [Appledore] harbor. This was just what the girls wanted, for now, with the boat listing to port they could all crowd over to the starboard side and get a perfect view of the passengers leaving the steamer, not 50 feet away. And then it happened. The boat slipped into the lee of the steamer; and wind pressure on the sail was cut off; the boat righted with a jerk, and because all the weight was on the starboard side, she kept right on listing to starboard until water was pouring, green and heavy, over the open gunwale. Being well ballasted to make her stiff when on the wind, she sank like a plummet."

It seems from various descriptions that the entire list of seventeen, including the skipper were carried down by the suction of the rapidly descending boat. No one was caught in the rigging, and no one fell beneath the hull. The Skipper said:

"'My God, girls, it's all over—we are all gone!' I yelled; and that was the last I saw of any of the party. As the boat sank we were all drawn under by the terrible whirl and suction, but as the craft struck the bottom the air in her forced me up to the surface again. I presume that the others also came to the top of the water, but I did not see any of the party.

"I was down for more than a minute, I should judge, and when I saw blue sky I was some distance from where we went under. Luckily a large soap box which had been in the boat was floating by and I put my arms around it. This was my salvation as I cannot swim a stroke, although I have worked on the water for more

153

ISLES OF SHOALS

than thirty years. I drifted shoreward and soon reached the rocks, which bumped and bruised me to some extent. I was taken from the water in an unconscious condition by two fishermen and carried to the hotel."

Oliver Adams was first to reach the floundering victims. He said:

"Lemuel Davis and I were near the Appledore Hotel when the party started out, and we waved them to turn back, but the boat kept on. They had been out about an hour when we saw the flaw strike the boat a good blow and over she went. With all possible haste Davis and I ran to the shore and launched a dory. The breakers were coming high and strong, but we got out there first. Davis had the oars and I never thought we would get to the drowning girls. It was an awful suspense.

"When we got to where she went down all were bunched. I grasped two of the girls, not knowing who they were and rowed rapidly to shore. I kept their heads out of the water as best I could, but it was a hard job to go through the breakers. We were about fifteen yards from the shore when I was thrown out of the boat, but still kept my hold on the girls. . . . After a time we succeeded in reaching dry land, and then we turned our efforts to resuscitating the two girls. It was then for the first time that I discovered that one of them was my sister Ena. I did not know that she was in the boat . . . After fully half an hour we succeeded in restoring Miss Haggerty . . . My sister was undoubtedly dead when she reached the shore. . .

"The last I saw of Alward and Farrington they were struggling and trying to hold several of the girls above water. Both were expert swimmers, but they could not hold out in such a sea against the odds."

The steamer *Sam Adams,* which had just discharged her passengers at the dock now made for the rescue with only her skipper, Charles Allen, and engineer, Peter Peterson, aboard. They threw a line to one girl who proved to be Lillian Bresnahan, and drew her aboard, but the second was too feeble to hold on, and sank. Winds and waves were driving the steamer onto the rocks, so she had to pull away from shore, and rescued no others.

By this time the waters were in tumult. Fishermen from Star and Smuttynose came in dories to join the frantic efforts of the Appledore boys. These boats, bobbing like corks on the choppy

ISLES OF SHOALS

sea managed to recover eight floating victims. These were brought to shore where Drs. Warren and Richter directed fruitless first aid. The bodies were carried on cots to the music room of the Appledore Hotel, and placed in a silent row for identification by friends and relatives from Star—nine in all, five missing, somewhere under the still savage waters.

Word had been cabled to Coroner Edward E. Shapleigh of Kittery and Undertaker H. W. Nickerson of Portsmouth, who left Portsmouth at about 9:15 on the steamer *Merryconeag*. After the bodies were identified they were carried on mattresses to the waiting *Merryconeag* and taken to Portsmouth where they were to be claimed by relatives.

The next day (July 18) Michael E. Hurley was summoned to undertake the recovery of five missing bodies. He assembled his own diving equipment, and early Saturday morning, with John Ford of Dover as tender, went down to explore the ocean bed. He found the whaleboat intact, and announced that Skipper Miles had not been at fault in handling his sails. Some had said he failed to free his sails in making his tack, and it was a tight sail which caused the boat to capsize, but Hurley found no tight sail. One at a time he discovered the sunken bodies, at a depth of about sixty feet, but it was not until the next afternoon that all had been recovered. Some faces were still recognizable, but others had been disfigured by the ravages of fish. All were taken to Portsmouth to join their silent companions, and wait to be taken home.

Guests at both hotels asked for no service on the evening of the tragedy. Appledore recovered more quickly after the last victim had been taken to the mainland, and the seas were calm once more. But the Oceanic could not be reconciled. Guests came from their rooms next morning in silence and seemed confused as they entered the dining-room where only a little handful of waitresses with haggard faces were there to serve them. Out of twenty-two sixteen were absent, fourteen never to return to their accustomed places. Orders were given with choked voices if at all. Many had no heart for eating but would rise without words and return to their rooms.

Days passed and new hands came to serve, but memory lingered long over those dark hours.

Dr. Park speaks for them all in his later review: "You say, why begin your reminiscenses with so sad a story? Had you been an

ISLES OF SHOALS

ardent Shoaler at that time could you have forgotten it? Could you have attended a single session for the next fifty years without at least once during the week recalling that fearful tragedy?"

3

THE PURCHASE OF STAR ISLAND

S TIME went on, the feeling of ownership grew more articulate among conference Shoalers. Delegates took greater interest in the history and development of the islands and became more aware of contemporary incidents. In 1901 they listened to the blasts on Smuttynose as the heart of the island was shaken loose and lifted by huge derricks for a breakwater between Smuttynose and Cedar. Three years later they witnessed an even larger project as the United States Government filled the gap between Cedar and Star with massive, irregular blocks of granite from Rockport quarries barged to the Shoals over twenty miles of open sea. Then they observed that heavy northeasters funnelled mountainous waves into the little cove between Cedar and Star and threw the south end of the new breakwater back into Gosport Harbor. Many times the Government sent heavy machinery to replace the boulders, but the storms continue with diabolical fury to toss them back even to this day.

The summer of 1914 was enlivened by two historical events—reconstruction of the John Smith monument and erection of the new Tucke monument.

The Smith monument erected in 1864 under the direction of Reverend Daniel Austin had fallen into sad disrepair. The *Society of Colonial Wars of New Hampshire* now placed a granite block of modest dimensions where the earlier shaft had stood on a three-cornered pedestal, and at the time of rededication placed the following inscription in bronze on the north face of the granite triangle.

"Captain John Smith, 1579-1631, after proving his valor in Europe and America became Governor of Virginia and Admiral of New England. While exploring this coast in the spring of 1614, made the first recorded visit to these islands, named by him Smith's Isles. This tablet is placed three hundred years later by the Society of Colonial Wars in the State of New Hampshire."

During that summer the Tucke monument was under construction. From rocking chairs on the Oceanic piazza guests had

ISLES OF SHOALS

an excellent view of barges unloading blocks of Rockport granite, which had been cut and finished in the Sargent and Sullivan quarries with meticulous care. They were approximately six-foot cubes, each weighing near fifteen tons. A narrow-guage railway was laid across the lawn north of the hotel, around the hill, past the ice ponds to the old village cemetery directly south of the Meetinghouse. Nothing on the islands was ever done with equal skill and precision. The whole enterprise was under the hand of Timothy P. Sullivan of Concord, who had supervised construction of the Congressional Library in Washington, the State Senate and New Hampshire Historical Society buildings in Concord, and the great dry dock at the Portsmouth Navy Yard.

It was Mr. Benjamin Ames Kimball who suggested to Mr. Edward Tuck, then living in Paris, that such a monument be erected, and who represented him at the dedication, which was planned for the same day as that of the renewed Smith monument. At ten o'clock of July twenty-ninth, 500 passengers boarded the steamer *Nassau* at Portsmouth to spend three hours at the island for the impressive ceremony.

Conferences grew and expanded with the seasons. The "Congregational Summer Conference Association" was formed in 1914 with Reverend Thomas Chalmers as chairman.

As early as 1910, delegates were talking openly about the possible advantage of owning one or more of the islands. Individuals began to collect funds in a small way before official action could be taken. Then came the holocaust on Appledore, and the movement toward ownership of Star Island gained speed.

War had broken out in Europe. News of war and the fire on Appledore spread like a pall over conference Shoalers. One thought seemed to possess them all: "We must keep Star Island."

The dramatic incidents which followed are narrated for us by Mr. Charles Lawrance, who shared with his father the anxieties and hilarities of the moment. Following are recorded comments made in the "Pink Parlor" of the Oceanic on August 29th, 1958:

"There was a shortage of money. Property of this type, on an island, was not too valuable—not a safe risk. The pressure was, I think, from the Bank Commissioners, as well as the desire of the banks to get their money back into circulation. But the pressure was so real that they were willing to take any customer that would

158

ISLES OF SHOALS

meet their price. We found that the mortgage on the Island was $16,000, and there was only one other possible customer interested in buying. Well, this other customer was not too desirable a citizen. He belonged to a group of men who operated road houses.

"One day my father was in his office at 25 Beacon Street in Boston when he had a telephone call from Portsmouth, informing him that Star Island would be sold within a period of twenty-four hours, and if the Unitarians wanted to buy they must act immediately, since the other party was ready to take over the mortgage. My father was so much disturbed by this news that he turned to one of his loyal friends of many years, a former parishioner in Winchester, Mr. Lewis Parkhurst, a partner in the firm of Ginn and Company, book publishers. Mr. Parkhurst had been a Shoaler himself for a number of years, and saw the necessity for immediate action. Without telling anyone what he was about he called the President of the Porstmouth Savings Bank, which held the mortgage, and said he would buy the Island himself, and insisted that the bank send a man to Boston at once with a letter showing that he had full authority to negotiate and close the sale. He must bring the mortgage papers, and have power to sign new papers.

"There was no Star Island Corporation at that time and the Isles of Shoals Summer Meetings Association was not incorporated, so we had no organization that could take title to the property.

"The bank representative appeared in due time at Mr. Parkhurst's office and presented his credentials. Mr. Parkhurst had called the Bank Commissioner in Concord, probably others too, so that he was sure of his grounds, and immediately made his offer, $16,000 for the Island, no less, no more. The man protested, the price was too low. The other party would pay more. Mr. Parkhurst repeated his offer, 'take it or leave it.' The man hedged, and said he would have to consult his principals. He couldn't close a deal like that! Mr. Parkhurst turned to the credentials and said, 'I have in this letter your full authority to negotiate and close the deal; is that right?' 'That's right.' Then said Mr. Parkhurst, 'You have my offer. The Bank Commissioners of Concord are asking that this be closed at once, and your bank holds the mortgage. My offer is still $16,000.'

"The representative still tried to stall for time and asked to use the telephone to call his principals, but Mr. Parkhurst said,

159

ISLES OF SHOALS

'My telephone is not available to you. Your authority is in this letter, and you are in my office now.' The man suggested that he would use a telephone outside, but Mr. Parkhurst looked him straight in the eye and said 'The moment you go out that door my offer ceases—$16,000 for the Island.'

"The man said, 'Well I can't do anything without cash.'

"Mr. Parkhurst smiled, reached into his desk drawer, pulled out a certified check for $16,000 made payable to the Savings Bank in Portsmouth. He also had a receipt for the agent to sign, and when he had received the mortgage papers properly conveyed, handed over the check."

It was now Mr. Parkhurst's island. He owned it and could hold it until Shoalers had formed a corporation competent to take over the title. He called Mr. Lawrance and there was much hilarity in the Lawrance home that evening.

Publicity for the Conferences of 1915 made no mention of the new ownership of Star Island. Indeed, we have not yet fixed the date of the transaction in Mr. Parkhurst's office, but we note the significant announcement that Mr. V. D. Harrington "will be the Hotel Manager at Star Island. He has spent ten seasons in various departments at Appledore and Oceanic hotels," the folder says, "and has, therefore, a thorough understanding of conditions at the Shoals. For the past eight years Mr. Harrington has been connected with Phillips Academy at Andover." (Until his death in 1945 he was business manager there.) Mr. Ramsdell's name does not appear after this date. Mr. Marvin had left in 1910 and was running the Hobkirk Inn at Camden, South Carolina.

Shoalers were now active in perfecting plans for a full-scale campaign to buy the island and establish its future. By-laws for a Star Island Corporation were drawn up and adopted on December third. Reverend William I. Lawrance was named president, Mr. Carl B. Wetherell, clerk and Mr. Isaac Sprague, treasurer. Mr. Wetherell had been treasurer of the Isles of Shoals Summer Meetings Association since 1912, and was now in a position to serve the islands in many capacities.

The newly formed corporation was not to have any denominational commitments, but was to be administered by a board of nine directors, six of whom should be Unitarians and the other three by inference Congregationalists, this representing roughly the proportion of Shoalers from these two fellowships.

160

ISLES OF SHOALS

In 1916 the Star Island Corporation received its charter from the Commonwealth of Massachusetts, under the stated purpose of holding and administering Star Island and such other property as the Corporation may acquire "for Religious, Educational and kindred purposes."

The campaign for funds did not wait for the Corporation to be formed, but was vigorously promoted during the summer of 1915. The first appeal was made by Caroline Lawrance (Mrs. William I.), who went out from the meeting held at Star Island when the vote was passed to form a Corporation, adorned herself in a mother-hubbard style of dress, and pinned a five-dollar bill over her heart. She challenged all guests to cover her with bills. Soon her mother-hubbard was a patchwork of fluttering bills, and the campaign was well under way before its committee was organized. Her daughter Mary was made chairman of the Young People's committee.

Mr. Carl Wetherell became chairman of the general committee. The first bulletin was sent out under the date of Autumn, 1915, carrying the exciting message that on October 15th, the fund had touched the mark of $13,225.

The Committee had announced that $40,000 should be raised to reimburse Mr. Parkhurst, restore the island, provide a steamboat, and establish a modest endowment.

It is doubtful if any Unitarian campaign has ever been so well conducted. The response was not only generous but enthusiastic. It seemed that everybody was working for the Shoals— churches, organizations, individuals. Mrs. Lawrance gave a series of lectures in many places and contributed the proceeds to the fund. Mr. Wetherell was on the road almost constantly, speaking at church functions, and helping churches in their local campaigns. Reverend Harold G. Arnold and Reverend Christopher R. Eliot gave a series of illustrated lectures "for the benefit of the Star Island Purchase Fund."

On December second a joint rally of Unitarians and Congregationalists was held at the Mt. Vernon Congregational Church in Boston. Reverend Samuel M. Crothers presided and introduced Mr. Parkhurst as "the man who saved Star Island for us—to save." Reverend Samuel A. Eliot warned the guests that this must not be a half-baked enterprise. "You must let subscribers know that the

161

ISLES OF SHOALS

whole $40,000 must be in hand by April 1, or the whole project fails."

It was announced that Mr. Parkhurst had given $5,000 to the fund, and Mr. Thomas Elliott told of another gift. He said on a later occasion:

"When it came to raising money, I was brought into contact with some very good friends, because I had charge of the real estate at Dartmouth College. Benjamin A. Kimball used to practically own the railroad, and I knew that he was an agent for Mr. Edward Tuck of Paris. So I saw him one day and told him the story and asked if Mr. Tuck would be interested to help. He replied: 'Naturally we would like to have the Island protected. If you will write a letter to Mr. Tuck, I'll see that he has it.'

"I got the letter in shape and sent it, and the next time I saw Mr. Kimball he had a check from Mr. Tuck for $5,000 toward the purchase of the Island."

By April twentieth the fund had reached $45,484.21, which was the official closing figure.

It was announced joyfully to the world that "Star Island, one of the Isles of Shoals, where summer meetings have been held for the last twenty years, has at last been purchased through the efforts of many lovers; it is now controlled by the Star Island Corporation and set apart forever to religious and educational purposes.

"The Oceanic Hotel has undergone extensive repairs and improvements. A new steamer, specially adapted to its route, has been acquired and put in commission in charge of a capable captain and crew. Mr. V. D. Harrington, the popular manager of the past seasons, has been retained in charge of the hotel."

In its "first annual message" the Star Island Corporation said:

"We paid $16,000 for the Island, spent $6,777.80 on repairs and improvements, invested $12,793.75 in interest-bearing bonds, and bought shares in the stock of the Star Island Steamboat Company to the value of $7,250, thus making the new boat, the *Sightseer* available for transportation. . . .

"Visitors to Star Island this year will note several improvements. Every carpet in the old hotel and cottages has been taken up and discarded, all old wall paper has been removed, and floors and walls have been painted. A contract has been signed providing for new plumbing and sanitation, the work being done by experts

ISLES OF SHOALS

highly recommended. An artesian well is being contracted for, with the hope that fresh water may be found in sufficient quantity to supply all needs.

"Eminent landscape architects have formulated a plan for the future development of the Island, so that such memorials may be offered with the assurance that they will fit into a permanent scheme. We hope for many such offerings. . . .

"To you, our loyal friends, who have made all these things possible, the Star Island Corporation extends grateful thanks.

For the Corporation

William I. Lawrance, President
Isaac Sprague, Treasurer
Carl B. Wetherell, Clerk"

The dedication of the Island was made the high feature of the conference season.

The Congregational Conferences which had their beginning in the earliest sessions at the Shoals, formed *The Isles of Shoals Congregational Association* in 1914, with the Rev. Thomas Chalmers as its first chairman. In 1929 the *Isles of Shoals Congregational Corporation* was chartered under Massachusetts laws to hold funds for the conferences. Thus through the years the "Congregational wing" has been a strong factor in building the great Shoals tradition. They are not mentioned separately in the foregoing pages because they are included in all the activities of the Star Island Corporation.

War clouds darkened during the winter of 1916, and on February first following, the United States broke off diplomatic relations with Germany, and on April sixth declared war. The Shoals were closed to all visitors. Arrangements were soon made to hold the conferences at Hotel Wentworth at New Castle, a most favorable site, where guests look across eight miles of ocean to see the Shoals clear against the eastern horizon. The conferences of 1917 and 1918 were held there.

L'ENVOI

This review of Island Lore and Legend goes to press as the Shoals are celebrating the three-hundred-fiftieth anniversary of John Smith's early visit. The New Hampshire Society of Colonial Wars has rededicated the triangular monument erected to his memory, and we are reminded that during three and a half centuries the islands have not only built a noble tradition among themselves but have entered deeply into the history of English-speaking people. Four times at least they have made effective contributions to mainland life and culture.

I   By creating a superior product, the famous dunfish, and by establishing the first trading post in New England, they became the center of the fishing industry in the New World.

II By refusing to pay the five-pound tax on each thirty tons of fish products, they thwarted the ambition of their overlords to make New England a feudal monopoly.

III By making Appledore Island, and notably Celia Thaxter's parlor, a focal point of inspiration for the leading artists, musicians, literary and professional men and women of the Atlantic seaboard, they had no small influence on the cultural life of the late 19th century.

IV By welcoming the new "religious, educational and kindred conferences" at the turn of the century, they became a source of strength and inspiration to thousands who have come to anchor in Gosport Harbor from the four corners of the earth.

Those who have returned through long succeeding years have watched the steady growth of these conferences from a season of two weeks in 1897 to ten weeks by mid-century. They have witnessed the beginning of New Gosport: Tucke Parsonage in 1927, Parker Hall, 1948, Newton Centre House, 1950, Sprague and Founders Cottages in 1953, Baker and Y.P.R.U. cottages in 1955, and the Vaughn Memorial building in 1960, with its rooms dedicated to Charles F. Vaughn and Celia Thaxter. For more power and light, a new service building was erected in 1960, and two Kleinschmidt converters were installed to purify sea water for hotel guests.

ISLES OF SHOALS

The story of this new development is more adequately told in the guidebook to the Shoals, *Ten Miles Out*, now in its fourth edition. Therein will be found the "Living History of the Isles of Shoals."

Since it is the honored tradition among historians to leave persons and events of current history to later writers, we close this volume with no further comment on more recent though no less important items of our own time. It is fitting, however, to recall the well-remembered words of Thomas H. Elliott, who ushered in the Conference era and was its guide and mentor for forty years. When confronted with serious problems he would say, "The Islands always rise to the emergency."

APPENDICES

APPENDIX I

OSCAR AND CEDRIC VIEW STAR ISLAND

From the high hill on Appledore Oscar and Cedric had a commanding view of the archipelago. Standing near the cairn which tradition said had been laid up by Captain John Smith, they looked across Gosport Harbor and saw Lemuel Caswell build his modest rooming house (1856), later to be incorporated into the New Oceanic Hotel (1875).

In the summer of 1859 they watched workmen from Portsmouth mount a new weathervane atop the steeple of the meetinghouse. This notable event appears in the Gosport town records: "At a considerable expense, the inhabitants of the Isles have put up a *beautiful vane* on our chapel. May their own hearts yield to the breathings of the Divine Spirit, as the vane does to the wind."

At the same time the Reverend Daniel Austin of Portsmouth contributed a bell, which still calls the pilgrims as it then called the fishermen, to morning and evening services.

Oscar wrote (November 17, '61) that Lem Caswell, Sarah's husband and the father of John Caswell, had cut his throat — had indeed made the attempt a year ago — the coffin was made in Oscar's shop at Appledore.

Cedric observed (March 1, 1863) that the Gosport Town Meeting was held last Tuesday, John C. Randall, moderator. Orin Caswell elected "representative of the mighty city of Gosport."

In '64 the brothers watched the erection of the monument on Star Island to commemorate the landing of John Smith, two hundred fifty years earlier. Perhaps they thought the new and more permanent marker was enough. In all events they permitted their own cairn to drift into the foundations of new cottages.

Cedric wrote to Celia (November 11, '65) "Willis Downs came running over the hill and told us that Charles Caswell (Pip's oldest brother) had just been picked up off Square Rock — drowned — coming out from Rye. This makes the sixth death from drowning this season." Three weeks earlier Captain Lear was found in a boat

ISLES OF SHOALS

with Brewster's head in his lap — dead. They had been adrift all day.

In '67 again from their hilltop the brothers watched Orin Caswell build another small hotel on Star Island which he named the Gosport House.

In the spring of '68 their gaze was fixed on Smuttynose where "Rumor says we have another accursed prize-fight," Cedric reported. "Alas that such a disgraceful and beastly exhibition should come off at the Islands." Two weeks later he wrote that the prize-fight had been given up. "The fog had one good effect, for it so disgusted the prizefighters that I guess they have given up. They were most horribly seasick, both coming out and going in, and the steamer from Boston got lost in fog and had to put back."

In '71 comes another spicy comment on Gosport elections, held this time in Rye, since Gosport citizens had gained permission to vote in Rye. "Amy and Pip have gone to Rye to the election. Amy generally gets drunk. When he went off to bid Mary a tender farewell after this fashion, 'Good-bye Mary, if we don't meet again here we shall in hell,' Mary was slightly discouraged by the prospect."

The next year another spicy note: "Mar. 8, 1872 — Lemmy and Elvin are the rival candidates for representative at Gosport, and I expect the meetinghouse will be knocked flat by the hardy voters. Elvin has been paying $30 a vote."

Mar. 15, "The Town Meeting at Gosport turned out to be a complete failure, for Captain Henry, Duckshooter and Chief Selectman, refused to have anything to do with it, and notwithstanding the curses of Elvin and the tears of Lemmy the whole thing resulted in a mizzle."

The last Town Meeting on Star Island was held March 14, 1876. Celia records the event without knowing that it was closing the official doors of Gosport as a town. She wrote Annie Fields: "Bad weather, but a steamer is coming out to bring people to see about voting at Star Island . . . Just think of the surprising fact that these brothers of mine, thirty years old and never voted in their lives and never wish to!"

The Town of Gosport was formally given up and the islands on the New Hampshire side of the state line (Star, Londoners and White) were annexed to the town of Rye, to which they still belong.

APPENDIX II

THE ISLANDS

In answer to many questions regarding the natural history of the islands — their area, altitude, geology, flora and fauna — the following notes are offered.

Observe first that in years past the islands have provoked sailor and savant alike to grotesque exaggeration. Hog Island was said to cover from 350 to 400 acres (actual size about 95). De Costa gives the elevation about 90 feet (government survey says not over 60). The deed to Star Island calls for 92 acres (more accurate estimate says not more than 40). However, since the islands never have been sold by the acre as farmland, nor by the foot as city lots, there is no guilt in the exaggerations. They are noted here and later estimates given, because there is no point in quoting inaccurate figures. Accuracy deepens interest, falsehood leads to disillusionment.

Geographically the Shoals lie within a quadrangle three miles north and south, by one and a half east and west. The nearest approach to mainland is about six and one half miles from Londoners to Straw Point on Rye Beach. The distance from the mouth of the Piscataqua to Gosport Harbor is about nine miles. Gosport Harbor is approximately half a mile wide. (Hereafter we shall omit the word "approximately," since all figures are mere estimates.)

AREA AND ALTITUDE

Appledore	95	acres	alt.	60 ft.
Cedar	15	”	”	15 ”
Duck	6	”	”	15 ”
Londoners	11	”	”	20 ”
Malaga	2.5	”	”	12 ”
Smuttynose	27.1	”	”	20 ”
Star	39	”	”	55 ”
Seavey	5	”	”	15 ”
White	6	”	”	40 ”

Total land surface of all islands 206 acres. (To visualize an acre note that a football field between goals is slightly more than an acre.)

169

ISLES OF SHOALS

LOCAL DISTANCES

Estimated in miles from Government maps.
From Star Island, (nearest point)

		Mi.
To — Cedar Island		.1
	Smuttynose	.3
	Appledore	.45
	Cannon Point	.57
	Londoners	.47
	White	.45
	Anderson's Ledge	.9
	Duck Island	1.8
	Boon Island	12.5
From Cedar Island		
To — Smuttynose		.17
	Cedar Island Ledge	.47
From Malaga		
To — Appledore		.17
From White Island		
To — Star Island dock		.7
	Anderson's Ledge	1.00
Gosport Harbor — deepest point	70 feet	

FLORA AND FAUNA

In 1940 Mr. Richard E. Schultes and Reverend Theodore L. Steiger made a survey of plant life. They were on the islands only five days (June 22-27) and listed 127 varieties, regretting that they could not return in late summer to continue the survey. They say:

"The environment for which all these plants have to be adapted in order to survive for more than one season is characterized by the high moisture content of the air in summer and the inexorable blasts of cold wind which sweep the Islands in winter. As a result there are no trees, but the herbaceous (i.e. not woody) plants — retreating in winter into the safety of underground dormancy — produce a rich carpet of vegetation with large flowers and deep colors in summer."

For a ten-year period (1929-1939) New Hampshire University conducted a summer school for advanced study in marine zoology at Appledore Island. Many theses were written on the flora and

170

ISLES OF SHOALS

fauna of the vicinity, with special attention to marine biology. These studies, now in the University Library at Durham, have greatly extended available data on natural history. The New Hampshire Audubon Society and the Appalachian Mountain Club conduct annual field trips to the islands and have added much to our lore on botany and ornithology. Agronomists have told us that our soil is all post-glacial, created by erosion and turned into humus by the rotting of its own vegetation, hence lacks the richness of older soils on the mainland. Soil for cultivated flower gardens is brought over by hardy guests in bags and buckets.

GEOLOGY

Strangely enough the most obvious and challenging subject — geology — has had little attention until recently. Early geologists were wont to toss off a few paragraphs to the effect that rock formations here resemble those on the mainland at Rye and Hampton, to which they are related. Later geologists have discovered that these islands have a story of their own — not simple and obvious, but extremely complex and difficult to interpret. Moreover this is a geologists's paradise, in that there are large denuded areas easy of access where a great variety of rock formations may be studied without drudgery of clearing soil.

It remained for Mrs. Katharine Fowler-Billings to make the first intensive study. Her excellent work, written in lucid style for the layman and illustrated with maps, charts, and photographs, was published in 1959 by the New Hampshire State Planning and Development Commission.

A ramble from the landing at the north shore of Star Island leads across a grassy field and up the rugged slope of the first hill, whose highest rock is less than sixty feet above the tide. This is the highest point of the island and commands the far horizon, broken only by the rounded dome of Appledore to the north. The trail leads on down the southern slope through a valley overgrown with rank grass and low bushes of sumac, bayberry, briars, and wild roses, then rises to the long ridge of a second hill. Here vegetation virtually ceases. The trail quickly emerges from a narrow belt of grass into a shambles of sharp, irregular boulders. The entire southern end of the island, nearly one fourth its whole area, lies bare and bleaching in the sun. There is no trail here. The visitor makes his way over and around the tumbled boulders to the third

ISLES OF SHOALS

summit—a rounded dome of solid rock—pegmatite—near the southern point of the island. The elevation here is not more than forty feet, yet the circling horizon is still unbroken except for the low hill to the north which we have just crossed. Note that their ridges point southwest toward their cousins in Rye and Hampton.

Some have thought that these hills and ridges, together with their neighbors on the other islands, were once the rugged summit of a high mountain which sank gradually into the sea. But such is not the case. These islands are a horizontal cross section of the base, not the summit, of a mountain whose origin dates back three or four hundred million years. The high alpine peak was eroded down to a modest hill and then sheared off by the last ice flow hardly more than ten thousand years ago. This rounded dome was once the central core, the stony heart, of the mountain whose summit lies on the bed of the Atlantic.

The southern dome, and all the naked rock at this end of the island, reveals by its character and structure the original rock whence it sprang. The dome itself and most of its environment is pegmatite; that is, granite in all its forms. Here are crystals ranging in size from microscopic grains to massive quartz and feldspar blocks as large as a football. Here also glinting in the sun are flecks of black (biotite) and white (muscovite) mica, bits of black tourmaline, and here and there rusty red fragments of garnet. These all remind us that this rock, once molten, cooled slowly, allowing various elements to form crystals, each after its own pattern. That may have been half a billion years ago, yet here they are bright and shining as if new born. No wonder geologists rave over them.

The evidence of glacial action is scattered over all the islands —grooves and scratches in the solid rock, glacial boulders (erratics) dropped here and there as the ice melted. There is a pothole on the north shore of Star Island, but more conspicuous than all else are the leveled slope of northwestern shores and the ragged high cliffs to the southeast. The glacier pushed down the valley of the Piscataqua, scraped and polished the western shores but "plucked" the eastern—breaking off huge boulders and carrying them far out to sea. Space does not permit a more detailed analysis of these fascinating rock formations. Their story is better told by Mrs. Billings. The time is ripe and the material mostly available for a definitive natural history of the Shoals.

APPENDIX III

MINISTERS
MISSIONARIES, TEACHERS, AGENTS

1637 - 1871

1637 - 1638	William Tompson
1639 - 1640	Joseph Hull
1640	Robert Jordan
1641 - 1642	Richard Gibson
1650 - 1662	John Brock
1663 - 1692	Samuel Belcher
1700	Samuel Moody
1702	Samuel Eburne
1705	Daniel Greenleafe
1707 - 1730	Joshua Moody
1731 - 1773	John Tucke
1773 - 1775	Jeremiah Shaw
*1799 -	Jacob Emerson
1800 -	John Low
*1801 - 1804	Josiah Stevens
1806 -	Daniel Lovejoy
1807 -	Enoch Whipple
1817 -	John Dutton
1822 -	Reuben Moody
1824 - 1826	Samuel Sewall
1834 -	Philip Cleland
1834 -	Stillman Pratt
1834 -	Clarindon Muzzy
1834 -	Robert Fuller
*1837 - 1847	Origin Smith
1842 -	Edwin Ritson
*1842 - 1844	Abner Hall
*1844 - 1847	Abraham Plumer
*1848 -	L. D. Blodgett
*1851 -	Oliver D. Eastman
*1853 - 1855	John Mason
*1853 -	Levi Lincoln Thaxter
*1856 - 1869	George R. Beebe

ISLES OF SHOALS

*1857 - 1868	Joshua Eaton
1868 - 1869	Henry H. Barber
1868 -	Mr. Hancock
1869 - 1870	Mr. Hughes
*1871 -	William Hewes

*Appointed by the *Society for Propagating the Gospel among the Indians and Others in North America.*

APPENDIX IV

ROSTER OF APPLEDORIANS

In his *Ninety Years at the Isles of Shoals* Oscar refers to Appledore as "a gathering place for distinguished people," and mentions thirty-five as if from memory. He did not have the hotel register in hand at the time, or he would have included many others. We have now the first two registers covering the years 1848 to 1866. What became of the subsequent books we do not know. Doubtless they were destroyed in the fire of 1914.

It has been possible however, to glean more names from other sources, chiefly correspondence, and offer them here with brief biographical notes as typical of those who visited the Shoals between the years of 1840 and 1894 and by their presence and interest entered the island tradition.

ADAMS, Charles Francis, statesman; b. Boston, Aug. 18, 1807, d. Nov. 21, 1886. Served in Mass. Gen. Court 1840-45, Cong. 1859-61, Minister to England 1861-68.

ADAMS, Charles Francis, Jr., atty., author; b. Quincy, Mass., May 27, 1835, d. Mar. 20, 1915. Harvard 1856. Entered law office of Richard Henry Dana and wrote his biog. in 1890. Became expert in railway traffic and was active in promoting first transcontinental railways. (The names of these two — father and son — first appear in the Appledore register July 18th 1848. They note that they arrived on the *Nautilus*.)

ALBEE, Rev. John, close friend of the Laightons; b. Bellingham, Mass., April 3, 1833, d. Washington, D.C., Mar. 24, 1915. Attended Harvard Divin. Sch. — did not graduate but served various churches. Wrote the biog. sketch of Celia which appears on pp. 161-74 of *The Heavenly Guest*.

ALDEN, Henry M., editor; b. Mt. Tabor, Vt., Nov. 11, 1836, d. New York, Oct. 7, 1919. Grad. Andover Theol, Sch. but never ordained. Advisor in chief and Mng. Editor of *Harper's Weekly* 1863-69. Editor *Harper's Magazine* 1869-1919.

ALDRICH. Thomas Bailey, author, editor; b. Portsmouth, N.H., Nov. 11, 1836, d. Boston, Mar. 19, 1907. Author: *The Bells,*

ISLES OF SHOALS

poems, 1855, *The Story of a Bad Boy*, 1870. Editor *Atlantic Monthly* 1881-90.

ANDERSON, Emma M. (Mrs. Larz). (See "Celia Thaxter and her Gardens" in *The Heavenly Guest*, pp. 115-23).

ANGIER, Rev. Joseph, minister, singer; b. Durham, N. H., April 24, 1808, d. April 12, 1871. Churches — New Bedford 1835-37, Milton, Mass. 1837-45, Troy, N.Y. 1851-52, Leicester, Mass. 1853-56, Haverhill, Mass. 1862-64.

BAILEY, Rear Admiral Theodorus, U. S. Navy; b. Chateaugay, N.Y., April 12, 1805, d. Washington, D.C., Feb. 10, 1877. Served in Mexican and Civil Wars, made Commander Portsmouth Navy Yard 1866.

BEECHER, Henry Ward, minister, editor; b. Litchfield, Ct., June 24, 1813, d. Brooklyn, N.Y., Mar. 8, 1887. Minister Plymouth Cong'l. Ch., Brooklyn. Grad. Lane Theol, Sch., Cincinnati, O., 1837. Editor N. Y. *Independent* 1861-63. Editor N.Y. *Outlook.*

BIGELOW, John, J. P., Horatio, and their families, appear frequently on the hotel register. Horatio was brother of Erastus, who invented looms for weaving Brussels and Wilton carpets. Around the mills established by Horatio and Erastus grew the present city of Clinton, Mass. Erastus was one of a small group who incorporated the Mass. Inst. of Tech. in 1866.

BOWDITCH, Henry Ingersoll, son of Nathaniel, noted Boston phys.; b. Salem, Mass. Aug. 9, 1808, d. Jan. 14, 1892. Prof. clinical med. Harvard.

BOWDITCH, J. Ingersoll, financier; brother of Henry I. & Nathaniel I.

BOWDITCH, Nathaniel Ingersoll, b. 1805, d. 1861. Wrote a life of Bowditch, later elaborated into a biog. by Henry I.

BRAUNER, Olaf Martinius, artist; b. Christiana, Norway, Feb. 9, 1869 m. Nikoline B. Berntsen, June 26, 1895. Instr. Mass. Normal Art Sch., Boston, 1892, Museum Sch., Boston, 1895. Prof. of painting Cornell Univ. 1900.

BROOKS, Phillips, Bishop of Mass.; b. Boston, Dec. 13, 1835, d. Boston, Jan. 23, 1893. Rector Trinity Ch., Boston, 1869-91.

BROWN, J. Appleton, artist; b. West Newbury, Mass. 1844, d.

ISLES OF SHOALS

1925. Illustrated "Landscapes in Am. Poetry" for Lucy Larcom, 1879. Studio in Boston 1868-74. Studio in N.Y. 1891.

BULL, Ole, violinist; b. Bergen, Norway, Feb. 5, 1810, d. Lyso, near Bergen, Aug. 17, 1880. Visited U.S. 1843-45 & 1852-57. Gave concerts at Appledore benefit Shoals Norwegian fishermen.

BUNNER, Henry Cuyler, journalist, poet, story writer; b. Oswego, N.Y., Aug. 3, 1855, d. Nutting, N.J., May 11, 1896. Editor *Puck,* earliest Amer. comic weekly. Author: *Airs from Arcady* poems, *Love in Old Clothes*, fiction.

BURNETT, Frances Hodgson, author; b. Manchester, Eng., Nov. 24, 1849, d. Long Island, N.Y., Oct. 29, 1924; m. Dr. L. M. Burnett of Washington, D.C., 1873. Author: *Little Lord Fauntleroy* 1886 (named for Cedric Laighton), *A Lady of Quality* 1896, *T. Tembarum* 1913.

BUTLER, Benjamin Franklin, Col., statesman; b. Deerfield, N.H., Nov. 5, 1818, d. Washington, D.C., Jan. 11, 1893. Mass. House 1853, U.S. Senate 1859, U.S. House 1867-79, Gov. Mass. 1882. Col. in Civil War.

CHURCHILL, Anna Quincy, M.D., daughter of Joseph R., b. Dorchester, Mass., May 31, 1884. Tufts Sch. of Med. 1917. Prof. Microscopic Anatomy, Tufts U., 36 yrs.

CHURCHILL, Joseph Richmond, jurist; b. Dorchester, Mass., July 29, 1845, d. Feb. 14, 1933. Justice of Municipal Court, Dorchester, 1871-1931. Celebrated as judge with longest active service on the bench in U. S. history (60 yrs.). Musician, botanist; gave herbarium of 15,000 sheets to Shaw Botanical Gardens, St. Louis, Mo.

CLARKE, Rev. James Freeman, clergyman and author; b. Hanover, N.H., April 4, 1810, d. Jamaica Plain, Mass., June 3, 1888. Ordained Boston, July 21, 1833. Church of the Disciples 1841-50, 1855-88.

CLIFFORD, Nathan, jurist; b. Rumney, N.H., 1803, d. 1881. Assoc. Justice U.S. Supreme Court 1858-81.

CUSHING, Caleb, atty., statesman; b. Salisbury, Mass., Jan. 17, 1800, d. Newburyport, Mass., Jan. 2, 1879. Mass. House 1825, Senate 1826, House 1828 and 1833, U.S. House 1835-43. First comm. to China 1844; negot. first treaty between China and U.S.;

177

ISLES OF SHOALS

U.S. Atty. Gen. under Franklin Pierce; U.S. minister to Spain 1874-77.

DANA, Richard Henry, atty., author; b. Cambridge, Mass., Aug. 1, 1815, d. Rome, Italy, Jan. 6, 1882. U.S. dist. atty. for Mass. 1860; Mass. House 1867-1868. Author: *Two Years Before the Mast* 1840.

DE HAAS, Maurice Frederick Hendrick, artist; b. Rotterdam, Dec. 12, 1832, d. Nov. 23, 1895. Mentioned by S.G.W. Benjamin in "The Atlantic Islands as Resorts of Health and Pleasure," *Harper's*, 1878, p. 220. His painting, "The Breaking-up of a Storm at Star Island" much admired.

DE NORMANDIE, Rev. James, minister; b. Newport, Pa., June 9, 1836, d. Boston, Oct. 6, 1924. Ordained Portsmouth, N.H. Oct. 1, 1862, served 1862-83; Roxbury, Mass. 1883-1917, Emeritus 1917-24.

EICHBERG, Julius, violinist; b. Dusseldorf, June 13, 1824, d. Boston, Jan. 18, 1893. Prof. in Conservatoire, Geneva, 1845; came to N.Y. 1857; to Boston, 1859. Dir. Boston Museum 7 yrs. Estab. Boston Conservatory of Music 1867. Composed operettas — four well known — *The Doctor of Alcantara, The Rose of Tyrol, The Two Cadis, A Night in Rome.*

FIELD, Kate, author, editor, writer; b.—— d. N.Y., 1895. Said by Laurence Hutton to be "the most promising young woman in her profession in America" (*Talks in a Library*, p. 382).

FIELDS, Annie Adams (Mrs. James T.), author; b. Boston, Jan. 6, 1834, d. Jan. 5, 1915, m. James T. Fields 1854. Author: *Under the Olive* 1880, *James T. Fields, Bio. Notes and Personal Sketches* 1881, *Authors and Friends* 1896, *Orpheus — A Masque* 1900, biog. sketch of Celia Thaxter in the *Atlantic Monthly*, and in *The Heavenly Guest* (pp. 86-114). Edited with Rose Lamb *The Letters of Celia Thaxter* 1895.

FIELDS, James T., author, editor, pub.; b. Portsmouth, N.H., Dec. 31, 1817, d. Boston, April 24, 1881. Firm of Ticknor & Fields 1846; Fields, Osgood & Co. 1868. Editor *Atlantic Monthly* 1862-70. Author: *Underbrush* 1877, *Yesterdays with Authors* 1872.

FISKE, John, philosopher, historian lecturer; b. Hartford, Ct., Nov. 30, 1842, d. Gloucester, Mass., July 4, 1901. Author: *Outlines of Cosmic Philosophy*, 1874.

ISLES OF SHOALS

GREELEY, Adolphus Washington, explorer, Maj Gen.; b. Newburyport, Mass., Mar. 27, 1844, d. Washington, D.C., Oct. 20, 1935. Commander *Lady Franklin Bay* 1881-84. Author: *Three Years of Arctic Service* 1909, *Handbook of Polar Discoveries* 1909, *Polar Regions of the 20th Cent.* 1928. A founder of the *National Geopraphic Society.*

HALE, Edward Everett, minister, author; b. Boston, April 3, 1822, d. Roxbury, Mass., June 10, 1909. Ordained April 26, 1846. Min. Church of the Unity, Worcester, Mass., 1846-56, South Cong'l Unitarian Church, Boston, 1856-1909. Chaplain U. S. Senate, 1903-09. Author: *My Double and How He Undid Me* 1859, *The Man without a Country* 1863, *Ten Times One is Ten* 1870, *In His Name* 1873 (origin of King's Daughters.)

HASSAM, Childe, artist; b. Dorchester, Mass., Oct. 7, 1859, d. East Hampton, L.I., Aug. 27, 1935. Medals won: Paris 1889, Chicago World's Fair 1893, Boston Art Club 1896, Phil. Art Club 1892, Carnegie Inst. 1898, Buffalo Pan American 1901, Pa. Acad. Fine Arts 1899 and 1920, Paris 1900, Phil. Sesqui-centennial 1926. Illus. Celia Thaxter's *Island Garden* 1894. Had studio on Appledore.

HAWTHORNE, Julian s. of Nathaniel; b. 1846, d. 1934. Wrote the standard Biog. *Nathaniel Hawthorne and His Wife* 1885, novels and short stories.

HAWTHORNE, Nathaniel, author, diplomat; b. Salem, Mass., July 4, 1804, d. Plymouth, N.H., May 19, 1864. Author: *The Scarlet Letter* 1850, *The House of Seven Gables* 1851, *The Marble Faun* 1859. Appt. U.S. Consul at Liverpool 1853; at Rome 1857.

HIGGINSON, Thomas Wentworth, col., minister, author; b. Cambridge, Mass., Dec. 22, 1823, d. Cambridge, May 9, 1911. Min. First Relig. Soc. Newburyport, Mass., 1847-49, Free Ch. in Worcester 1852-56. Col. 1st So. Carolina Volunteers. Author: *Cheerful Yesterdays* 1898, *Contemporaries* 1899, *Atlantic Essays* 1871.

HOWELLS, William Dean, author, editor, diplomat; b. Martin's Ferry, O., Mar. 1, 1837, d. N.Y., May 11, 1920. Author: *The Campaign Life of Lincoln* 1860, *The Rise of Silas Lapham* 1885. Editor-in-chief *Atlantic Monthly* 1874-81. Consul at Venice 1860-65.

HUBBARD, Henry, atty.; eminent lawyer, Gov. of N.H. 1842-43.

HUIDEKOPER, Edgar b. 1812, d. 1862. Estab. Fund.

ISLES OF SHOALS

HUNT, William Morris, artist; b. Brattleboro, Vt. Mar. 31, 1824, d. Isles of Shoals, Sept. 8, 1879.

HUTTON, Laurence, author, educator; b. N. Y. City, Aug. 8, 1843, d. Princeton, N.J., June 10, 1904. Editor *Harper's Magazine* 1886-98. Author: *Talks in a Library* 1905 (see poem dedicated to L. H. in *The Heavenly Guest*, p. 46).

JENNESS, John Scribner, atty., author: *The Isles of Shoals* 1873, second edition, 1915.

JEWETT, Sarah Orne, author; b. South Berwick, Me., Sept. 3, 1849, d. South Berwick, June 14, 1909. Author: *Deephaven* 1877, *A Country Doctor* 1884, *The Country of the Pointed Firs* 1896. Edited Celia Thaxter's Poems 1896.

KANE, Elisha Kent, explorer; b. Phil., Feb. 3, 1820, d. Havana, Cuba, Feb. 16, 1857. Arctic explorer, awarded gold medal by Congress 1855. Member Royal Geog. Soc. London; awarded Queen's medal.

LAMB, Rose, artist; with Annie Fields, edited Celia Thaxter's letters 1895.

LAMSON, Alvan, Rev., minister, author; b. Weston, Mass., Nov. 18, 1792, d. Dedham, Mass., July 18, 1864. Ordained Dedham, Oct. 29, 1818, resigned 1860. Wrote *Church of the First Three Centuries* 1860.

LARCOM, Lucy, poet, educator; b. Beverly, Mass., Mar. 5, 1824, d. April 17, 1893. Teacher in Wheaton Coll. 1854-62.

LONGFELLOW, Samuel, minister, hymn writer; b. Portland, Me., June 18, 1819, d. Oct. 3, 1892. Ordained at Fall River, Mass., 1848; minister Germantown, Pa. 1878-82. Author: Hymns; edited with Samuel Johnson, Service Books.

LORING, Edward Greeley, ophthalmologist; b. Boston, Sept. 28, 1837, d. N.Y. City, April 23, 1888. Developed first practical ophthalmoscope 1874. Author of texts on ophthalmology.

LOWELL, James Russell, author, diplomat; b. Cambridge, Mass., Feb. 22, 1819, d. Cambridge, Aug. 12, 1891. Admitted to Bar 1840, m. Maria White Oct. 27, 1844, m. Frances Dunlap 1856. Ambassador to England 1880-85. Smith prof. modern languages, Harvard 1856-76. First editor *Atlantic Monthly* 1857-61; an editor *North Amer. Review* 1864-72. Author: *A Fable for Critics* 1848,

ISLES OF SHOALS

The Vision of Sir Launfal 1848, *The Biglow Papers, Pictures from Appledore* 1854.

MAREAN, Emma E., editor *Christian Register.* Secured signatures from authors of Hymns in the Shoals Hymn Book.

MASON, Lowell, composer; b. Medfield, Mass., Jan. 8, 1792, d. Orange, N.J., Aug. 11, 1872. Pres. Handel and Haydn Soc.; founded Boston Acad. of Music 1832.

MASON, William, pianist; b. Boston, Jan. 24, 1829, d. N.Y., July 14, 1908. Boy prodigy, toured Europe as concert pianist at early age.

MITCHELL, Silas Weir, author, physician; b. Phil., Feb. 15, 1829, d. Jan 4, 1914. M.D. Jefferson Med. Coll. 1850, prescribed "The Rest Cure." Wrote poems, novels, medical works.

MOULTON, Louise Chandler, author; b. Pomfret, Ct., April 10, 1835, d. Boston, Aug. 10, 1908. Author: *Bedtime Stories* 1873, *Juno Clifford* (novel) 1873. Presided over the most noted salon in Boston.

MURFEE, Mary Noailles, author (pen name Charles Egbert Craddock); b. Murfeesboro, Tenn., 1850, d. 1922. Wrote early stories of mountain life, *Atlantic Monthly; In the Tennessee Mountains* 1884, *The Prophet of the Great Smoky Mountains* 1888.

PAGE, Walter Hines, editor, diplomat; b. Carey, N.C., Aug. 15, 1855, d. Dec. 27, 1918. Editor of the *Forum* 1890-95; of the *Atlantic Monthly* 1896-99. Partner in pub. firm of Doubleday, Page, and Co. 1899. Founded mag. *World's Work* 1900, Ambassador to Great Britain 1913.

PAINE, John Knowles, pianist, composer; b. Portland, Me., Jan. 9, 1839, d. Cambridge, Mass. April 25, 1906. Prof. of Music at Harvard from 1875.

PEABODY, Andrew P. minister; b. Beverly, Mass., Mar. 19, 1811, d. Mar 10, 1893. Ordained Portsmouth, N.H., Oct. 24, 1833, served there until 1860. Plummer Prof. of Christian Morals at Harvard 1860-81. Supervised Gosport Chapel. Proprietor and editor *North American Review* for ten years. Acting pres. of Harvard 1862 and again 1868-69.

PHELPS, Elizabeth Stuart, author; b. Andover, Mass., Aug. 13,

ISLES OF SHOALS

1815, d. Nov. 30, 1852; m. Austin Phelps 1842 (mother of Elizabeth Stuart Phelps Ward).

PIERCE, Franklin, atty. statesman; b. Hillsboro, N.H., Nov. 23, 1804, d. Concord, N.H., Oct. 8, 1869. A. B. Bowdoin Coll. 1824, with Nathaniel Hawthorne and Henry W. Longfellow. N.H. House 1829, Speaker 1831-32; U.S. House 1834; U.S. Senate 1837; Fed. Dist. Atty. 1842. Enlisted as a private in War with Mexico 1846. Pres. U.S. 1852-56.

RICHARDS, C. A. bus. exec.; pres. Metropolitan Railroad.

RILEY, James Whitcomb, poet; b. Greenfield, Ind., Oct. 7, 1849, d. Indianapolis, July 22, 1916. Mem. Am. Acad. of Arts and Letters. Birthday made an official holiday in Ind. 1915. Author: *The Old Swimmin'-Hole, Little Orphant Annie, Home Folks.*

ROBBINS, Ellen, artist; b. July 1, 1828, d. 1905. Teacher of art in Watertown and Boston. Noted for still-life and flower arrangements. Commissioned to paint a frieze in the Browning Room at Wellesley College.

SANBORN, Franklin Benjamin, author; b. Hampton Falls, N.H., Dec. 15, 1831, d. Feb. 24, 1917. With Amos Bronson Alcott and William T. Harris, established Concord Sch. of Philos. 1879. Author: Lives of John Brown, Henry D. Thoreau, Samuel Gridley Howe, Ralph W. Emerson, Nathaniel Hawthorne, and others. Edited *Springfield Republican* 1868-1914.

SCUDDER Horace Elisha, editor and writer (1838-1902). Edited the *Atlantic Monthly* 1890-98. Directed the *American Commonwealth Series* and the *Cambridge Edition of the Poets* for Houghton Mifflin. Author: juvenile stories, biographies of Bayard Taylor and James Russell Lowell.

SHAW, Justin H., judge. Wrote biog. sketch of Celia Thaxter in *The Heavenly Guest,* pp. 141-54.

SPOFFORD, Harriet Prescott, author; b. Calais, Me., Apr. 3, 1835, d. Aug. 14, 1921. First article in *Atlantic Monthly* 1859. m. atty. Richard Smith Spofford, Jr. 1865.

STATLER, E. M. Oscar observes, "It has been said that the success of the great hotel man Statler is due to his close study of the methods of the Laighton family at Appledore." Roger W. Babson notes in his Autobiography: "He was a wonderful man, modest, upright

ISLES OF SHOALS

and progressive. He revolutionized the hotel business in America." (*Actions and Reactions,* Harper & Bros. 1935, p. 110).

STEDMAN, Edmund Clarence, author, editor, financier; b. Hartford, Ct., Oct. 8, 1833, d. N.Y., June 18, 1908. Editor and news writer for N.Y. *Tribune* and N.Y. *World.* Edited *A Victorian Anthology* 1895, *An American Anthology* 1900, N.Y. Stock Exchange 1869-1900.

STEDMAN, Henry R., physician; physician at Appledore the summer following graduation from Med. Sch. Met and later married Mabel, daughter of Rev. John Weiss. Head of Bournewood Hosp. (for mental illness) 300 South St., Brookline, Mass. (formerly Woodburn Hosp. at Forest Hills).

STOWE, Harriet Beecher, author; b. Litchfield, Ct., June 14, 1811, d. Hartford, Ct., July 1, 1896. Author: *Uncle Tom's Cabin* 1852, *The Minister's Wooing* 1859, *Pearl of Orr's Island* 1862.

TROWBRIDGE, John Townsend, author; b. Ogden, N.Y., Sept. 18, 1827, d. Feb. 12, 1916. Author: Short stories and poems, Jack Hazard Series, Toby Trafford Series, *The Drummer Boy* 1863, *Cudjo's Cave* 1864, *Darius Green and his Flying Machine.* Edited *Our Young Folks.* Wrote boy's books under pseudonym Paul Creyton.

TUCK, Amos., atty., politician; b. Parsonsfield, Me., Aug. 2, 1810, d. Exeter, N.H., Dec. 11, 1879. Served in N.H. Legislature 1842, U.S. House 1847. Friend of Lincoln. Father of Edward Tuck who gave Tucke Monument to Star Island.

TURNER, Ross, artist; b. Westport, N.Y., June 29, 1847, d. Feb. 12, 1915. Studied in Germany and Italy. Wrote *Art for the Eye, School Room Decorations.* Had studio at Appledore.

VANNAH, Kate, musician; composed music for Celia Thaxter's "Good-Bye Sweet Day" (see poem dedicated to K. V. in *The Heavenly Guest* p. 44.

WARD, Elizabeth Stuart Phelps, novelist; b. Andover, Mass., Aug. 31, 1844, d. Newton, Mass., Jan. 28, 1910. m. Dr. H. D. Ward 1888, Author: *Gates Ajar* 1868, *Chapters from a Life* 1897, *Songs of the Silent World,* Poems.

WARD, Samuel Gray, Boston Banker and patron of art. Emerson's most intimate friend, to whom he wrote the *Letters to a Friend,* published by Charles Eliot Norton. Confidante of Celia Thaxter.

ISLES OF SHOALS

WARNER, Charles Dudley, author; b. Plainfield, Mass., Sept. 12, 1829, d. Hartford, Ct., Oct. 26, 1900. Editor *Library of the World's Best Literature.* Author: *My Summer in a Garden* 1870, *My Winter on the Nile* 1876.

WARREN, William, physician.

WEISS, Rev. John, minister, author; b. June 1818, d. Boston, Mass., Mar. 9, 1879. Ordained Watertown, Mass., Oct. 25, 1843; m. Sarah Fiske Jennison Apr. 9, 1844. Served Watertown 1843-47, New Bedford, Mass., 1847-58. Retired from ministry 1859 and took up residence in Milton and later Boston.

WHITING, Arthur, composer and concert pianist; b. Cambridge, Mass., June 20, 1861, d. Beverly, Mass., July 26, 1936. Played with the Boston Symph. Orchestra and Kneisel Quar., both of which performed works of his. Introduced in Cambridge a series of lecture-recitals to promote musical appreciation.

WHITNEY, Anne, poet and sculptor; b. Watertown, Mass., 1821, d. 1915. Among her celebrated sculptures are: Leif Ericson, the Fenway, Boston; Charles Sumner, Harvard Square, Cambridge; Harriet Beecher Stowe, Hartford, Conn.; Shakespeare, now owned by Mrs. Wilson F. Payne of Needham, Mass.; Samuel Adams, Washington; Lady Godiva, owned by Harriet Martineau.

WHITTIER, John Greenleaf, poet; b. Haverhill, Mass., Dec. 17, 1807, d. Hampton Falls, N.H., Sept. 7, 1892.
(See poems dedicated to J.G.W. in *Poems* by Celia Thaxter, pp. 139, 167, 192 and in *The Heavenly Guest,* p. 25.)

WOODBURY, Charles Levi, prominent Boston Atty.; a frequent visitor at the Laighton's, both at White Island and at Appledore.

APPENDIX V

WESTERN SKYLINE FROM STAR ISLAND

Shoalers take well earned satisfaction in lounging on the western piazza of the Hotel whence they gaze over the sunlit ocean into the dim shadows of the mainland. There spreads the continent of North America as if it were sliding over the rim of the world into the nebulous unknown. The immediate shoreline, just seven miles away, is dotted with tiny flecks of white which in a vague way we assume to be summer cottages on little stretches of sandy beach. A few landmarks catch the eye — the Wentworth Hotel in New Castle off to the northwest, and the dark pencil of the water-tower at Great Boars Head in Hampton almost directly southwest. Rolling hills, blue in the distance, form an undulating horizon. Out of prolonged reverie someone emerges with the inevitable questions, "What mountains do we see from here? What could we see on a clear day?"

Many years ago well informed guests began to make uninformed guesses and some drew charts naming all the points which might be visible to an infrared camera. It is disconcerting to study such a chart and then discover that most of the celebrated peaks are completely hidden by the intervening lower hills. Only three or four are within our range of vision. We have therefore assembled all available data, made calculations and drawn maps to satisfy ourselves as to the true names and locations of these domes. We have developed a real fondness for many little hills unknown to fame which add so much to the mystery and charm of that western horizon.

For your convenience we drew a circle with the west end of the piazza as center, and marked the circumference with the conventional 360 degrees. By sighting along a radial line you may identify the distant hill. For example, Hotel Wentworth is 314° — and so also is Blue Job Mountain 28 miles beyond. Which means that on a clear day you may see the rounded dome of Blue Job rising above the Wentworth.

The continental horizon line visible from the Shoals extends in a crescent from Cape Neddick 12 miles north to Cape Ann 20 miles south. A straight line drawn from one to the other would pass over the Shoals about a mile east of where we are now sitting. There-

ISLES OF SHOALS

fore on our chart we show Cape Neddick as 5° and Cape Ann as 175°, because they are both a trifle east of us.

Both these points are hidden from us at the moment. Cape Neddick is behind Appledore and Cape Ann is cut off by the southwest corner of our hotel. If the hotel were square with the compass we could see Cape Ann from here, but it faces slightly east of north, which falsifies our sense of direction. The distance, elevation and degree are given in parentheses after each place name, thus, Thachers Light (22.8 – 166 – 175) means that it is 22.8 miles from here, 166 ft. high and may be located by sighting along radial 175.

Thachers (22.8 - 166 - 175) and Straitsmouth (21.3 - 46 - 175) were long known as the twin lights of Cape Ann. In those days we saw them almost as one with Thachers on the left. Halibut Point (20 - 130 - 180) is our nearest point of land on the south. Pigeon Hill is the highest elevation on Halibut Pt. Back of it and to the right about 1° is Pools Hill (23 - 235 - 182). The depression to the right is Annisquam at the mouth of the Annisquam River, the beginning of Ipswich Bay. In 1605 Champlain called this a "cul de sac."

In 1614 Captain John Smith drew the first credible map of this area and gave the name Tragabigzanda to the Cape in honor of the Turkish princess who befriended him while he was a captive in Constantinople. Three rocks off the cape were named Turbashaw, Grualgo and Bonny Mulgro in rcognition of the three Turks whom he slew in single combat. But the name of Princess Tragabigzanda soon gave place to that of Queen Ann.

Next on the horizon is Old Town Newbury (19 - 180 - 220) and then Turkey Hill (20 - 120 - 230) in Newburyport. These low lying hills are seldom distinguishable, but there they are if you care to identify them.

We have inadvertantly passed by the long stretch of Plum Island, the mouth of the Merrimack River and Salisbury Beach, all in Massachusetts and entered New Hampshire just after passing Turkey Hill in Newburyport. The state line passes between the summits of Po and her nearest neighbor, Chair.

Po Hill in Salisbury, called Powow Hill on all current maps, (18 - 330 - 243) is in the words of Celia Thaxter, "the last prominent hill to the south on our horizon." It was one of Whittier's

ISLES OF SHOALS

favorite haunts, and he and Celia often began their letters, "Po Hill greets Appledore," or "Appledore greets Po."

What appears to be the right shoulder of Po are Chair (17 - 328 - 248), Sawyer (19 - 316 - 242) and Bugsmouth (20.75 - 310 - 252). Their blending summits give the impression of a slightly undulating sky line. Immediately before them, are Grape (17 - 210 - 247) and Great (14.5 - 244 - 255).

Morse Hill (21.5 - 314 - 258) and Moulton Ridge (18.5 - 287 - 262) lead the horizon into a slight depression in the middle of which on an exceptional day the peak of Mt. Monadnock (75 - 3166 - 263) may be seen. Then, almost obscuring Monadnock are Rollins Hill (13.75 - 223 - 273) and Bunker, leading to the taller twins, Jewett (15 - 300 - 283) and Stratham (14.5 - 290 - 288). Above them on a clear day the summit of Pawtuckway (31 - 1011 - 288) will hang as a blue shadow.

Descending from Stratham, forming its right shoulder, is Great Hill (18 - 220 - 293). Then there is another mild depression with nothing in the foreground, but the dome of Saddleback (33 - 1180 - 295) in the distance. The right side of this depression continues on with the low lying Wednesday Hill (22 - 252 - 298) and Demeritt (22 - 200 - 304) leading to the taller Hicks (21 - 300 - 308) which is almost hidden by the much smaller Pudding Hill (20 - 220 - 311).

To the right of Pudding and rising above it though farther away, is Green Hill (25 - 389 - 312) and then the dome of Rochester Heights (29 - 500 - 314) partly hidden by Long (24 - 300 - 318). When the ground haze has cleared again, Blue Job (35 - 1356 - 314) will rise majestically. This clump of hills will seem to hang directly over the Wentworth Hotel.

Another clump of rounded domes hovers over Gerrish Island — the area on the coast line between Whaleback Light and Brave Boat Harbor. These are Frosts (15.5 - 315 - 324), Third (15.5 - 360 - 329) and Raitt (15.5 - 280 - 328). To their right is Jewett (18.5 - 310 - 330) and then Powderhouse (20 - 297 - 333). There may be a slight depression to their right, and there on the clearest of days will appear a blue mound that will hang like a cloud on the horizon. If it does not move — if no wind blows it away, it is Mt. Washington (95 - 6288 - 341). It is well up on the western slope of Agamenticus, and may have as a tiny shoulder on the right the romantic Bauneg Beg (29 - 866 - 342).

ISLES OF SHOALS

But the most commanding dome on the entire horizon is the celebrated Agamenticus (18 - 692 - 348). It is the most conspicuous landmark on the Atlantic seaboard from Blue Hill near Boston to Nova Scotia. The graceful dome slopes to the northeastward into Second (18.5 - 410 - 350) and Third (18 - 300 - 353). In the nearer foreground is York Hill (14.5 - 220 - 357) and then the gentle slope of Cape Neddick (12 - 50 - 5). But Neddick and a large area of Agamenticus are hidden behind the western slope of Appledore.

The boundary line between New Hampshire and Maine is easily followed. It goes through Gosport Harbor directly to the mouth of the Piscataqua River, between Fort Point and Whaleback Lights.

Note that there are three pairs of unrelated hills bearing the same name, Great Hill in Hampton Falls and Newmarket, Jewett in Stratham and So. Berwick and Third in Eliot and York.

The nearest approach to mainland from the Shoals is from Londoners to Straw Point in Rye, 6¼ miles. But from the hotel piazza it is seven miles to Straw Point and exactly the same to Whaleback Light. The sailing distance from Gosport Harbor to the wharf in Portsmouth is just over ten miles.

ISLES OF SHOALS
CHART OF THE HILLS
Distances in miles and elevation in feet estimated from Government maps.

Hill	Town	Dist.	Elev.	Degree
1. Thachers Hill	Rockport, Mass.	22.8	166	175
2. Straitsmouth Light	Rockport, Mass.	21.3	46	175
3. Pigeon Hill (Halibut Pt.)	Rockport, Mass.	20	130	180
4. Pools Hill	Rockport, Mass.	23	235	182
5. Mount Ann	Gloucester, Mass	24	272	195
6. Old Town Newbury	Newbury, Mass,	19	180	220
7. Turkey Hill	Newburyport, Mass.	20	120	230
8. Po Hill (Powow)	Salisbury, Mass.	18	330	243
9. Grape Hill	Salisbury, Mass.			
	Seabrook, N.H.	17	210	247
10. Sawyer	So. Hampton, N.H.	19	316	242
11. Chair Hill	So. Hampton, N.H.	17	328	248
12. Bugsmouth Hill	So. Hampton, N.H.	20.75	310	252
13. Great Hill	Hampton Falls, N.H.	14.5	244	255
14. Morse Hill	Kensington, N.H.	21.5	314	258
15. Moulton Ridge	Kensington, N.H.	18.5	287	262
16. Monadnock	Jaffrey & Dublin, N.H.	75	3166	263
17. Rollins	Stratham, N.H.	13.75	223	273
18. Bunker	Stratham, N.H.	15.5	210	278
19. Jewett	Stratham, N.H.	15	300	283
20. Pawtuckway	Deerfield, N.H.	31	1011	288
21. Stratham	Stratham, N.H.	14.5	290	288
22. Great Hill	Newmarket, N.H.	18	220	293
23. Saddleback	Norwoood, N.H.	33	1180	295
24. Wednesday	Lee, N.H.	22	252	298
25. Demeritt	Lee, N.H.	22	200	304
26. Hicks	Madbury, N.H.	21	300	308
27. Pudding Hill	Madbury, N.H.	20	220	311
28. Blue Job	Farmington, N.H.	35	1356	314
29. Green Hill	Barrington, N.H.	25	389	312
30. Rochester Heights	Rochester, N.H.	29	500	314
31. Long Hill	Somersworth, N.H.	24	300	318
32. Garrison	Dover, N.H.	20.5	300	321
33. Frosts	Eliot, Maine	15.5	315	324
34. Raitt	Eliot, Maine	15.5	280	328
35. Third Hill	Eliot, Maine	15.5	360	329
36. Jewett	South Berwick, Maine	18.5	310	330
37. Powderhouse	South Berwick, Maine	20	297	333
38. Washington	New Hampshire	95	6288	341
39. Bauneg Beg	Berwick, Maine	29	866	342
40. Agamenticus	York, Maine	18	692	348
41. Second Hill	York, Maine	18.5	410	350
42. Third Hill	York, Maine	18	300	353
43. York Hill	York, Maine	14.5	220	357
44. Cape Neddick	York, Maine	12	50	5

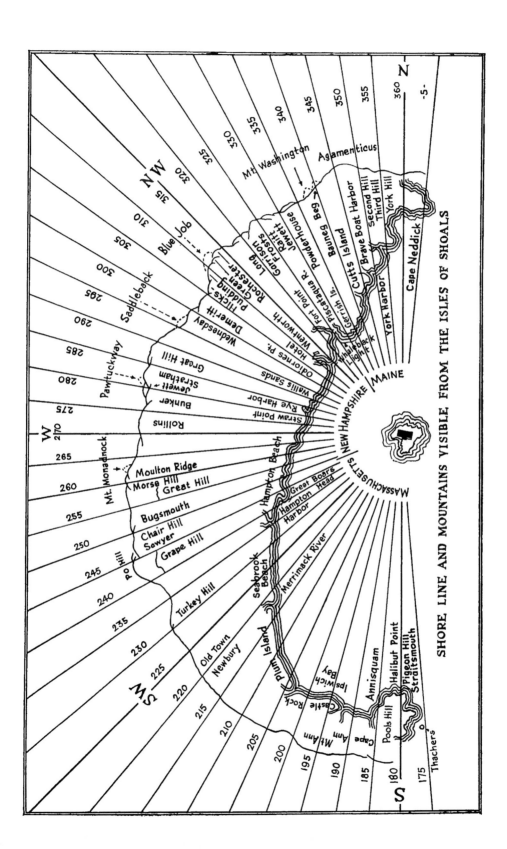

APPENDIX VI

ERRATIC SPELLING

For permanent record we have tried to determine the spelling of proper names according to (1) recognized authorities, (2) personal family use, (3) general usage. There are exceptions to all three, hence in some instances there seems to be no single "correct" usage. Our preference given first.

Argall, Sir Samuel. Often incorrectly Argal.

Endel, Michael and Richard. Sometimes Endle.

Gibbons, Ambrose. Sometimes Gibbins.

Ingebretson, George. Seldom appears correctly. Variants are Ingebredson, Inglebritzen, Ingebertsen, Inglebridsen. Correct spelling was given by a lineal descendant.

Kelley, Roger and Mary. Often given as Kelly.

Londoners Island. Following variants appear often: Londoner's, Londoners', Londoner, Londonner, and present usage by owners, *Lunging.*

Morse, Rev. Jedediah. Often Jedidiah — equally correct.

New Castle. Note that most early colonial place names were written as two words, North Hampton, Smutty Nose; whereas in current usage it is one word — Newcastle, Smuttynose, etc.

Pepperrell, Sir William. Original family spelling seems to have included all possible letters, and is so given in Sanborn's Hist. of N.H and Enc. Brit. but most current writers omit one "r"

Plumer, Rev. Abraham. Often given as Plummer, but his signature in Gosport Town Records has only one "m". Note also that the Gov. of N.H. was Plumer.

Richmond's Island. Mistakenly written Richman's.

Seeley, William, Richard, and George. All three signed a petition as Sealy, but authorities say Seeley.

Stevens, Rev. Josiah. Appears as Stephens on the stone at Star Island, but authorities use Stevens.

Strawbery Banke. This spelling was most frequently used, and since the name was dropped in 1653, we see no reason to

ISLES OF SHOALS

modernize, although later historians frequently use Strawberry Bank. The name first appears as Strabery.

Thomson, David. But Thompson's Island in Boston Bay was named for the same man.

Tompson, Rev. William. Note that this Tompson has no "h," but uses "p," whereas David uses "h" but no "p."

Tucke, Rev. John. Current usage for Tuck descendants omits final "e," but John signed his name both ways. Monument at Star uses John Tucke.

Willy, Capt. Edward. Often given incorrectly as Willey.

BIBLIOGRAPHY

Barnaby, Henry Clay. *My Wanderings.* Chapel Publishing Co., 1913.

Beck, Horace P. *The Folklore of Maine.* J. B. Lippincott Company, 1957.

Benjamin, S. G. W. *The Atlantic Islands as Resorts of Health and Pleasure.* Harper & Brothers, 1878.

Carter, Robert. *A Summer Cruise on the Coast of New England.* Crosby and Nichols, 1864.

Crawford, Mary C. *The Romance of Old New England Rooftrees.* L. C. Page & Co., 1903.

DeCosta, Rev. B. F. *Rambles in Mount Desert* (Chapter on Shoals). A. D. F. Randolph and Co., 1871.

Downs, John W. *Sprays of Salt.* Private Printing, 1944.

Drake, Samuel Adams. *The Pine-Tree Coast.* Estes & Lauriat, 1891.

------, *New England Legends and Folk Lore.* Little, Brown & Company, 1900.

------, *Nooks and Corners of the New England Coast.* (Chapters on Shoals) Harper and Brothers, 1876.

Fields, Annie. *Celia Thaxter and Whittier.* Harpers, 1893.

Fields, James T. *Yesterdays with Authors.* Houghton Mifflin Co., 1871.

Hawthorne, Nathaniel. *The American Note-Books.* Houghton Mifflin & Co., 1881. Yale University Press, 1932.

Herrmann, Paul. *Conquest by Man.* Harper & Bros., 1954.

Higginson, Mary Thacher. *Biography of Thomas Wentworth Higginson.* Houghton Mifflin Co., 1914.

Higginson, Thomas Wentworth. *Letters and Journals of Thomas Wentworth Higginson.* Edited by Mary Thacher Higginson. Houghton Mifflin Co., 1921.

------, *Cheerful Yesterdays.* Houghton Mifflin Co., 1898.

------, *Atlantic Essays.* James R. Osgood and Co., 1871.

Hutton, Laurence. *Talks in a Library.* G. P. Putnam's Sons, 1905.

Jenness, John Scribner. *The Isles of Shoals.* Hurd & Houghton, 1873. Houghton Mifflin Co., 1915.

Knowlton, Helen. *The Art of William Morris Hunt.*

Laighton, Oscar. *Ninety Years at the Isles of Shoals.* Andover Press, 1929. Beacon Press, 1930.

Lamb, Harold. *New Found World.* Doubleday and Co., 1955.

Lawrence, Robert P. *New Hampshire Churches.* Claremont, N.H., 1856.

Massachusetts Historical Society. *Collection.* Hall, 1801.

Mitchell, Edward P. *Memoirs of an Editor.* Charles Scribner's Sons, 1924.

Pearson, Edmund. *Murder at Smuttynose.* Doubleday, Page & Co., 1926.

Sanborn, Frank B. *New Hampshire.* Houghton Mifflin & Co., 1904.

Shannon, Martha A. S. *Boston Days of William Morris Hunt.* Marshall Jones Company, 1923.

ISLES OF SHOALS

Shipton, Clifford K. *Biographical Sketches of Those Who Attended Harvard 1722-1725.* Harvard University Press.

Smith, Captain John. *Travels and Works.* Edited by Edward Arber. John Grand, Edinburg 1910.

Smith, Bradford. *Captain John Smith.* J. B. Lippincott Co., 1953.

Snow, Edward Rowe. *Famous Lighthouses of New England.* Yankee Publishing Co., 1945.

------, *Pirates and Buccaneers of the North Atlantic.* Dodd, Mead & Co., 1950.

------, *Secrets of the North Atlantic Islands.* Dodd, Mead and Company, 1950. 1950.

Spofford, Harriet Prescott. *A Little Book of Friends.* Little, Brown and Company, 1917.

Stearns, Frank Preston. *Sketches from Concord and Appledore.* G. P. Putnam's Sons, 1895.

Thaxter, Celia. *Among the Isles of Shoals.* James R. Osgood, 1873 and later.

------, *Poems by Celia Thaxter.* Houghton Mifflin Co., 1895 and 1916.

------, *Stories and Poems for Children.* Houghton Mifflin Co., 1895.

------, *An Island Garden.* Houghton Mifflin Co., 1894.

------, *Letters of Celia Thaxter.* Edited by Annie Fields and Rose Lamb. Houghton Mifflin Co., 1895.

Thaxter, Celia and Others. *The Heavenly Guest.* Smith and Couts Co. Andover, Mass., 1935.

Thaxter, Rosamond. *Sandpiper, The Life and Letters of Celia Thaxter.* Wake Brook House, 1961. Marshall Jones, 1963.

Usher, Roland G. *The Pilgrims and their History.* The Macmillan Co., 1920.

Weiss, Frederick L. *The Colonial Clergy and the Colonial Churches of New England.* Lancaster, Mass. 1936.

Westbrook, Perry D. *Acres of Flint.* Scarecrow Press, 1951.

Willison, George F. *Saints and Strangers.* Reynal and Hitchcock, 1945.

York County Records. *Report of the Trial and Conviction of Louis H. F. Wagner.* William S. Noyes Co., 1874.

PAMPHLETS

Bigelow, Rev. E. Victor. *Brief History of the Isles of Shoals.* Conference, 1923.

Brewster, Lewis W. *The Isles of Shoals.* Portsmouth, N.H., 1905 and 1910.

Cornish, Rev. Louis C. *The Story of the Isles of Shoals.* Beacon Press, 1916 and 1926.

Gage, Rev. William Leonard. *The Isles of Shoals in Summer Time.* Case, Lockwood and Brainard Co., Hartford 1875.

Gosport Town Records, 1731-1876. (New England Historical Society, 1913- and 1914).

Montegeu, M. Tzl, M.D. *Ancient and Modern Isles of Shoals.* G. Alex. Emery, 1872.

195

ISLES OF SHOALS

New Hampshire Historical Society. *Memorial to John Tucke and John Smith.* 1914.

Society for Promoting Religious Instruction at the Isles of Shoals. *Annual Reports and Tracts.*

Society for Propagating the Gospel Among the Indians and Others in North America. *Annual Reports and Pamphlets.*

PICTURE CREDITS

White Island by Moonlight, *by John Hanson.*

John Smith Monument (1914), Caswell Cemetery, Beebe Cemetery, Graves of Anethe and Karen Christensen in South Cemetery, Portsmouth, Gosport Meetinghouse, Gosport Village, A Conference Group, White Island Light, Betty Moody's Cave, Illingworth Rock Garden, Gosport Harbor (N.Y. Yacht Club), Old Man of the Sea, *by Edward Rutledge.*

Air View of Star Island, *by Philip Marston.*

The Viking, *by James Wentz.*

Maren's Rock on Smuttynose and Sullivan Cottage on Appledore, *by Harry Sullivan.*

Crandall Cottage on Lunging Island, *by Prudence Randall.*

Foye Cottages on Cedar Island, *by Robert Williams, Jr.*

St. Hilaire Cottage on Appledore, *by Charles Schoolicas.*

Castle Rock on Appledore, *by Katharine Glidden Hooke.*

Old Prints of Levi L., Celia, Roland, Karl and John Thaxter, Appledore Hotel in flames, *kindness of Rosamond Thaxter.*

John Weiss, *kindness of Mrs. Albert Hale.*

Cedric Laighton, *kindness of Barbara Laighton Durant.*

Gloucester Fisherman, *drawing by Oscar Laighton.*

INDEX

Names of distinguished guests at the Shoals during the Laighton era — 1839-1914 — which do not appear in the Index, may be found in the Roster of Appledorians, Appendix IV, pages 175-184.

Names of ministers and agents who served at the Shoals from 1637 to 1871 are listed in Appendix III, page 173.

Names of hills and mountains visible from Star Island are given in Appendix V, pages 185-190.

A

Academy on Hog Island, 19
Acadia, 4
Adams, Ella and Oliver, 152
Agamenticus, 7, 39, 189
Albany, State capitol, 115
Albee, John, 124, 149
Alcohol, consumption, 52, 54
Alfred, Maine, trial of Louis Wagner, 113
Allen, Charles, 154
Allen, Prentice, school, 95
Altitude and area of islands, 169
Alward, (waitresses tragedy), 154
American Note-Books by Hawthorne, 81
Among the Isles of Shoals
published in *Atlantic Monthly*, 103
Horace Greeley's tribute, 131
Anderson, Mrs. Larz, 120
house on Appledore, 140
Andover (Mass.) Seminary, 52
Andrews, Charles M., 6
Animals
cows, 23, 45
dog, Ringe, 104
goats, 14, 15, 63
sheep, 68
Appledore Hotel
built, 75
mortgaged, 140
burned, 141
Appledore Island
area, 169
Laightons bought, 49
- - - - built houses on, 69, 74
- - - - rechristened, 174, 117
- - - - moved to, 75

- - - - threatened to sell, 135
bought by Star Island Corp., 142
(See also Hog Island)
Appledore Land and Building Co., 141
Appledore township, created, 25; dissolved, 27
Appledorians, roster of, 175-184
Argall, Samuel, 30
Arnold, Rev. Harold G,. 161
Artichoke Mills, 87
Athorne, property on Appledore, 143
Atlantic Monthly
Land-Locked, 86
Annie Fields' essay, 92
A Memorable Murder, 103
Among the Isles of Shoals, 131
Audubon Society, 83, 171, 133
Austin, Rev. Daniel
monument to John Smith, 8
bell for meetinghouse, 167
Avery, Henry, 31

B

Babb, Philip
island named for, 3
taverner, 22, 23
as a ghost, 31 sq.
Babb's Cove, conveyed to U.S. Govt., 141
Baker Cottage, 164
Baker, Nathaniel, absentee landlord, 28
Baring Brothers, blocked sale of Appledore, 135
Barton, Rev. William E., 149
Basso, Hamilton, 6
Bay of Maine, 30

ISLES OF SHOALS

Becker, Fabius, 68 sq.
  to White Island
  at wedding 80
Beethoven, 137
Belcher, Rev. Samuel, 25, 41
Bernsten, Mina and Niccolina, 127, 136
Berry, N., 68
Beverly, Oak Knoll, 133
Bigelow, Mrs., 86
Billerica, Mass., 148
Billings, Katharine Fowler, 171
Birds
  canaries, 67
  fawn gull, 83
  parrot, 91
  Celia's correspondence with Torrey, 134
Bjornson, 104
Blackbeard, (pirate), 31 sq.
Blagdon, James, 27
Blake, Celia's letter to, about Levi, 118
Blithedale Romance, 81
Boats
  early fishing 2
  listed by Jenness, 2
  Arbella, 16
  Charles, 38
  Clara Bella, 106
  Conception, 47
  Gift of God, 5
  Lion's Whelp, 17
  Lucy, 50
  Merryconeag, 155
  Nassau, 158
  Penacook, 141
  Pinafore, 120
  Piscataqua, 142
  Pocahontas, 63, 64
  Sagunto, 47
  Sam Adams, 154
  Sightseer, 162
  Springbird, 75
  Spy, 75
  Viking, 148
Boon Island, 153
Boston Evening Transcript, 150
Boston, magistrates, 15
Boundaries
  Bay Colony, 16
  Shoals Harbor, 17
  Mass. to Casco Bay, 18

  new meaning, 25
Bowditch, Nathaniel, 61
Bowditch, Henry I., consulted by Celia, 95
Bowditch, J. Ingersoll, building on Appledore, 140
Bowdoin, 72
Brattleboro, Vermont, Hunt's burial, 117
Breakwater, 157
Brewster, drowned, 168
British Empire, 6
Brock, Rev. John, 40
Brook Farm, 81
"Brothers and Sisters", 72
Brown, J. Appleton, 116, 122, 137, 138, 140
Browning, Robert, 73, 85, 91, 115, 118
Bull, Ole, 124
Burge, Ray, bought Brewster Cottage on Appledore, 142
Burke, James, dory stolen, 113
Burrill, Mrs. Maria J., 78
Burrington, Bartholomew, 19
Burslem, early settler, 16
Burying grounds
  Appledore I.
    Laighton family, 100, 138
  Smuttynose I.
    Haley family, 49
    Spanish sailors, 47
  Star I.
    Beebe children, 149
    Caswell family, see illustration
    Old Village, 158

C

Cadiz, *Conception* from, 47
Caliban, 149
California St., Newtonville house bought for Levi, 83
  advertised, 99
  up for sale, 117
Carleton, Thomas, 6
Carlyle, Thomas, 73
Carman,, Bliss, estimate of Celia, 92
Cary, Alice, 130
Casco Bay, 16
  boundary, 18
Caswell, Amos and Rebecca, 44
Caswell, Charles, 167
Caswell, Ed., 138
Caswell, John, 167

199

ISLES OF SHOALS

Caswell, Lemuel, cut his throat, 167
Caswell, Orin, 168
Caswell, Sarah, 167
Cedar Island, named, 3
  trees, 7
Chalmers, Rev. Thomas, 158
Champernowne, 117
Champlain, Samuel de, 4
Champlain, Lake, 17
Charles I, 24
  beheaded, 18
Charles II, 27
Charles River, 16
Chastes, Aymar de, 4
Cheever, at White Island, 69
China painting, 89
Chopin, Preludes, 120
Christensen, Anethe, Ivan, Karen, 105
Christian Register, 150
Claflin, Mary E., *Personal Recollections of John Greanleaf Whittier*, 132
Clark, Clarence H., takes Bowditch cottage, 140
Clark, Eleanor, house on Appledore, 140
Clark, J. S., 86
Clark, Mary Cowden, 136
Cleaves, Samuel, 62
Cleland, P. S., 52
Coffman, F. L., *1001 Post, Buried or Sunken Treasures*, 37
Collins, Nellie, 152
Colonial Wars, N. H. Society of, 8
Columbus, 2
Conferences, first sessions, 148 sq.
Congregational Summer Conference Assoc., 158
Congressional Library, 158
Coues, S. E., 64
Court of Pascataquack, 14
Craven, Wesley Frank, 6
Crothers, Rev. Samuel M., 161
Cucking stool, 20
Culture, island, 55
Currier, Charles, bought Cedric Laighton cottage, 142
Curtis, William, 19
Cushing, Caleb, 69, 72
Cutt, John, Richard and Robert on Smuttynose, 23
Cutt, John., Pres. of N.H., 26

Cutt, Richard, owned Star Island, 26
Cutting, John, 14

D

Dana, R. H.,
  quoted, 64
  visitors T. B. Laighton on Smuttynose, 69
  author, 72
Dartington, 117
Davis, Lemuel, 154
Death penalty, abolished, 114
Democratic-Republican, 62
DeCosta, B. F., 8
  describes Fort Star, 28
Dedham, John Thaxter in, 97
DeNormandie, James, 138
DeQuincy, Thomas, 56
Derby, Lucy, 137
Dialect, 55 sq.
Diamond, Andrew, absentee landlord, 28
Dickens, Charles
  comment on Islanders, 1
  dinner for, 91
  impressed by Celia's writing, 103
Dimick, Rev. F. L., 53
Dingley, son of Gov., 152
Distances
  local, 170
  of hills and mountains, 185 sq.
Donovan, James A., bought Appledore, 142
Dover, joined Massachusetts, 18
  Oyster River, 39
Downs, Rebora, 19
Downs, John B., 68
Downs, Willis, 167
Drake, Samuel Adams, 8
  doubts Sagunto story, 47
  story of Babb's ghost, 31
Duck Island, named, 3
  ghosts, 37
  whale 71
Dunfish, 9
Dutton, Rev. John, 51

E

Eastman, Rev. Oliver, 82
Eburne, Rev. Samuel, 41
Eden, Gov. of Carolina, 33
Eichberg, Julius, in Celia's parlor, 123
  Julius and Sophie, 136

200

ISLES OF SHOALS

Elections, Gosport, 168
Eliot, Rev. Christopher R., 161
Elliott, Thomas H., 147
Ely, J., teacher, 53
Emerson, Rev. Jacob, 50
Emerson, Ralph Waldo, 72
  essay read at Appledore, 123
Emery, Samuel, 243
Ericson, Leif, 2
Exeter, joined Massachusetts, 18

F

Fairyland, Appledore, 64, 75, 85
Falls, Capt., 62
Fays (of Cambridge,) 73
Fields, Annie Adams, biographical
  notes about Celia, 85, 122, 137, 138
  Celia's letters to, about
    despondency, 90
    Eliza's death, 101
    Wm. M. Hunt, 116
    Champernowne, 117
    last letters, 136
Fields, James T., letter from
  Dickens, 1
  editor, *Atlantic Monthly*, 86
  library, 121
Fish, at the Shoals, (for extended
  list see Guide Book, *Ten Miles
  Out*)
Fishermen, Norwegian, 104
Fishing, John Brock's story, 41
Fishing industry
  earliest, 2
  "dunfish", 9
  price quoted, 10
  fish flakes, 9
  tax protested, 13
  mackerel, 70
Fletcher, Gov., 28
Flora and fauna, 170
Flowers, in Celia's parlor, 121
Folkways, 57
Folsom, George, 86, 97
Ford, John, diver, 155
Forde, Stephen, abusing constable,
  19
  tragedy, 21
Fort Star, 28
  dismantled, 44
Founders Cottage, 164
Fox, Feroline, Celia's letters to, 101,
  133, 136
Fox, Rev. T. B., 51

Freeman, Mabel, married to Roland
  Thaxter, 133

G

Gazette, Boston, note on Spanish
  ship, 47
Gazette, New Hampshire, 62
Gee, Peters, 21
Geology of islands, 171
Gibbon, Ambrose, 33
Gibson, Rev. Richard, 39
Gilbert, Raleigh, 5
Goodwin, Ichabod, 64
Goodwin, Capt. James, 71, 75
Gorgeana, court at, 15, 20
Gorges, Sir Ferdinando, 5, 9
  partnership with Mason, 11
  character, 12
  hailed into court, 13
  dominion of, 17
  attempt to revoke Charter, 18
  uncle of Francis Champernowne,
    117
Gorges, Robert, appointed Gov-
  ernor, 13
Gosnold, Bartholomew, 4
Gosport, made a township, 27
  dissolved, 168
  town records, 50 sq.
  dialect, 55
Gosport Church records, 43, sq.
  call to John Tucke, 43
Gosport elections, 168
Gosport Harbor, 61
Gosport House, 167
Gosport Village, rebuilt, 164
Government of Shoals, 10
Granville, Henry, 31
Greeley, Horace, 130
Greeley, Wm. Roger, account of
  tragedy, 152
  discovers sconces in meeting-
    house, 149
Greenland, Dr. Henry, 20, 30
Greenleaf, Abner, 62
Greenleaf, Abner, Jr., 62
Greenleafe, Rev. Daniel, 41
Grossman, Ignatius, 96, 97, 136
Grubb, Gabriel, 19
Guast, Pierre du, 4
Gulf of Maine, 2
Gull wings, 83
Guns, for Shoals, 28
  taken to Newburyport, 44

201

ISLES OF SHOALS

H

Hale, Mrs. Albert, 138
Hale, Edward Everett, 73
Haley, family on Smuttynose, 50
Haley, Benjamin, 49
Haley, Samuel, discovered silver
  bars, 33
  epitaph, 49
  house, described by Celia Thax-
  ter, 46
  "King of the Islands", 46 sq.
Haley, Samuel Jr., took title to
  Hog Island, 48
Haley, Miss Susanna, married to
  Josiah Stevens, 51
Haley's harbor, 46, 107
Haley's Island, 48
Hall, Rev. Abner, 54
Hamilton, Gail, 129
Hampton, N.H. joined Massachu-
  setts, 18
Harrington, V. D., 160, 162
Harvard University, attended by
  Thaxters, 72, 115
  Randall Hall, 141
Hassam, Childe, studio, 137, 138,
  140
Hastings, Warren, 6
Hatfield, Mass., destroyerd, 19
Hawthorne, Nathaniel,
  Story of Babb's ghost, 31
  Comments on Gosport, 43
  classmate of Pierce, 71
  American Note-Books, 81
  "Miranda of the Islands" 85
  in Celia's Parlor, 126
Heavenly Guest
  tributes to Celia, 93
  article by Maud McDowell, 122
Henry IV, 4
Herjulfson, Bjarni, 2
Hesperides, 120
"He will come again", 35
Higginson, Thomas Wentworth
  consulted by Levi Thaxter, 72
  first to see "Utopia", 74
  impressed by Celia, 78
  called to Worcester, 79
  letter to Annie Fields, 92
Hilaire, Ralph St., bought cottage
  on Appledore, 142
Hills and mountains, 185 sq.
Hingham, Mass., 72

Hobkirk Inn, 160
Hodges, Nicholas, 19
Hog Island
  first named, 4
  part of Appledore township, 25
  academy on, 19
  abandoned, 26
  bought by Samuel Haley, 48
  bought by Thomas B. Laighton,
  49, 62
  buildings erected by T.B.L., 69
  as a sanitorium, 73
  Thaxters buy interest in, 74
  name changed to Appledore, 74,
  117
Hontvet, John Maren, Matthew,
  104-105
Hotel Clifford, Boston, 133
Hou, Alfred, sold house on California St., 83
House of Seven Gables, 81
Hoxie, Elizabeth, Celia's letters to,
  about Karl and John, 95, failing
  health, 136
Hubbard, *History of New England,*
  21
Huguenot, 4
Hull, Rev Joseph, 39
Hunt, William Morris, 115 sq.
  sketches in Celia's parlor, 122
Hurley, Michael, diver, 155
Hutton, Laurence, 104
  estimate of Celia, 125

I

Indian raids, 26, 29
Ingebretson family, 104
  Emil, 106
  Jorg, 111
Ipswich bay, 4
Islanders, their isolation, 1
  law unto themselves, 3
  independence of, 15
  character of, 19 sq.
Island Garden, Celia's, 136
Isles of Shoals, area and altitudes,
  169
  "rock in the sea", 1
  named, 3 sq.
  logged by Champlain, 4
  number of, 8
  government of, 10
  ownership of, 11

ISLES OF SHOALS

Isles of Shoals Congregational Corporation, 163
Isles of Shoals Hotel Co., 141
Isles of Shoals Summer Meetings Association, 150

J

Jacksonville, Levi's visit to, 97
James I of England, 11
Jamestown, Va., 5, 7
Jaquith, Abby, 148
Jarvis, H. Wood, 6
Jeffrey, early settler, 16
Jenner, Rev. Thomas, 20
Jenness, John Scribner
  listed fishing boats, 2
  independence of Islanders, 15
  disparagement of Shoalers, 19
Jewett, Sarah Orne, 91
  Celia's letter to, about health, 136
  edited Celia's poems, 137
Johnson, Abbie W., property on Appledore, 142
Jordan, Rev. Robert, 39
Joslyn, Henry, climbed church tower, 26
Josselyn, John, 21

K

Kean, Charles, actor, 72, 73
Kelly, Abraham, 19
Kelly brothers, William, Roger and John, 24
Kelley, Mary, 20
Kennebec river, 13
Kidd, William, 30
Kimball, Benjamin Ames, 158, 162
Kimball, Daniel S., to sell Appledore, 142
King, Anna Eichberg, Celia's letter to, about illness, 135
"King of the Islands"
  Capt. Haley, 46
  Thomas B. Laighton, 61, 100
King Philip's War, 19
Kings, the (of Salem), 73
Kismet, 131
Kittery, Maine, 17
  home of Pepperrells, 24
  Champernowne, 117

L

Laconia Co., 17
Laighton, Cedric
  born, 66

Mufti, 83
  letter about Land-Locked, 86
  at Hotel Clifford, 133
  care of Celia's parlor, 139
  to Florida, and death of, 140
Laighton, Celia - See Thaxter, Celia
Laightoi, Eliza, married, 62
  at White Island, 64 sq.
  Cedric born to, 66
  visits Watertown, 83
  cried over Land-Locked, 88
  visits White Mountains, 101
  death, 101
Laighton, Helen, 62
Laighton, Joseph, 69
Laighton, Mark, 61, 64
Laightoi, Oscar, born, 62
  writes *Ninety Years at the Isles of Shoals*, 74
  story of Babb's ghost, 32
  account of storm, 79
  comment on Celia's death, 137
  builds coffin, 167
Laighton, Ruth, 133
Laighton, Thomas Bell
  bought four islands, 49
  "King of the Islands", 61
  to White Island, 62
  selectman at Portsmouth, 67
  care of islanders, 68
  moved to Smuttynose, 48, 69
  erected houses on Appledore, 69
  partnership with Levi L. Thaxter, 71 sq.
  illness, 83
  death, 100
Laighton's threat to sell Appledore, 135
Lamb, Charles, 150
Lamb, Rose, 92, 136, 137
Land-Locked, 85, 87, 128
Landlords, absentee, 28
Lane, A. J., 141
Larcom, Lucy. 91, 128
Laurig, Norway, 104
Lawrance, Caroline, 161
Lawrance, Charles, 158
Lawrance, Mary, 158
Lawrance, William I., 159
Lawson, Mary, Celia's letter to, 96, 99
Levett, Sir Christopher, first visit to Shoals, 9

203

ISLES OF SHOALS

Lewis, Thomas, 39
Leyden group, 12
Life magazine, buried treasure, 37
Living History, 153
Locksley Hall, 74
London Company, 3, 5
Londoners, island named, 3
  trading post, 9
Longfellow, Henry W., 73, 91
Longfellow, Samuel, 73
  letter about Celia, 78
Louisburg, battle of, 24
Lovejoy, Rev. Daniel, 51
"Lovely lonely rock", 65
Lovewell's War, 29
Low, Rev. John, 50
Lowell, James Russell, 73, 86, 126
Lowell Courier Citizen, 148

M

Magnalia, quoted, 40
Maine coast explored, 4
Maine, province of, 9, 13, 17, 18
Maine, State Prison, 114
Malaga Island named, 3
  Haley's sea wall, 46
  purchased by Thomas B. Laighton, 62
Map, John Smith's, 7
March, Captain, 28
Marean, Emma E., correspondent, 150
Mariana, 12
Martha's Vineyard, 2, 10
Marvin, Harry, 140, 148, 160
Mason, John, partnership with Gorges, 11, 12,
  died, 17
Mason, Rev. John, 82
Mason, John Tufton, 26
Mason, William (musician), 120, 137, 138
Massachusetts Bay Colony, 10
  first meeting, 16
  boundary, 18
  assumed authority, 24
Massachusetts General Court, 18, 47
Massachusetts grant to Samuel Haley, 48
Massachusetts Historical Collection, 39
Mather, Rev. Cotton, 31, 40, 42
Matthews, Samuel, 19
Maverick, Antipas, 15

Mayes, Frank B., house on Appledore, 140
Mayflower Compact, 12, 16
Mayhew, Thomas, visits Shoals, 10
McDowell, Maud Appleton, description of Celia's parlor, 121, 122
McLean, Hon. George P., 152
Meetinghouse
  on Smuttynose, 39
  on Star, - first 1, 27
    second, 1, 34, 45, 50
    third, 50, 53, 149
Merrimack river, 12, 16
Mid-Ocean House, 71
Migration, from Hog to Star, 26
Miles, Capt. Frederick, 152
Ministers, rosters of, 173
Minot's Ledge Light, 79
Miranda of the Islands, 85
Mitchell, Bartholomew, 19
Monhegan Island, 7
Monuments, John Smith cairn on Appledohre, 167
  John Smith monument on Star, 8, rebuilt, 167, rededicated, 164
  John Tucke monument, built, 158.
Moody, Betty, 29
Moody, Rev. Joshua, 1, 34, 41
Moody, Rev. Reuben, 51
Moody, Rev. Samuel, 41
Mordell, Albert, *Quaker Militant, John Greenleaf Whittier*, 129
Morse, Rev. Jedediah, 42, 50
Morton, Thomas, 16
Morton's Memorial, 18
Mountains and hills, 185 sq.
Moxom, Rev. Philip S., read Thaxter poems, 149
Mt. Vernon Church, 161
Mt. Washington Seminary, 78
Muchmore, Anna, 44
Muzzy, C. F., 52

N

Naples, Bay of, 132
Nature, 65, 79
  Celia's only teacher, 125
Nature's Nobleman, 6
Neptune's Hall on Appledore, 85
Newbury, Mass., 41
Newburyport, guns from Star, 44
  aiding Shoals, 50, 52

ISLES OF SHOALS

New Castle, Star annexed to, 27, 168

New Church, School, Cambridge, Kart attended, 95

New Engand, indebted to John Smith, 6, 8

New England Council formed, 12

New England Historical and Genealogical Register, 44

Newfound Land, 11

New France, 8

New Hampshire, created royal province, 23, 26

New Hampshire Audubon Society, 171

New Hampshire Gazette, 62, 72

New Hampshire Historical Society bldg., 158

New Hampshire Society of Colonial Wars, 8, 157, 164

New Hampshire State Planning Commission, 171

New Hampshire University, 171

Newport, R.I., 47

Newton, Nancy, 68

Newton Centre House, 164

Newtonville, California St., house bought for Levi Thaxter, 83

Nickerson, H. W., undertaker, 155

Ninety Years at the Isles of Shoals, 74

North cottage, Appledore,
Levi's bachelor quarters, 77
Karl's birthplace, 81

North Middlesex Conference, 147

Norton's Woods, Cambridge, 135

Norumbega, 7

Norwegian Cove, 85

Norwegians at Shoals, 104, 126

Nova Scotia, Levi visits, 97

O

Oak Knoll, Beverly, 133

Oceanic Hotel, 103, 152, 167

Ocracoke Island, 33

Oliver brothers, William, Benedict and Richard, 24

Olivier, Richard, 19

Oyster River (Dover, N.H.), 39

P

Page, John, Gov., 62

Paine, John Knowles, 124

Paracelsus, quoted, 98

Park, Rev. Charles E., account of tragedy, 153

Parker Hall, 164

Parkhurst,, Lewis, 159, 162

Parkman, Rev. Dr., 54

Parliament, dissolved, 13

Parsonage, Tucke, moved to York, 45

Parsonage, built for Josiah Stevens, burned in 1905, 51
Celia lived in, 83

Parsonage, Tucke, built in 1927, 164
Thomas H. Elliott in, 147

Partnership formed, (Thomas B. Laighton and Levi L. Thaxter), 74
dissolved, 76

Pascataquack, court at, 14

Patchwork, Celia hated, 85

Peabody, Miss, 53

Peabody, Rev. Andrew P., 54, 82

Pearson, Edmund, *Murder at Smuttynose*, 104

Pierce, Clementine B., teacher, 53

Pendleton, Bryan, 22

Pepperrell, Sir William, knighted, 24

Phelps, Elizabeth Stuart, estimate of Celia, 90, 91

Phillips Academy, Andover, 160

Pickard, Samuel T., Whittier's biographer, 128, 129 quote from Celia, 131

Pidgin, Rev. William, 51

Pierce, Franklin, 71, 81

Piers built at Appledore and Star, 103

Pigeons, extinct, 75

Pilgrims, Leyden group, 12

Pirate ship (Mermaiden), 20

Pirate silver, discovered by Haley, 46

Pirates, 30 sq.

Piscataqua, boundary, 17

Plumer, Rev., 54

Plymouth Company, 5

Plymouth, England, 11, 12

Plymouth, Mass., 8

Pocahontas, wreck of, 63

Po Hill, 131

Poor, John, builds Oceanic, 103

Popham, Sir John, 5

205

ISLES OF SHOALS

Population, 9, 18, 23, 44, 50
Port Royal, 4
Portsmouth, Celia's residence, 134
Portsmouth England, 11
Portsmouth Evening Times, 113
Porstmouth Navy Yard, at Appledore fire, 141
Porstmouth Savings Bank, 159
Portsmouth Unitarian Church, 54, 82
Portsmouth Whaling Company, 62, 64
Ports of Piscataqua, 64
Post Master, 62
Pound, Thomas, 31
Pratt, S., 52
Pre-Raphaelitism, 82
Preston, Peter, 154
Prize fight, 168
Proctor, Edna Dean, 129
Province of Maine, 9, 49
Puritans, 11, 20
Pusley, Widow, on Smuttynose, 45
Pym, Coke, and Selden, in Parliament, 13

Q
Queen of the islands, 123
Quelch, Capt. John, (pirate), 31, 37, 38

R
Raids, Indian, 26
Raitt, Nellie, 152
Raleigh, Sir Walter, 4
Ramsdell, Charles, 141, 160
Randal, Louisa and Eliza, 68
Randall, Hall, Cambridge, 141
Randall, John, to Smuttynose, 74
Randall, Walter, challenged constable, 26
Red house, scene of murder, 107
burned, 114
Remmick, 74
Revolution and the Shoals, 44 sq.
Reynolds, John, 14
Rhodes, Cecil, 6
Richmond's Island, 39
Richter, M. Emil, M.D., cottage on Appledore, 140
tragedy of waitresses, 155
Rift, the presumed, 93
Riley, Jesse, bought cottage on Appledore, 142
Ritson, Rev. Edwin, 54

Robbins, Allen L., 114
Rockport granite, 158
Roller block, 61
Royalist settlements, 12
Rye, N.H., Star assigned to, 17, 168
Levi, sailed to, 77
Charles Caswell drowned, comin from, 167
Rymes, Christopher, investment in Appledore, 135
Rymes, Eliza, married to Thomas B. Laighton, 62
Rymes, William, at Smuttynose, 68
took letters to Portsmouth, 69
built houses on Appledore, 74

S
Saco, Maine, 39
Sagadahoc, Popham settlement, 5
murder in, 114
Sagunto, 47
Sailors, Spanish, named Malaga, 3
St. Augustine, Florida, Levi visits, 97
St. Burian, Cornwall, 39
St. Croix Island, fort, 4
St. Lawrence River, northern boundary, 12
St. Sepulchre's Church, John Smith buried in, 8
Salem, Mass., home of Joseph White, 3, 44
boundary line, 12
Salisbury Beach, Whittier on, 130
Saltonstall, Wm. G. *Ports of Piscataqua,* 64
Saltonstall, Leverett, 73
Santore, Carmen, executed, 114
Sargent and Sullivan quarries, 158
Saturday Club, Dickens dinner, 91
Saunders, Robert, 30
Scarlet Letter, 81
School at Gosport, 53
Miss Underhill, 76
Schultes, Richard E., 170
Scott, Capt. (pirate), 31
his widow, 34, 36
Seavey Island, named, 3
Seeley, John, 15
Seeley brothers, William, Richard and John, 24, 46
William, ensign, 25
Service Building 164
Settlers at Shoals, 10
Royalist, 12, 13

206

ISLES OF SHOALS

Sewall, Rev. Samuel, 52, 53
Shapleigh, Nicholas, 22
Shaw, Rev. Jeremiah, 44
Shaw, Justine H. Judge, 67
Shipton, Clifford K., life of John
  Tucke, 44
Shoals, named, 3 sq .
  early settlers, 14
  presented for neglect, 27
  petition for township status, 25
  rebel against tax, 26
  independent, 27
  petition for protection, 28
  not pirates, 30
  exiled to mainland, 45
Shute, Gov. Samuel, 1
Smith, Bradford, quoted, 6
Smith, Captain John, 2
  Admiral of New England, 6
  character, 12
  monument on Star, 8
  monument rebuilt, 157
  cairn on Appledore, 141
Smith, Rev. Origin, 54
Smyth's Isles, 7
Smuttynose Island, named, 3
  brick church, 19
  early settlers, 22, 23
  Blackbeard's honeymoon, 33
  Haley's Island, 46, 48
  population, 50
  purchased by Thomas B. Laigh-
    ton, 62
  Thomas B. Laighton's residence,
    69
  Randall moved to, 74
  Wagner murder, 103
  prize fight, 168
Society of Colonial Wars, 157
*Society for Promoting Religious In-
  struction at the Isles of Shoals*, 53
Societly for Propagating the Gospel,
  50, 82, 173
Somebody, Rev. Seth, 80
Southampton, Earl of, 4
South Virginia Company, 5, 6
Spanish sailors, 3
  drowned, 47 sq.
Spofford, Harriet Prescott, 124
Sprague, Isaac, 160
  Sprague cottage, 164
Standish, Miles, 16
Stannard, Harold, 6

Star Island, named, 3
  John Smith monument, 8
  owned by Richard Cutt, 26
  first meetinghouse, 27
  stone meetinghouse 50
  purchase of, 158 sq.
  dedicated, 163
Star Island Corporation, formed, 161
  bought Appledore Hotel Reserva-
    tion, 142
  now owns 95% of Appledore
Stedman, H. R., M.D., 138
Steiger, Rev. Theodore L., 170
Stevens, Rev. Josiah, 50, 51
Stickney and Poor, 103
Stoddard, Mary Gertrude, married
  to John Thaxter, 133
Storeys, the, (of Cambridge), 73
Storm of 1635, 18
  Northeaster of 1839, 63
  Storm of 1851, 79
Strawbery Banke, 15
  joined Massachusetts, 18
  derelicts, 21
  home of Richard Cutt, 23
Straw Point, Rye, 169
Sullivan, Harry, cottage on Apple-
  dore, 143
Sullivan, Timothy P., 158
Summer Day, The, 129

T

Talks in a Library, 104
Tax, Province, 1
  on fish, 13
  on Shoalers, 26
Teach, Edward (Blackbeard), 31
Temperance Society, 54
Ten Miles Out, 165
Tennyson, Alfred, 73
Tent on the Beach, The, 128, 130
Thaxter, Celia
  Life and Career
    born at Portsmouth, N.M., 62
    childhood at White Island, 63,
      65
    residence on Smuttynose, 46
    school at So. Boston, 78
    engaged to Levi L. Thaxter, 78
    wedding at Appledore, 79
    Karl born at Appledore, 81
    residence on Star Island, 82
    John born at Artichoke Mills,
      82

207

ISLES OF SHOALS

Celia's parrot, 91
residence at Newtonville, 83, 117
marooned at Appledore, 96
residence in Boston, 133
social life in Boston, 91
the so-called "rift", 93
joined the Audubon Society, 133
dreads leaving Karl, 134
parlor at Appledore, 120 sq.
residence at Kittery Point, 117
funeral at Appledore, 131
Character and Personality
"Flower of the Rocks", 78
"Miranda of the Islands", 85
"Queen of the Islands", 85
"Queen of the Islands", 123
Comments by C. T. Young and Elizabeth Stuart Phelps, 90; A. W. E. Macy, 93; analysis, 94; Laurence Hutton, 104; 125; John Albee, 124; Maud McDowell, 122; Charles Dickens, 1; Harriet Prescott Spofford, 124.
Letters to
Mr. Blake, 118; Cedric, 83, 86; Annie Field, 90, 99, 101, 116, 117; Feroline Fox, 89, 101, 133; Elizabeth Hoxie, 95, 96, 136; Sarah Orne Jewett, 136; Mary Lawson, 97, 99; Bradford Torrey, 134, 136; Mrs. S. G. Ward, 133; 134; Whittier, 134; Jennie Usher, 79
Publications
Land-Locked, 85
Sandpiper, 100
Among the Isles of Shoals, 10, 48, 63, 103
A Memorable Murder, 103, 104, 111
An Island Garden, 136
Letters published, 92
Collected poems, 137
Thaxter, John, born, 82
married, 133
Thaxter, Jonas, at Celia's wedding, 80
off to California, 78
Thaxter, Karl
born at Appledore, 81

"Comfort critter", 82
at New Church School, 95
Celia's anxiety for, at Hotel Clifford, 133
Thaxter, Levi, Sr., mortgage on Appledore, 74
bought house on California St., 83
Thaxter, Levi Lincoln
first visit to Shoals, 70, 71
home in Watertown, 72
letter to Thomas B. Laighton, 73
partnership with T. B. L., 74
partnership dissolved, 76
built cottage on Appledore, 77
married, 79
missioner to Star, 82
inheritance, 83
Browning scholar, 91
character, 94
failing health, 96
excursions, 97
began journal, 97
illness, 99
death, 118
eulogy, 118
Thaxter, Mrs. Lucy, legacy, 83
Thaxter, Lucy, at Celia's wedding, 80
Thaxter, Roland
born, 95
married, 133
Browning epitaph, 118
home at "Norton's Woods," 135
Prof. at Harvard, 135
edited Celia's letters, 92
Thaxter, Rosamond, biography of Celia, 93
bought cottage on Appledore, 142
Thomaston, Maine, 114
Thoreau, Henry David, 73
Thurlow, Captain, 75
Ticknor and Fields, 86
Titcomb, B. B., 82
Toads, Celia's episode, 134
Thompson, Rev. William, 39
Torrey, Bardford, 134, 136, 137
Town Meeting, last, 168
Township of Appledore, 25
Tragedy of waitresses, 152
Transcript, Boston Evening, 150
Treasure, found by Haley, 46
Trees, scrubby old Cedars, 3
no trees at all, 9

ISLES OF SHOALS

Haley's orchard, 46
Tuck, Edward, 158
  contributes to Star Island fund, 162
Tucke, Rev. John, 43 sq.
  grave discovered, 50
Tucke, Mary Dole, 44
Tucker, Grace, 20
Tucker, the tailor, 18
Tuckerman, Samuel, 62
Tuckerman, of Boston, 73
Turks, beheaded by Smith, 8
Turner, Ross, studio on Appledore, 140
Tuttle, Charles W., 8
Twombly, Helen, 152
Two Years Before the Mast, 72
Tyng, Dudley A., visited Shoals, 46, 50

U

Underhill, Capt., 21
Underhill, Nancy J., 76
University of New Hampshire, summer school, 170
United States, life saving station on Appledore, 141
Usher, Jennie, Celia's letter to, 79
Utopia, 11, 74

V

Vaughn Memorial, 164
Vaughan, William, 23
Vinland, 2
Viking, 148
Virginia Companies formed, 4
Vision of Sir Launfal, 73

W

Wagner, Louis H. F., murder at Smuttynose, 104
Waitresses, tragedy of, 152
Walton, Mark, moves Tucke parsonage to York, 45
Wanewright, Francis, absentee landlord, 28
Ward, Mrs. S. G., Celia's letters to, 133, 135
Warnerton, Thomas, 21
Warren, Dr. Joseph W., copied Gosport records, 44
  note on Sagunto, 47
  tragedy of waitresses, 155
Water, spring on Hog Island, 3
  artesian well attempted, 163
  Kleinschmidt converters, 164

Watertown, Mass., 72, 74, 78, 98
Weathervane, 167
Wedding, Celia and Levi, 79
  Fabius Becker, 68
Weirs, N.H., 147
Weiss, Rev. John, 67
  first visit to islands, 71
  first to register, 75
  perpetual clown, 79
  Celia's letter to, 89
Wentworth, Gov. John, last visit to Shoals, 45
Wentworth Hotel, 110, 163
West, Francis, Lieut. Gov., 13
Wetherell, Carl B., 160 sq.
Weymouth, George, 4
Weymouth, Mass., 39
Whale, stranded on Duck Island, 71
Whaling Company, 62
Whaling - Pocahontas, 64
Wheeler, Philip W., 114
Whipple, Rev. Enoch, 51
White, Capt. Joseph, born on Hog Island, 3
  son murdered, 44
White, Maria, 73
White Island, named, 3
  buried treasure, 38
White Island Light, 47, 130
  Thomas B. Laighton appointed to, 62
  Becker took charge, 74
White Mountains, Eliza visits, 101
Whiting, Arthur, 124
Whittier, John Greaanleaf
  comment on Dickens, 1, 88, 103
  in Celia's parlor, 123, 126
  love for Shoals, 129-132
  lines to Celia, 131
Whittle, Judge, 33
Wilkinson, Daniel 114
Williams, Frank, 70, 73, 74
Willy, Capt. Edward, 28
Winnipesaukee, 16, 147
Winthrop, Gov. John, 16, 39
Winthrop House, Boston, 133
Withington, Rev. Leonard, 53
Women at Shoals, 14, 15
Woodbury, Levi, 69
Worcester, Mass., Higginson's new pastorate, 79
Workingmen's reading club, 61
World War I, 163

209

ISLES OF SHOALS

Wormwood, Wm., 15

Y

Yeaton, Richard, selectman, 1
York Beach, 76

York, Maine, 39
Y.P.R.U. Cottage, 164
Young, C. T., estimate of Celia, 90

About the Author

Lyman V. Rutledge was a retired Unitarian minister, and a celebrated author of Isles of Shoals titles.

Beginning in 1911, he summered on the islands and devoted many years to the Shoals movement in which he served as president of the Isles of Shoals Unitarian Association, director and executive director of the Star Island Corporation.

In 1949 he wrote *Ten Miles Out* – the official guide book for the islands now in a fourth edition.

During fifty-five years in the ministry, Mr. Rutledge served churches in Billerica, Cambridge, Dorchester, and Dedham, Massachusetts and in Dublin, New Hampshire. He was appointed by two Massachusetts governors to recess commissions: Juvenile Delinquency by Governor Bradford, and Minimum Wage Laws by Governor Dever.

For twenty years he was chaplain of the Norfolk County House of Corrections and for twenty-five chaplain of his Masonic Lodge. In Rotary he served as Governor of his district.

Mr. Rutledge has been president of the Unitarian Sunday School Society, Unitarian Social Service Council, Unitarian Temperance Society, the Greater Boston Sunday School Union and was councilor-in-chief of the Southern New England Council and vice president of the Massachusetts Historical League.